The Ultimate TSA Guide

Published by *RAR Medical Services Limited, trading as* **Infinity Books**
www.uniadmissions.co.uk
info@uniadmissions.co.uk
+44 (0) 208 068 0438

About the Authors

Jon studied Economics and Management at St Hugh's College, Oxford, between 2013 and 2016. He sat the Thinking Skills Assessment and **scored full marks** in section 1 of the paper, placing him in the **top 0.1% of candidates** who sat the assessment that year.

Jon has worked with UniAdmissions since 2014, working primarily as a personal tutor for a number of applicants across the entire application process. He has also provided Thinking Skills Assessment preparation courses within schools, and remains very familiar with all aspects of the paper.

Although Jon has moved into finance since graduation, he remains involved with tutoring as much as time allows. He regularly visits Oxford in his free time, and hopes to return for further study at some point in the future.

Rohan is the **Director of Operations** at *UniAdmissions* and is responsible for its technical and commercial arms. He graduated from Gonville and Caius College, Cambridge and is a fully qualified doctor. Over the last five years, he has tutored hundreds of successful Oxbridge and Medical applicants. He has also authored twenty books on admissions tests and interviews.

Rohan has taught physiology to undergraduates and interviewed medical school applicants for Cambridge. He has published research on bone physiology and writes education articles for the Independent and Huffington Post. In his spare time, Rohan enjoys playing the piano and table tennis.

The Ultimate TSA Guide

300 Practice Questions

Rohan Agarwal
Jonathan Madigan

UniAdmissions

The Basics

What is the TSA?

The Thinking Skills Assessment is an aptitude test taken by students who are applying to certain courses at Cambridge and Oxford. Cambridge applicants sit the TSA Cambridge and Oxford applicants sit the TSA Oxford.

What does it test?

SECTION	SKILLS TESTED	QUESTIONS	TIMING
ONE	Problem-solving skills, including numerical and spatial reasoning. Critical thinking skills, including understanding argument and reasoning using everyday language.	50 MCQs	90 minutes
TWO	Ability to organise ideas in a clear and concise manner, and communicate them effectively in writing. Questions are usually but not necessarily medical.	One Essay from Four	30 minutes

NB: **TSA Oxford** consists of sections 1 + 2; **TSA Cambridge** and **TSA UCL** consist of only section 1.

Why is the TSA used?

The TSA is considered by tutors alongside your grades (both achieved and predicted), personal statement, references, and interview, in order to determine whether you should get an offer. Different colleges and admission tutors will give different weighting to each of these components, and therefore there is no sure-fire way to know how much consideration will be given in each application.

In general, Oxbridge applicants tend to be a bright bunch and therefore usually have excellent grades. This means that competition is fierce – meaning that the universities must use the TSA to help differentiate between applicants.

Who has to sit the TSA?

Exam	Course
TSA Oxford	Students applying for the following subjects at Oxford **MUST** take the TSA: Economics and Management Experimental Psychology Chemistry Human Sciences Philosophy and Linguistics Philosophy, Politics and Economics (PPE) Psychology and Linguistics Psychology and Philosophy
TSA Cambridge	Students applying for Land Economy **MAY** have to take the TSA depending on the college they apply to.
TSA UCL	Students applying for European Social and Political Students **MUST** take the TSA.

When do I sit TSA?

The TSA takes place in the first week of November every year, normally on a Wednesday Morning.

Can I resit the TSA?

No, you can only sit the TSA once per admissions cycle.

Where do I sit the TSA?

You can usually sit the TSA at your school or college (ask your exams officer for more information). Alternatively, if your school isn't a registered test centre or you're not attending a school or college, you can sit the TSA at an authorised test centre.

How much does it cost?

The TSA is usually free although there may be a small administration charge from the centre.

If I reapply, do I have to resit the TSA?

You only need to resit the TSA if you are applying to Oxford or Cambridge for a course that requires the TSA again. You cannot use your score from any previous attempts.

How is the TSA Scored?

Section 1 is scored on a scale of approximately 1 – 100. In general, the average TSA score for an applicant to Cambridge is in the high 50s. Only 10% of students score above 70.

When do I get my results?

TSA results are released in early January of the following year.

How is the TSA used?

Whilst the personal statement and references might give a good indication of a candidate's motivation or enthusiasm, the TSA score is one of only two pieces of quantitative information available to tutors about the academic ability of candidates, alongside grades. It can often be hard to differentiate between candidates given that the majority will receive high numbers of A and A* grades during their time at school. The TSA results provide Oxbridge tutors with a **way of differentiating between applicants** who may otherwise look very similar.

There is no set score a candidate must receive in the assessment in order to receive an offer, but most tutors will set a rough threshold which candidates must meet in order to be seriously considered. Nevertheless, tutors understand that everyone has bad days and if a TSA score seem disproportionately low for an otherwise strong candidate they are likely to look into why this occurred, rather than dismissing the application entirely.

It is not uncommon for tutors to **refer to the TSA at interview**. Some will ask for the applicant's opinion of how the exam went, or disclose their score to them. Others may ask a candidate a number of TSA style questions, in order to verify that the score they received reflects their ability. At Oxford, where the writing task makes up Section 2 of the paper, candidates are sometimes **asked questions on the essay** they submitted. This process is used by tutors to gain a better understanding of how you think; don't assume that you are being questioned on your TSA because you scored particularly low (or indeed particularly high!).

General Advice

Start Early

It is much easier to prepare if you practice little and often. **Start your preparation well in advance**; ideally by mid September but at the latest by early October. This way you will have plenty of time to complete as many papers as you need to and won't have to panic and cram just before the test, which is a much less effective and more stressful way to learn.

Prioritise

Some questions can be long and complex – and given the intense time pressure you need to know your limits. It is essential that you **don't get stuck with very difficult questions**. If a question looks particularly long or complex, move on and mark it for review. You don't want to be caught 5 questions short at the end just because you took more than 3 minutes in answering a challenging multi-step problem-solving question. If a question is taking too long, choose a sensible answer and move on. Remember that **each question carries equal weighting** and therefore, you should adjust your timing in accordingly. With practice and discipline, you can get very good at this and learn to maximise your efficiency.

Positive Marking

There are no penalties for incorrect answers in the TSA; you will gain one for each right answer and will not get one for each wrong or unanswered one. This provides you with the luxury that you can always guess should you absolutely be not able to figure out the right answer for a question or run behind time. Since each question provides you with 4 to 6 possible answers, you have a 16-25% chance of guessing correctly. Therefore, if you aren't sure (and are running short of time), then guess and move on. Before 'guessing' you should try to **eliminate a couple of answers** to increase your chances of getting the question correct.

For example, if a question has 5 options and you manage to eliminate 2 options- your chances of getting the question increase from 20% to 33%!

Avoid losing easy marks on other questions because of poor exam technique. Similarly, if you have failed to finish the exam, take the last 10 seconds to guess the remaining questions to at least give yourself a chance of getting them right.

Practice

This is the best way of familiarising yourself with the style of question and the timing for this section. You are unlikely to be familiar with the style of questions in the TSA when you first encounter them.

Practising questions will put you at ease and make you more comfortable with the exam. The more comfortable you are, the less you will panic on the test day and the more likely you are to score highly. Initially, **work through the questions at your own pace**, and spend time carefully reading the questions and looking at any additional data. When it becomes closer to the test, make sure you practice the questions under exam conditions.

Past Papers

Official past papers and answers for the TSA Oxford are freely available at **www.uniadmissions.co.uk/tsa-past-papers**. If you are sitting the TSA Cambridge/UCL, you should still attempt the TSA Oxford papers as they are the same style and difficulty. Once you've completed the questions in this book, you should attempt as many past papers as possible (at least 4).

You will undoubtedly get stuck when doing some past paper questions – they are designed to be tricky and the answer schemes don't offer any explanations. Thus, you're highly advised to acquire a copy of *TSA Past Paper Worked Solutions* – a free ebook is available online (see the back of this book for more details). For a final boost to your preparation, you can find an additional 4 practice papers at **www.uniadmissions.co.uk/tsa-practice-papers**.

Keywords

If you're stuck on a question; pay particular attention to the options that contain

Top tip! Ensure that you take a watch that can show you the time in seconds into the exam. This will allow you have a much more accurate idea of the time you're spending on a question.

Scoring Tables

Use these to keep a record of your scores – you can then easily see which paper you should attempt next (always the one with the lowest score).

SECTION 1	1st Attempt	2nd Attempt	3rd Attempt
2008			
2009			
2010			
2011			
2012			
2013			
2014			
2015			
2016			

Extra Practice

If you're blessed with a good memory, you might remember the answers to certain questions in the past papers – making it less useful to repeat them again. If you want to tackle extra mock papers which are fully up-to-date then check out **www.uniadmissions.co.uk/tsa-practice-papers** for **4** x full mock papers with worked solutions.

These are normally £60 but as thanks for purchasing this book, you can get them for £40 instead. Just enter "*TSAWS20*" at checkout.

SECTION 1	1st Attempt	2nd Attempt	3rd Attempt
Practice Paper A			
Practice Paper B			
Practice Paper C			
Practice Paper D			

Repeat Questions

When checking through answers, pay particular attention to questions you have got wrong. If there is a worked answer, look through it carefully until you feel confident that you understand the reasoning, and then repeat the question without help to check that you can do it. If only the answer is given, have another look at the question and try to work out why that answer is correct. This is the best way to learn from your mistakes, and means you are **less likely to make similar mistakes** when it comes to the test. The same applies for questions which you were unsure of and made an educated guess which was correct, even if you got it right. When working through this book, make sure you **highlight any questions you are unsure of**, this means you know to spend more time looking over them once marked.

No Calculators

You aren't permitted to use calculators in the TSA – thus it is essential that you have **strong numerical skills**. For instance, you should be able to rapidly convert between percentages, decimals and fractions. You will seldom get questions that would require calculators but you would be expected to be able to arrive at a sensible estimate. Consider for example:

Estimate 3.962 x 2.322:
3.962 is approximately 4 and 2.323 is approximately 2.33 = 7/3.
Thus, $3.962 \times 2.322 \approx 4 \times \frac{7}{3} = \frac{28}{3} = 9.33$

Since you will rarely be asked to perform difficult calculations, you can use this as a signpost of if you are tackling a question correctly. For example, if you end up in the situation where you have to divide 8,079 by 357- this should raise alarm bells because calculations in the TSA are rarely this difficult.

A word on timing...

"If you had all day to do your TSA, you would get 100%. But you don't."

Whilst this isn't completely true, it illustrates a very important point. Once you've practiced and know how to answer the questions, the clock is your biggest enemy. This seemingly obvious statement has one very important consequence. **The way to improve your TSA score is to improve your speed.** There is no magic bullet. But there are a great number of techniques that, with practice, will give you significant time gains, allowing you to answer more questions and score more marks.

Timing is tight throughout the TSA – mastering timing is the first key to success. Some candidates choose to work as quickly as possible to save up time at the end to check back, but this is generally not the best way to do it. TSA questions have a lot of information in them – each time you start answering a question it takes time to get familiar with the instructions and information. By splitting the question into two sessions (the first run-through and the return-to-check) you double the amount of time you spend on familiarising yourself with the data, as you have to do it twice instead of only once. This costs valuable time.

In addition, candidates who do check back may spend 2–3 minutes doing so and yet not make any actual changes. Whilst this can be reassuring, it is a false reassurance as it has little effect on your actual score. Therefore it is usually best to **pace yourself very steadily**, aiming to spend the same amount of time on each question and finish the final question in a section just as time runs out. This reduces the time spent on re-familiarising with questions and maximises the time spent on the first attempt, gaining more marks.

It is essential that you **don't get stuck with the hardest questions** – no doubt there will be some. In the time spent answering only one of these you may miss out on answering three easier questions. If a question is taking too long, choose a sensible answer and move on. Never see this as giving up or in any way failing, rather it is the smart way to approach a test with a tight time limit. With practice and discipline, you can get very good at this and learn to maximise your efficiency.

Use the Options

Some questions may try to overload you with information. When presented with large tables and data, it's essential you look at the answer options so you can focus your mind. This can allow you to **reach the correct answer a lot more quickly**. Consider the example below:

The table below shows the results of a study investigating antibiotic resistance in staphylococcus populations. A single staphylococcus bacterium is chosen at random from a similar population. Resistance to any one antibiotic is independent of resistance to others.

Calculate the probability that the bacterium selected will be resistant to all four drugs:

Antibiotic	Number of Bacteria tested	Number of Resistant Bacteria
Benzyl-penicillin	10^{11}	98 10^2
Chloramphenicol	10^9	1200 10^3
Metronidazole	10^8	256 $2 \times 10^?$
Erythromycin	10^5	2 2

A	1 in 10^6	**C**	1 in 10^{20}	**E**	1 in 10^{30}
B	1 in 10^{12}	**D**	1 in 10^{25}	**F**	1 in 10^{35}

Looking at the options first makes it obvious that there is **no need to calculate exact values**- only in powers of 10. This makes your life a lot easier. If you hadn't noticed this, you might have spent well over 90 seconds trying to calculate the exact value when it wasn't even being asked for.

In other cases, you may actually be able to use the options to arrive at the solution quicker than if you had tried to solve the question as you normally would i.e. using trial and error.

In general, it pays dividends to **look at the options briefly** and see if they can be help you arrive at the question more quickly. Get into this habit early – it may feel unnatural at first but it's guaranteed to save you time in the long run.

SECTION 1

This is the first section of the TSA and as you walk in, it is inevitable that you will feel nervous. Make sure that you have been to the toilet because once it starts you cannot simply pause and go. Take a few deep breaths and calm yourself down. Remember that panicking will not help and may negatively affect your marks- so try and avoid this as much as possible.

You have 90 minutes to answer 50 questions in section 1. The questions generally fall into two categories:

➤   Problem Solving
➤   Critical Thinking

Whilst the TSA is renowned for being difficult to prepare for, there are **powerful shortcuts and techniques that you can use** to save valuable time on these types of questions.

You have 108 seconds per question; this may sound like a lot but given that **you're often required to read and analyse passages or graphs**- it can often not be enough. Some questions in this section are very tricky and can be a big drain on your limited time. The students who fail to complete this section are those who get bogged down on a particular question.

Therefore, it is vital that you start to get a feel for which questions are going to be easy and quick to do and which ones should be left till the end. The best way to do this is through practice and the questions in this book will offer extensive opportunities for you to do so.

SECTION 1: Critical Thinking

TSA Critical thinking questions require you to understand the constituents of a good argument and be able to pick them apart. The majority of TSA Critical thinking questions tend to fall into 5 major categories:

1. Identifying Conclusions
2. Identifying Assumptions + Flaws
3. Strengthening and Weakening arguments
4. Matching Arguments
5. Applying Principles

Having a good grasp of language and being able to filter unnecessary information quickly and efficiently is a vital skill at Oxbridge – you simply do not have the time to sit and read vast numbers of textbooks cover to cover, you need to be able to **filter the information** and realise which part is important and this will contribute to your success in your studies

Only use the Passage

Your answer must only be based on the information available in the passage. Do not try and guess the answer based on your general knowledge as this can be a trap. For example, if the passage says that spring is followed by winter, then take this as true even though you know that spring is followed by summer.

Take your Time

Unlike the problem solving questions, **critical thinking questions are less time pressured**. Most of the passages are well below 300 words and therefore don't take long to read and process. Thus, your aim should be to understand the intricacies of the passage and **identify key information** so that you don't miss crucial information and lose easy marks.

Identifying Conclusions

Students struggle with these type of questions because they confuse a premise for a conclusion. For clarities sake:

- A **Conclusion** is a summary of the arguments being made and is usually explicitly stated or heavily implied.
- A **Premise** is a statement from which another statement can be inferred or follows as a conclusion.

I.e. a conclusion is shown/implied/proven by a premise. Similarly, a premise shows/indicates/establishes a conclusion. Consider for example: *My mom, being a woman, is clever as all women are clever.*

Premise 1: My mom is a woman + **Premise 2:** Women are clever = **Conclusion:** My mom is clever.

This is fairly straightforward as it's a very short passage and the conclusion is explicitly stated. Sometimes the latter may not happen. Consider: *My mom is a woman and all women are clever.*
Here, whilst the conclusion is not explicitly being stated, both premises still stand and can be used to reach the same conclusion.

You may sometimes be asked to identify if any of the options cannot be "reliably concluded". This is effectively asking you to identify why an option **cannot** be the conclusion. There are many reasons why but the most common ones are:

1. Over-generalising: *My mom is clever therefore all women are clever.*
2. Being too specific: All kids like candy thus my son also likes candy.
3. Confusing Correlation vs. Causation: *Lung cancer is much more likely in patients who drink water. Hence, water causes lung cancer.*
4. Confusing Cause and Effect: *Lung cancer patients tend to smoke so it follows that having lung cancer must make people want to smoke.*

Note how conjunctives like hence, thus, therefore and it follows give you a clue as to when a conclusion is being stated. More examples of these include: 'it follows that', 'implies that', 'whence', 'entails that'.
Similarly, words like 'because', 'as indicated by', 'in that', 'given that', and 'due to the fact that' usually identify premises.

Assumptions + Flaws:

Other types of critical thinking questions may require you to identify assumptions and flaws in a passage's reasoning. Before proceeding it is useful to define both:

- An assumption is a reasonable assertion that can be made on the basis of the available evidence.
- A flaw is an element of an argument which is inconsistent to the rest of the available evidence. It undermines the crucial components of the overall argument being made.

Consider for example: *My mom is clever because all doctors are clever.*

Premise 1: Doctors are clever. **Assumption:** My mom is a doctor. **Conclusion:** My mom is clever.

Note that the conclusion follows naturally even though there is only one premise because of the assumption. I.e. the argument relies on the assumption to work. Thus, if you are unsure if an option you have is an assumption or not, just ask yourself:

1) *Is it in the passage?* If the answer is **no** then proceed to ask:
2) *Does the conclusion rely on this piece of information in order to work?* – If the answer is **yes** – then you've identified an assumption.

Top tip! Don't get confused between premises and assumptions. A **premise** is a statement that is explicitly stated in the passage. An **assumption** is an inference that is made from the passage.

You may sometimes be asked to identify flaws in argument – it is important to be aware of the types of flaws to look out for. In general, these are broadly similar to the ones discussed earlier in the conclusion section (over-generalising, being too specific, confusing cause and effect, confusing correlation and causation). Remember that **an assumption may also be a flaw**.

For example consider again: *My mom is clever because all doctors are clever.*

What if the mother was not actually a doctor? The argument would then breakdown as the assumption would be incorrect or **flawed**.

Strengthening and Weakening Arguments:

You may be asked to identify an answer option that would most strengthen or weaken the argument being made in the passage. Normally, you'll also be told to assume that each answer option is true. Before we can discuss how to strengthen and weaken arguments, it is important to understand "what constitutes a good argument:

1. **Evidence:** Arguments which are heavily based on value judgements and subjective statements tend to be weaker than those based on facts, statistics and the available evidence.
2. **Logic:** A good argument should flow and the constituent parts should fit well into an overriding view or belief.
3. **Balance:** A good argument must concede that there are other views or beliefs (counter-argument). The key is to carefully dismantle these ideas and explain why they are wrong.

Thus, when asked to strengthen an argument, look for options that would: Increase the evidence basis for the argument, support or add a premise, address the counter-arguments.

Similarly, when asked to weaken an argument, look for options that would: decrease the evidence basis for the argument or create doubt over existing evidence, undermine a premise, strengthen the counter-arguments.

In order to be able to strengthen or weaken arguments, you must completely understand the passage's conclusion. Then you can start testing the impact of each answer option on the conclusion to see which one strengthens or weakens it the most i.e. is the conclusion stronger/weaker if I assume this information to be true and included in the passage.

Often you'll have to decide which option strengthens/weakens the passage most – and there really isn't an easy way to do this apart from lots of practice. Thankfully, you have plenty of time for these questions.

Matching Arguments:

Some questions will test your ability to identify similarities between two arguments about different topics. The similarity you are looking for is in the **structure or the pattern of the argument**. A question of this type will ask you to find the option that most closely parallels the format of the example argument.

Consider the example:

"James' grades have improved a lot recently. Either he is putting more effort into his homework or he has been less distracted in lessons. I know for a fact that James' hasn't been doing his homework, so it must be that he's paying more attention in class."

Which of the following most closely parallels the reasoning used in the above argument?

The first step is to identify the structure of the example argument. You may be able to do this by identifying key points, and how they are arranged within the passage.

In this case, the structure of the argument is as follows:
X = James is putting more effort into homework
Y = James is paying more attention in class

➢ Either X is true or Y is true.
➢ X cannot be true.
➢ Therefore Y must be true.

The second step in answering the question is to identify which of the answers offers an argument that most accurately **represents the structure of the example reasoning**. Some of the answers may follow relatively similar structures, but contain small discrepancies which make the answer incorrect.

In the case of the example, the correct answer may be along the lines of: "My car is currently broken. Either it has a faulty exhaust, or the ignition isn't working properly. When I took it to the garage, the mechanic confirmed that the ignition was fully functioning. Therefore the issue must be with the exhaust."

Identifying Principles:

Some questions are designed to examine an applicant's capacity to identify the underlying principle within an argument.

A **principle** is a general recommendation which can be applied to a number of cases. When faced with questions of this sort, you are expected to extract the fundamental principle from the single case presented in the passage, and then to see where this principle has been applied in other cases.

The principle you are searching for will not be explicitly stated in a problem of this nature, so you must attempt to obtain it for yourself. To do this, you must first have a solid understanding of what the passage is saying, including both the conclusions reached and the reasoning behind them.

Consider the following example:

"Some people criticise government policy which aims to provide training for young people looking to find work, on the basis that increased training is not enough to reduce the problem of unemployment. Those critics are correct in identifying that more needs to be done, beyond increased training programs, for unemployment levels to fall. However no policy should be discouraged purely because it fails to provide a complete solution to a problem. Any idea which has a beneficial impact should be embraced, even if that impact is relatively small."

The argument is suggesting that people are wrong to criticise a policy just because it does not completely solve an issue. The passage suggests that as long as the policy has some positive impact on the problem, it may be worth pursuing. This is the **key principle** to be taken from this question.

Using this principle, you should be able to identify the correct answer. In this case, one answer that accurately reflects the principle in the passage may be:

"The use of warning labels on cigarette packets should not be discouraged just because they will not single-handedly solve the problem of high levels of smokers."

Top tip! Though it might initially sound counter-intuitive, it is often best to read the question *before* reading the passage. Then you'll have a much better idea of what you're looking for and are therefore more likely to find it quicker.

Critical Thinking Questions

Question 1-5 are based on the passage below:

People have tried to elucidate the differences between the different genders for many years. Are they societal pressures or genetic differences? In the past it has always been assumed that it was programmed into our DNA to act in a certain more masculine or feminine way but now evidence has emerged that may show it is not our genetics that determines the way we act, but that society pre-programmes us into gender identification. Whilst it is generally acknowledged that not all boys and girls are the same, why is it that most young boys like to play with trucks and diggers whilst young girls prefer dollies and pink?

The society we live in has always been an important factor in our identity, take cultural differences; the language we speak the food we eat, the clothes we wear. All of these factors influence our identity. New research finds that the people around us may prove to be the biggest influence on our gender behaviour. It shows our parents buying gendered toys may have a much bigger influence than the genes they gave us. Girls are being programmed to like the same things as their mothers and this has lasting effects on their personality. Young girls and boys are forced into their gender stereotypes through the clothes they are bought, the hairstyle they wear and the toys they play with. The power of society to influence gender behaviour explains the cases where children have been born with different external sex organs to those that would match their sex determining chromosomes. Despite the influence of their DNA they identify to the gender they have always been told they are. Once the difference has been detected, how then are they ever to feel comfortable in their own skin? The only way to prevent society having such a large influence on gender identity is to allow children to express themselves, wear what they want and play with what they want without fear of not fitting in.

Question 1:

What is the main conclusion from the first paragraph?

A. Society controls gender behaviour.
B. People are different based on their gender.
C. DNA programmes how we act.
D. Boys do not like the same things as girls because of their genes.

Question 2:

Which of the following, if true, points out the flaw in the first paragraph's argument?

A. Not all boys like trucks.
B. Genes control the production of hormones.
C. Differences in gender may be due to an equal combination of society and genes.
D. Some girls like trucks.

Question 3:

According to the statement, how can culture affect identity?

A. Culture can influence what we wear and how we speak.
B. Our parents act the way they do because of culture.
C. Culture affects our genetics.
D. Culture usually relates to where we live.

Question 4:

Which of these is most implied by the statement?

A. Children usually identify with the gender they appear to be.
B. Children are programmed to like the things they do by their DNA.
C. Girls like dollies and pink because their mothers do.
D. It is wrong for boys to have long hair like girls.

Question 5:

What does the statement say is the best way to prevent gender stereotyping?

A. Mothers spending more time with their sons.
B. Parents buying gender-neutral clothes for their children.
C. Allowing children to act how they want.
D. Not telling children if they have different sex organs.

Question 6:

Samantha requires 3 As at A Level to be accepted onto a University course. Samantha is accepted onto the University course, therefore she must have achieved 3 As at A Level.

Which of the following statements most closely follows the reasoning used in this paragraph?

A. A train must pass through Clapham Junction before arriving at Victoria Station. The train passes through Clapham Junction, therefore it will shortly arrive at Victoria Station.
B. If Darlington football club defeat Spennymoor, they will win the league. Darlington defeat Spennymoor, therefore they will win the league.
C. Zeeshan has sold his old car. If he buys a new one, he will go on holiday to London. Zeeshan has gone on holiday to London, therefore he must have bought a new car.
D. Lucy is afraid of flying, but needs to travel on an aeroplane in order to visit Egypt. Lucy has recently visited Egypt, therefore she must have travelled on an aeroplane.
E. If the A1 is open, Andrew will be able to drive to Scotland. However, the A1 is closed due to a traffic collision, so Andrew cannot drive to Scotland.

Questions 7-11 are based on the passage below:

New evidence has emerged that the most important factor in a child's development could be their napping routine. It has come to light that regular napping could well be the deciding factor for determining toddlers' memory and learning abilities. The new countrywide survey of 1000 toddlers, all born in the same year showed around 75% had regular 30-minute naps. Parents cited the benefits of their child having a regular routine (including meal times) such as decreased irritability, and stated the only downfall of occasional problems with sleeping at night. Research indicating that toddlers were 10% more likely to suffer regular night-time sleeping disturbances when they regularly napped supported the parent's view.

Those who regularly took 30-minute naps were more than twice as likely to remember simple words, such as those of new toys, than their non-napping counterparts, who also had higher incidences of memory impairment, behavioural problems and learning difficulties. Toddlers who regularly had 30 minute naps were tested on whether they were able recall the names of new objects the following day, compared to a control group who did not regularly nap. These potential links between napping and memory, behaviour and learning ability provides exciting new evidence in the field of child development.

Question 7:
If in 100 toddlers 5% who did not nap were able to remember a new teddy's name, how many who had napped would be expected to remember?

A. 8   B. 9   C. 10   D. 12

Question 8:
Assuming that the incidence of night-time sleeping disturbances is the same in for all toddlers independent of all characteristics other than napping, what is the percentage of toddlers who suffer regular night-time sleeping disturbances as a result of napping?

A. 7.5%   C. 14%   E. 50%
B. 10%   D. 20%

Question 9:

Using the information from the passage above, which of the following is the most plausible alternative reason for the link between memory and napping?

A. Children who have bad memory abilities are also likely to have trouble sleeping.
B. Children who regularly nap, are born with better memories.
C. Children who do not nap were unable to concentrate on the memory testing exercises for the study.
D. Parents who enforce a routine of napping are more likely to conduct memory exercises with their children.

Question 10:

Which of the following is most strongly indicated?

A. Families have more enjoyable meal times when their toddlers regularly nap.
B. Toddlers have better routines when they nap.
C. Parents enforce napping to improve their toddlers' memory ability.
D. Napping is important for parents' routines.

Question 11:

Which of the following, if true, would strengthen the conclusion that there is a causal link between regular napping and improved memory in toddlers?

A. Improved memory is also associated with regular mealtimes.
B. Parents who enforce regular napping are more inclined to include their children in studies.
C. Toddlers' memory development is so rapid that even a few weeks can make a difference to performance.
D. Among toddler playgroups where napping incidence is higher and more consistent memory performance is significantly improved compared to those that do not.

Question 12:

Tom's father says to him: 'You must work for your A-levels. That is the best way to do well in your A-level exams. If you work especially hard for Geography, you will definitely succeed in your Geography A-level exam'.

Which of the following is the best statement Tom could say to prove a flaw in his father's argument?

A. 'It takes me longer to study for my History exam, so I should prioritise that.'
B. 'I do not have to work hard to do well in my Geography A-level.'
C. 'Just because I work hard, does not mean I will do well in my A-levels.'
D. 'You are putting too much importance on studying for A-levels.'
E. 'You haven't accounted for the fact that Geography is harder than my other subjects.'

Question 13:

Today the NHS is increasingly struggling to be financially viable. In the future, the NHS may have to reduce the services it cannot afford. The NHS is supported by government funds, which come from those who pay tax in the UK. Recently the NHS has been criticised for allowing fertility treatments to be free, as many people believe these are not important and should not be paid for when there is not enough money to pay the doctors and nurses.

Which of the following is the most accurate conclusion of the statement above?

A. Only taxpayers should decide where the NHS spends its money.
B. Doctors and nurses should be better paid.
C. The NHS should stop free fertility treatments.
D. Fertility treatments may have to be cut if finances do not improve.

Question 14:

'We should allow people to drive as fast as they want. By allowing drivers to drive at fast speeds, through natural selection the most dangerous drivers will kill only themselves in car accidents. These people will not have children, hence only safe people will reproduce and eventually the population will only consist of safe drivers.'

Which one of the following, if true, most weakens the above argument?

A. Dangerous drivers harm others more often than themselves by driving too fast.
B. Dangerous drivers may produce children who are safe drivers.
C. The process of natural selection takes a long time.
D. Some drivers break speed limits anyway.

Question 15:

In the winter of 2014 the UK suffered record levels of rainfall, which led to catastrophic damage across the country. Thousands of homes were damaged and even destroyed, leaving many homeless in the chaos that followed. The Government faced harsh criticism that they had failed to adequately prepare the country for the extreme weather. In such cases the Government assess the likelihood of such events happening in the future and balance against the cost of advance measures to reduce the impact should they occur versus the cost of the event with no preparative defences in place.

Until recently, for example, the risk of acts of terror taking was low compared with the vast cost anticipated should they occur. However, the risk of flooding is usually low, so it could be argued that the costs associated with anti-flooding measures would have been pre-emptively unreasonable. Should the Government be expected to prepare for every conceivable threat that could come to pass? Are we to put in place expensive measures against a seismic event as well as a possible extra-terrestrial invasion?

Which of the following best expresses the main conclusion of the statement above?

A. The Government has an obligation to assess risks and costs of possible future events.
B. The Government should spend money to protect against potential extra-terrestrial invasions and seismic events.
C. The Government should have spent money to protect against potential floods.
D. The Government was justified in not spending heavily to protect against flooding.
E. The Government should assist people who lost their homes in the floods.

Question 16:

Sadly the way in which children interact with each other has changed over the years. Where once children used to play sports and games together in the street, they now sit alone in their rooms on the computer playing games on the Internet. Where in the past young children learned human interaction from active games with their friends this is no longer the case. How then, when these children are grown up, will they be able to socially interact with their colleagues?

Which one of the following is the conclusion of the above statement?
A. Children who play computer games now interact less outside of them.
B. The Internet can be a tool for teaching social skills.
C. Computer games are for social development.
D. Children should be made to play outside with their friends to develop their social skills for later in life.
E. Adults will in the future play computer games as a means of interaction.

Question 17:

Between 2006 and 2013 the British government spent £473 million on Tamiflu antiviral drugs in preparation for a flu pandemic, despite there being little evidence to support the effectiveness of the drug. The antivirals were stockpiled for a flu pandemic that never fully materialised. Only 150,000 packs were used during the swine flu episode in 2009, and it is unclear if this improved outcomes. Therefore this money could have been much better spent on drugs that would actually benefit patients.

Which option best summarises the author's view in the passage?
A. Drugs should never be stockpiled, as they may not be used.
B. Spending millions of pounds on drugs should be justified by strong evidence showing positive effects.
C. We should not prepare for flu pandemics in the future.
D. The recipients of Tamiflu in the swine flu pandemic had no difference in symptoms or outcomes to patients who did not receive the antivirals.

Question 18:

High BMI and particularly central weight are risk factors associated with increased morbidity and mortality. Many believe the development of cheap, easily accessible fast-food outlets is partly responsible for the increase in rates of obesity. An unhealthy weight is commonly associated with a generally unhealthy lifestyle, such a lack of exercise. The best way to tackle the growing problem of obesity is for the government to tax unhealthy foods so they are no longer a cheap alternative.

Why is the solution given, to tax unhealthy foods, not a logical conclusion from the passage?

A. Unhealthy eating is not exclusively confined to low-income families.

B. A more general approach to unhealthy lifestyles would be optimal.

C. People do not only choose to eat unhealthy food because it is cheaper.

D. People need to take personal responsibility for their own health.

Question 19:

As people are living longer, care in old age is becoming a larger burden. Many people require carers to come into their home numerous times a day or need full residential care. It is not right that the NHS should be spending vast funds on the care of people who are sufficiently wealthy to fund their own care. Some argue that they want their savings kept to give to their children; however this is not a right, simply a luxury. It is not right that people should be saving and depriving themselves of necessary care, or worse, making the NHS pay the bill, so they have money to pass on to their offspring. People need to realise that there is a financial cost to living longer.

Which of the following statements is the main conclusion of the above passage?

A. We need to take a personal responsibility for our care in old age.

B. Caring for the elderly is a significant burden on the NHS.

C. The reason people are reluctant to pay for their own care is that they want to pass money onto their offspring.

D. The NHS should limit care to the elderly to reduce their costs.

E. People shouldn't save their money for old age.

Question 20:

There is much interest in research surrounding production of human stem cells from non-embryo sources for potential regenerative medicine, and a huge financial and personal gain at stake. In January 2014, a team from Japan published two papers in *Nature* that claimed to have developed totipotent stem cells from adult mouse cells by exposure to an acidic environment. However, there has since been much controversy surrounding these papers. Problems included: inability by other teams to replicate the results of the experiment, an insufficient protocol described in the paper and issues with images in one of the papers. It was dishonest of the researchers to publish the papers with such problems, and a requirement of a paper is a sufficiently detailed protocol, so that another group could replicate the experiment.

Which of the following statements is most implied?

A. Research is fuelled mainly by financial and personal gains.
B. The researchers should take responsibility for publishing the paper with such flaws.
C. Rivalry between different research groups makes premature publishing more likely.
D. The discrepancies were in only one of the papers published in January 2014.

Question 21:

The placebo effect is a well-documented medical phenomenon in which a patient's condition undergoes improvement after being given an ineffectual treatment that they believe to be a genuine treatment. It is frequently used as a control during trials of new drugs/procedures, with the effect of the drug being compared to the effect of a placebo, and if the drug does not have a greater effect than the placebo, then it is classed as ineffective. However, this analysis discounts the fact that the drug treatment still has more of a positive effect than no action, and so we are clearly missing out on the potential to improve certain patient conditions. It follows that where there is a demonstrated placebo effect, but treatments are ineffective, we should still give treatments, as there will therefore be some benefit to the patient.

Which of the following best expresses the main conclusion of this passage?

A. In situations where drugs are no more effective than a placebo, we should still give drugs, as they will be more effective than not taking action.
B. Our current analysis discounts the fact that even if drug treatments have no more effect than a placebo, they may still be more effective than no action.
C. The placebo effect is a well-recognised medical phenomenon.
D. Drugs may have negative side effects that outweigh their benefit.
E. Placebos are better than modern drugs.

Question 22:

The speed limit on motorways and dual carriageways has been 70 mph since 1965, but this is an out-dated policy and needs to change. Since 1965, car brakes have become much more effective, and many safety features have been introduced into cars, such as seatbelts (which are now compulsory to wear), crumple zones and airbags. Therefore, it is clear that cars no longer need to be restricted to 70 mph, and the speed limit can be safely increased to 80 mph without causing more road fatalities.

Which of the following best illustrates an assumption in this passage?

A. The government should increase the speed limit to 80 mph.
B. If the speed limit were increased to 80mph, drivers would not begin to drive at 90 mph.
C. The safety systems introduced reduce the chances of fatal road accidents for cars travelling at higher speeds.
D. The roads have not become busier since the 70 mph speed limit was introduced.
E. The public want the speed limit to increase.

Question 23:

Despite the overwhelming scientific proof of the theory of evolution, and even acceptance of the theory by many high-ranking religious ministers, there are still sections of many major religions that do not accept evolution as true. One of the most prominent of these in western society is the Intelligent Design movement, which promotes the religious-based (and scientifically discredited) notion of Intelligent Design as a scientific theory. Intelligent Design proponents often point to complex issues of biology as proof that god is behind the design of human beings, much as a watchmaker is inherent in the design of a watch.

One part of anatomy that has been identified as supposedly supporting Intelligent Design is fingerprints, with some proponents arguing that they are a mark of individualism created by God, with no apparent function except to identify each human being as unique. This is incorrect, as fingerprints do have a well documented function – namely channelling away of water to improve grip in wet conditions – in which hairless, smooth skinned hands otherwise struggle to grip smooth objects. The individualism of fingerprints is accounted for by the complexity of thousands of small grooves. Development is inherently affected by stochastic or random processes, meaning that the body is unable to uniformly control its development to ensure that fingerprints are the same in each human being. Clearly, the presence of individual fingerprints does nothing to support the so-called-theory of Intelligent Design.

Which of the following best illustrates the main conclusion of this passage?
A. Fingerprints have a well-established function.
B. Evolution is supported by overwhelming scientific proof.
C. Fingerprints do not offer any support to the notion of Intelligent Design.
D. The individual nature of fingerprints is explained by stochastic processes inherent in development that the body cannot uniformly control.
E. Intelligent design is a credible and scientifically rigorous theory.

Question 24:

If the blue party wins the general election, they will implement all of the policies of their manifesto, including an increase in the number of soldiers enlisted in the army. If the army has more soldiers, it will build a new military base in Devon to accommodate them. Therefore, if the blue party wins the election, a new military base will be built in Devon.

Which of the following most closely follows the reasoning used in this argument?

A. If David does not pay his road tax, his car will be confiscated by the local council. If David's car is confiscated, he will not be able to travel to work. Therefore, if David does not pay his road tax, he will lose his job.

B. If a car passes a speed camera whilst travelling at more than 70mph, it will be photographed by the speed camera. If a car is photographed by a speed camera, a speeding ticket will be sent to the owner. Therefore, if John's car is driving along the road at 80mph, he will receive a speeding ticket.

C. If Omar does well in his A Level exams, he will be accepted at Durham University to study classics. If he is accepted at Durham University, he will graduate in Durham Cathedral. Therefore, if Omar does well in his exams, he will graduate in Durham Cathedral.

D. Grace is travelling home from Birmingham. However, the fuel on her car is running low. In order to make it home, she needs to refuel her car. In order for her to refuel her car, she has to leave the motorway and visit a petrol station. Grace arrives home, therefore she must have visited a petrol station

E. If Country X is further south than Country A, crops will be planted earlier in the year than they are in Country A. If crops are planted earlier, they will be ripe sooner in the year. Crops in Country X are ripe earlier in the year than crops in Country A. Therefore, Country X must be further south than France.

Question 25:

A train is scheduled to depart from Newcastle at 3:30pm. It stops at Durham, Darlington, York, Sheffield, Peterborough and Stevenage before arriving at Kings Cross station in London, where the train completes its journey. The total length of the journey between Newcastle and Kings Cross was 230 miles, and the average speed of the train during the journey (including time spent stood still at calling stations) is 115mph. Therefore, the train will complete its journey at 5:30pm.

Which of the following is an assumption made in this passage?

A. The various stopping points did not increase the time taken to complete the journey.
B. The train left Newcastle on time.
C. The train travelled by the most direct route available.
D. The train was due to end its journey at Kings Cross.
E. There were no signalling problems encountered on the journey.

Question 26:

There have been many arguments over the last couple of decades about government expenditure on healthcare in the various devolved regions of the UK. It is often argued that, since spending on healthcare per person is higher in Scotland than in England, that therefore the people in Scotland will be healthier.

However, this view fails to take account of the different needs of these 2 populations of the UK. For example, one major factor is that Scotland gets significantly colder than England, and cold weakens the immune system, leaving people in Scotland at much higher risk of infectious disease. Thus, Scotland requires higher levels of healthcare spending per person simply to maintain the health of the populace at a similar level to that of England.

Which of the following is a conclusion that can be drawn from this passage?

A. The higher healthcare spending per person in Scotland does not necessarily mean people living in Scotland are healthier.
B. Healthcare spending should be increased across the UK.
C. Wales requires more healthcare spending per person simply to maintain population health at a similar level to England.
D. It is unfair on England that there is more spending on healthcare per person in Scotland.
E. Scotland's healthcare budget is a controversial topic.

Question 27:

Vaccinations have been hugely successful in reducing the incidence of several diseases throughout the 20th century. One of the most spectacular achievements was arguably the global eradication of Smallpox, once a deadly worldwide killer, during the 1970s. Fortunately, there was a highly effective vaccine available for Smallpox, and a major factor in its eradication was an aggressive vaccination campaign. Another disease that is potentially eradicable is Polio.

However, although there is a highly effective vaccine for Polio available, attempts to eradicate it have so far been unsuccessful. It follows that we should plan and execute an aggressive vaccination campaign for Polio, in order to ensure that this disease too is eradicated.

Which of the following is the main conclusion of this passage?

A. Polio is a potentially eradicable disease.
B. An aggressive vaccination campaign was a major factor in the eradication of smallpox.
C. Both Polio and smallpox have been eradicated by vaccination campaigns.
D. We should execute an aggressive vaccination campaign for Polio.
E. The eradication of smallpox remains one of the most spectacular achievements of medical science.

Question 28:

The Y chromosome is one of 2 sex chromosomes found in the human genome, the other being the X chromosome. As the Y chromosome is only found in males, it can only be passed from father to son. Additionally, the Y chromosome does not exchange sections with other chromosomes (as happens with most chromosomes), meaning it is passed on virtually unchanged through the generations. All of this makes the Y chromosome a fantastic tool for genetic analysis, both to identify individual lineages and to investigate historic population movements. One famous achievement of genetic research using the Y chromosome provides further evidence of its utility, namely the identification of Genghis Khan as a descendant of up to 8% of males in 16 populations across Asia.

Which of the following best illustrates the main conclusion of this passage?

A. The Y chromosome is a fantastic tool for genetic analysis.
B. Research using the Y chromosome has been able to identify Genghis Khan as the descendant of up to 8% of men in many Asian populations.
C. The Y chromosome does not exchange sections with other chromosomes.
D. The Y chromosome is a sex chromosome.

Question 29:

In order for a bacterial infection to be cleared, a patient must be treated with antibiotics. Rachel has a minor lung infection, which is thought by her doctor to be a bacterial infection. She is treated with antibiotics, but her condition does not improve. Therefore, it must not be a bacterial infection.

Which of the following best illustrates a flaw in this reasoning?

A. It assumes that a bacterial infection would definitely improve after treatment with antibiotics.

B. It ignores the other potential issues that could be treated by antibiotics.

C. It assumes that antibiotics are necessary to treat bacterial infections.

D. It ignores the actions of the immune system, which may be sufficient to clear the infection regardless of what has caused it.

E. It assumes that antibiotics are the only option to treat a bacterial infection.

Question 30:

The link between smoking and lung cancer has been well established for many decades by overwhelming numbers of studies and conclusive research. The answer is clear and simple, that the single best measure that can be taken to avoid lung cancer is to not smoke, or to stop smoking if one has already started.

However, despite the overwhelming evidence and clear answers, many smokers continue to smoke, and seek to minimise their risk of lung cancer by focusing on other, less important risk factors, such as exercise and healthy eating. This approach is obviously severely flawed, and the fact that some smokers feel this is a good way to reduce their risk of lung cancer shows that they are delusional.

Which of the following best illustrates the main conclusion of this passage?

A. Many smokers ignore the largest risk factor, and focus on improving less important risk factors by eating healthily and exercising.

B. Some smokers are delusional.

C. The biggest risk factor of lung cancer is smoking.

D. Overwhelming studies have proven the link between smoking and lung cancer.

E. The government should ban smoking in order to reduce the incidence of lung cancer.

Question 31:

The government should invest more money into outreach schemes in order to encourage more people to go to university. These schemes allow students to meet other people who went to university, which they may not always be able to do otherwise, even on open days.

Which of the following is the best conclusion of the above argument?

A. Outreach schemes are the best way to encourage people to go to university.
B. People will not go to university without seeing it first.
C. The government wants more people to go to university.
D. Meeting people who went to a university is a more effective method than university open days.
E. It is easier to meet people on outreach schemes than on open days.

Question 32:

The illegal drug cannabis was recently upgraded from a class C drug to class B, which means it will be taken less in the UK, because people will know it is more dangerous. It also means if people are caught, possessing the drug they will face a longer prison sentence than before, which will also discourage its use.

Which **TWO** statements if true, most weaken the above argument?

A. Class C drugs are cheaper than class B drugs.
B. Upgrading drugs in other countries has not reduced their use.
C. People who take illegal drugs do not know what class they are.
D. Cannabis was not the only class C drug before it was upgraded.
E. Even if they are caught possessing class B drugs, people do not think they will go to prison.

Question 33:

Schools with better sports programmes such as well-performing football and netball teams tend to have better academic results, less bullying and have overall happier students. Thus, if we want schools to have the best results, reduce bullying and increase student happiness, teachers should start more sports clubs.

Which one of the following best demonstrates a flaw in the above argument?

A. Teachers may be too busy to start sports clubs.
B. Better academic results may be a precondition of better sports teams.
C. Better sports programmes may prevent students from spending time with their family.
D. Some sports teams may be seen to encourage internal bullying.
E. Sport teams that do not perform well lead to increase bullying.

Question 34:

The legal age for purchasing alcohol in the UK is 18. This should be lowered to 16 because the majority of 16 year olds drink alcohol anyway without any fear of repercussions. Even if the police catch a 16-year-old buying alcohol, they are unable to enforce any consequences. If the drinking limit was lowered the police could spend less time trying to catch underage drinkers and deal with other more important crimes. There is no evidence to suggest that drinking alcohol at 16 is any more dangerous than at 18.

Which one of the following, if true, most weakens the above argument?

A. Most 16 year olds do not drink alcohol.
B. If the legal drinking age were lowered to 16, more 15 year olds would start purchasing alcohol.
C. Most 16 year olds do not have enough money to buy alcohol.
D. Most 16 year olds are able to purchase alcohol currently.

Question 35:

There has been a recent change in the way the government helps small businesses. Whilst previously small businesses were given non-repayable grants to help them grow their profits, they can now only receive government loans that must be repaid with interest when the business turns a certain amount of profit. The government wants to support small businesses but studies have shown they are less likely to prosper under the new scheme as they have been deterred from taking government money for fear of loan repayments.

Which one of the following can be concluded from the passage above?

A. Small businesses do not want government money.

B. The government cannot afford to give out grants to small businesses anymore.

C. All businesses avoid accumulating debt.

D. The action of the government is more likely to do more harm than good to small businesses.

E. Big businesses do not need government money.

Questions 36-41 are based on the passage below:

Despite the numerous safety measures in place within the practice of medicine, these can fail when the weaknesses in the layers of defence aligns to create a clear path leading to often disastrous results. This is known as the 'Swiss cheese model of accident causation'. One such occurrence occurred where the wrong kidney was removed from a patient due to a failure in the line of defences designed to prevent such an incident occurring.

When a kidney is diseased it is removed to prevent further complications, this operation, a 'nephrectomy', is regularly performed by experienced surgeons. Where normally the consultant who knew the patient would have conducted the procedure, in this case he passed the responsibility to his registrar, who was also well experienced but had not met the patient previously. The person who had copied out the patient's notes had poor handwriting had accidentally written the 'R' for 'right' in such a way that it was read as an 'L' and subsequently copied, and not noticed by anyone who further reviewed the notes. The patient had been put asleep before the registrar had arrived and so he proceeded without checking the procedure with the patient, as he normally would have done. The nurses present noticed this error but said nothing, fearing repercussions for questioning a senior professional.

A medical student was present whom, having met the patient previously in clinical, tried to alert the registrar to the mistake he was about to make. The registrar shouted at the student that she should not interrupt surgery; she did not know what she was talking about and asked her to leave. Consequently the surgery proceeded with the end result being that the patient's healthy left kidney was removed, leaving them with only their diseased right kidney, which would eventually lead to the patient's unfortunate death. Frightening as these cases appear what is perhaps scarier is the thought of how those reported may be just the 'tip of the iceberg'.

When questioned about his action to allow his registrar to perform the surgery alone, the consultant had said that it was normal to allow capable registrars to do this. 'While the public perception is that medical knowledge steadily increases over time, this is not the case with many doctors reaching their peak in the middle of their careers.' He had found that his initial increasing interest in surgery had enhanced his abilities, but with time and practice the similar surgeries had become less exciting and so his lack of interest had correlated with worsening outcomes, thus justifying his decision to devolve responsibility in this case.

Question 36:

Which of the following, if true, most weakens the argument above?

A. If incidences are severe enough to occur they will be reported.
B. Doctors undergo extensive training to reduce risks.
C. Thousand of operations happen every year with no problems.
D. Some errors are unavoidable.
E. The patient could have possibly passed away even if the operation had been a complete success.

Question 37:

Which one of the following is the overall conclusion of the statement?

A. The error that occurred was a result of the failure of safety precautions in place.
B. Surgeries should only be performed by surgeons who know their patients well.
C. The human element to medicine means errors will always occur.
D. The safety procedures surrounding surgical procedures need to be reviewed.
E. Some doctors are overconfident.

Question 38:

Which of the following is attributed as the original cause of the error?

A. The medical student not having asserted herself.
B. The poor handwriting in the chart.
C. The hierarchical system of medicine.
D. The registrar not having met the patient.
E. The patient being asleep.
F. The lack of the surgical skill possessed by the registrar.
G. The registrar's poor attitude.

Question 39:

What does the 'tip of the iceberg' refer to in the passage?

A. Problems we face every day.
B. The probable large numbers of medical errors that go unreported.
C. The difficulties of surgery.
D. Reported medical errors.
E. Problems within the NHS.

The following graphs are needed for Questions 40-41:

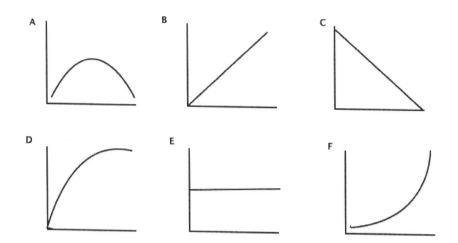

Question 40:

Which graph best describes the consultants' performance versus emotional arousal over his career?

A. A   B. B   C. C   D. D   E. E   F. F

Question 41:

Which graphs best describe the medical knowledge acquired over time?

	Public's Perception	Consultant's Perception
A	B	B
B	B	D
C	B	F
D	D	B
E	D	D
F	D	F
G	F	B
H	F	D
I	F	F

Question 42:

Sadly, in recent times, the lack of exercise associated with sedentary lifestyles has increased in the developed world. The lack of opportunity for exercise is endemic and these countries have also seen a rise of diseases such as diabetes even in young people. In these developed countries, bodily changes such as increased blood pressure, that are usually associated with old age, are rapidly increasing. These are however still uncommon in undeveloped countries, where most people are physically active throughout the entirety of their lives.

Which one of the following can be concluded from the passage above?

A. Exercise has a greater effect on old people than young people.

B. Maintenance of good health is associated with lifelong exercise.

C. Changes in lifestyle will be necessary to cause increased life expectancies in developed countries.

D. Exercise is only beneficial when continued into old age.

E. Obesity and diabetes are the result of lack of exercise.

Questions 43 -45 are based on the passage below:

'Midwives should now encourage women to, as often as possible, give birth at home. Not only is there evidence to suggest that normal births at home are as safe those as in hospital, but it removes the medicalisation of childbirth that emerged over the years. With the increase in availability of health resources we now, too often, use services such as a full medical team for a process that women have been completing single-handedly for thousands of years.

Midwives are extensively trained to assist women during labour at home and capable enough to assess when there is a problem that requires a hospital environment. Expensive hospital births must and should move away from being standard practice, especially in an era where the NHS has far more demands on its services that it can currently afford.'

Question 43:

Which one of the following is the most appropriate conclusion from the statement?

A. People are over dependent on healthcare.

B. Some women prefer to have their babies in hospital.

C. Having a baby in hospital can actually be more risky than at home.

D. Childbirth has been over medicalised.

E. Encouraging women to have their babies at home may relieve some of the financial pressures on the NHS.

F. We should have more midwives than doctors.

Question 44:

Which one of the following if true most weakens the argument presented in the passage above?

A. Some women are scared of home births.

B. Home births are associated with poorer outcomes.

C. Midwives do not like performing home visits.

D. Some home births result in hospital births anyway.

Question 45:

Which one of the following describes what the statement cites as the cause for the 'medicalisation of childbirth'?

A. Women fear giving birth without a full medical team present.

B. Midwives are incapable of aiding childbirth without help.

C. Giving birth at home is not as safe as it used to be.

D. Excessive availability of health services.

Question 46:

We need to stop focussing so much attention on the dangers of fires. In 2011 there were only 242 deaths due to exposure to smoke, fire and flames, while there were 997 deaths from hernias. We need to think more proportionally as these statistics show that campaigns such as 'fire kills' are not necessary as comparison with the risk from the death from hernias clearly shows that fires are not as dangerous as they are perceived to be.

Which of the following statements identify a weakness in the above argument?
1. More people may die in fires if there were no campaigns about their danger and how to prevent them.
2. The smoke of a fire is more dangerous than it flames.
3. There may be more people with hernias than those in fires.

A. 1 only
B. 2 only
C. 3 only
D. 1 and 2 only

E. 1 and 3 only
F. 2 and 3 only
G. 1, 2 and 3

Question 47:

A survey of a school was taken to find out whether there was any correlation between the sports students played and the subjects they liked. The findings were as follows: some football players liked Maths and some of them liked History. All students liked English. None of the basketball players liked History, but all of them, as well as some rugby players liked Chemistry. All rugby players like Geography.

Based on the findings, which one of the below must be true?
A. Some of the footballers liked Maths and History.
B. Some of the rugby players liked three subjects.
C. Some rugby players liked History.
D. Some of the footballers liked English but did not like Maths and History.
E. Some basketball players like more than 3 subjects.

Question 48:

The control of illegal drug use is becoming increasingly difficult. New 'legal highs' are being manufactured which are slightly changed molecularly from illegal compounds so they are not technically illegal. These new 'legal drugs' are being brought onto the street at a rate of at least one per week, and so the authorities cannot keep up.

Some health professionals therefore believe that the legality of drugs is becoming less relevant as to the potentially dangerous side effects. The fact that these new compounds are legal may however mean that the public are not aware of their equally high risks.

Which of the following are implied by the argument?

1. Some health professionals believe there is no value in making drugs illegal.
2. The major problem in controlling illegal drug use is the rapid manufacture of new drugs that are not classified as illegal.
3. The general public are not worried about the risks of legal or illegal highs.
4. There is no longer a good correlation between risk of drug taking and the legal status of the drug.

A. 1 only
B. 2 only
C. 1 and 4
D. 2 and 4
E. 2 and 3
F. 1, 2, 3 and 4

Question 49:

WilderTravel Inc. is a company which organises wilderness travel holidays, with activities such as trekking, mountain climbing, safari tours and wilderness survival courses. These activities carry inherent risks, so the directors of the company are drawing up a set of health regulations, with the aim of minimising the risks by ensuring that nobody participates in activities if they have medical complications meaning that doing so may endanger them.

They consider the following guidelines:

'Persons with pacemakers, asthma or severe allergies are at significant risk of heart attack in low oxygen environments'. People undertaking mountain climbing activities with WilderTravel frequently encounter environments with low oxygen levels. The directors therefore decide that in order to ensure the safety of customers on WilderTravel holidays, one step that must be taken is to bar those with pacemakers, asthma or allergies from partaking in mountain climbing.

Which of the following best illustrates a flaw in this reasoning?

A. Participants should be allowed to assess the safety risks themselves, and should not be barred from activities if they decide the risk is acceptable.

B. They have assumed that all allergies carry an increased risk of heart attack, when the guidelines only say this applies to those with severe allergies.

C. The directors have failed to consider the health risks of people with these conditions taking part in other activities.

D. People with these conditions could partake in mountain climbing with other holiday organisers, and thus be exposed to danger of heart attack.

Question 50:

St John's Hospital in Northumbria is looking to recruit a new consultant cardiologist, and interviews a series of candidates. The interview panel determines that 3 candidates are clearly more qualified for the role than the others, and they invite these 3 candidates for a second interview. During this second interview, and upon further examination of their previous employment records, it becomes apparent that Candidate 3 is the most proficient at surgery of the 3, whilst Candidate 1 is the best at patient interaction and explaining the risks of procedures. Candidate 2, meanwhile, ranks between the other 2 in both these aspects.

The hospital director tells the interviewing team that the hospital already has a well-renowned team dedicated to patient interaction, but the surgical success record at the hospital is in need of improvement. The director issues instructions that therefore, it is more important that the new candidate is proficient at surgery, and patient interaction is less of a concern.

Which of the following is a conclusion that can be drawn from the Directors' comments?

A. The interviewing team should hire Candidate 2, in order to achieve a balance of good patient relations with good surgical records.
B. The interviewing team should hire Candidate 1, in order to ensure good patient interactions, as these are a vital part of a doctor's work.
C. The interviewing team should ignore the hospital director and assess the candidates further to see who would be the best fit.
D. The interviewing team should hire Candidate 3, in order to ensure that the new candidate has excellent surgical skills, to boost the hospital's success in this area.

Question 51:

Every winter in Britain, there are thousands of urgent callouts for ambulances in snowy conditions. The harsh conditions mean that ambulances cannot drive quickly, and are delayed in reaching patients. These delays cause many injuries and medical complications, which could be avoided with quicker access to treatment. Despite this, very few ambulances are equipped with winter tyres or special tyre coverings to help the ambulances deal with snow. Clearly, if more ambulances were fitted with winter tyres, then we could avoid many medical complications that occur each winter.

Which of the following is an assumption made in this passage?

A. Fitting winter tyres would allow ambulances to reach patients more quickly.
B. Ambulance trusts have sufficient funding to equip their vehicles with winter tyres.
C. Many medical complications could be avoided with quicker access to medical care.
D. There are no other alternatives to winter tyres that would allow ambulances to reach patients more quickly in snowy conditions.

Question 52:

Vaccinations have been one of the most outstanding and influential developments in medical history. Despite the huge successes, however, there is a strong anti-vaccination movement active in some countries, particularly the USA, who claim vaccines are harmful and ineffective.

There have been several high-profile events in recent years where anti-vaccine campaigners have been refused permission to enter countries for campaigns, or have had venues refuse to host them due to the nature of their campaigns. Many anti-vaccination campaigners have claimed this is an affront to free speech, and that they should be allowed to enter countries and obtain venues without hindrance. However, although free speech is desirable, an exception must be made here because the anti-vaccination campaign spreads misinformation to parents, causing vaccination to rates to drop.

When this happens, preventable infectious diseases often begin to increase, causing avoidable deaths of innocent members of the community, particularly so in children. Thus, in order to protect innocent people, we must continue to block the anti-vaccine campaigners from spreading misinformation freely by pressuring venues not to host anti-vaccination campaigners.

Which of the following best illustrates the principle that this argument follows?

A. Free speech is always desirable, and must not be compromised under any circumstances.

B. The right of innocent people to protection from infectious diseases is more important than the right of free speech.

C. The right of free speech does not apply when the party speaking is lying or spreading misinformation.

D. Public health programmes that achieve significant success in reducing the incidence of disease should be promoted.

Question 53:

In order for a tumour to grow larger than a few centimetres, it must first establish its own blood supply by promoting angiogenesis. Roger has a tumour in his abdomen, which is investigated at the Royal General Hospital. During the tests, they detect newly formed blood vessels in the tumour, showing that it has established its own blood supply. Thus, we should expect the tumour to grow significantly, and become larger than a few centimetres. Action must be taken to deal with this.

Which of the following **best** illustrates a flaw in this reasoning?

A. It assumes that the tumour in Roger's abdomen has established its own blood supply.

B. It assumes that a blood supply is necessary for a tumour to grow larger than a few centimetres.

C. It assumes that nothing can be done to stop the tumour once a blood supply has been established.

D. It assumes that a blood supply is sufficient for the tumour to grow larger than a few centimetres.

Question 54:

In this year's Great North Run, there are several dozen people running to raise money for the Great North Air Ambulance (GNAA), as part of a large national fundraising campaign. If the runners raise £500,000 between them, then the GNAA will be able to add a new helicopter to its fleet. However, the runners only raise a total of £420,000. Thus, the GNAA will not be able to get a new helicopter.

Which of the following **best** illustrates a flaw in this passage?

A. It has assumed that the GNAA will not be able to acquire a new helicopter without the runners raising £500,000.

B. It has assumed that that GNAA wishes to add a new helicopter to its fleet.

C. It has assumed that the GNAA does not have better things to spend the money on.

D. It has assumed that some running in the Great North Run are raising money for the GNAA.

Question 55:

Many courses, spanning Universities, colleges, apprenticeship institutions and adult skills courses should be subsidised by the government. This is because they improve the skills of those attending them. It has been well demonstrated that the more skilled people are, the more productive they are economically. Thus, government subsidies of many courses would increase overall economic productivity, and lead to increased growth.

Which of the following would most weaken this argument?

A. The UK already has a high level of growth, and does not need to accelerate this growth.
B. Research has demonstrated that higher numbers of people attending adult skills courses results in increased economic growth.
C. Research has demonstrated that the cost of many courses (to those taking them) has little effect on the number of people undertaking the courses.
D. Employers often seek to employ those with greater skill-sets, and appoint them to higher positions.

Question 56:

Pluto was once considered the 9th planet in the solar system. However, further study of the planet led to it being reclassified as a dwarf planet in 2006. One key factor in this reclassification was the discovery of many objects in the solar system with similar characteristics to Pluto, which were also placed into this new category of 'Dwarf Planet'. Some astronomers believe that Pluto should remain classified as a planet, along with the many entities similar to Pluto that have been discovered. Considering all of this, it is clear that if we were to reclassify Pluto as a planet, and maintain consistency with classification of astronomical entities, then the number of planets would significantly increase.

Which of the following best illustrates the main conclusion of this passage?
A. If Pluto is classified as a planet, then many other entities should also be planets, as they share similar characteristics.
B. Some astronomers believe Pluto should be classified as a planet.
C. Pluto should not be classified as a Planet, as this would also require many other entities to be classified as planets to ensure consistency.
D. If Pluto is to be classified as a planet, then the number of objects classified as planets should increase significantly.

Question 57:

2 trains depart from Birmingham at 5:30 pm. One of the trains is heading to London, whilst the other is heading to Glasgow. The distance from Birmingham to Glasgow is three times larger than the distance from Birmingham to London, and the train to London arrives at 6:30 pm. Thus, the train to Glasgow will arrive at 8:30pm.

Which of the following is an assumption made in this passage?

A. Both trains depart at the same time.
B. Both trains depart from Birmingham.
C. Both trains travel at the same speed.
D. The train heading to Glasgow has to travel three times as far as the train heading to London.

Question 58:

Carcinogenesis, oncogenesis and tumorigenesis are various names given to the generation of cancer, with the term literally meaning 'creation of cancer'. In order for carcinogenesis to happen, there are several steps that must occur. Firstly, a cell (or group of cells) must achieve immortality, and escape senescence (the inherent limitation of a cell's lifespan). Then they must escape regulation by the body, and begin to proliferate in an autonomous way. They must also become immune to apoptosis and other cell death mechanisms. Finally, they must avoid detection by the immune system, or survive its responses. If a single one of these steps fails to occur, then carcinogenesis will not be able to occur.

Which of the following is a conclusion that can be reliably drawn from this passage?

A. Several steps are essential for carcinogenesis.
B. If all the steps mentioned occur, then carcinogenesis will definitely occur.
C. The immune system is unable to tackle cells that have escaped regulation by the body.
D. There are various mechanisms by which carcinogenesis can occur.
E. The terminology for the creation of cancer is confusing.

Question 59:

P53 is one of the most crucial genes in the body, responsible for detecting DNA damage and halting cell replication until repair can occur. If repair cannot take place, P53 will signal for the cell to kill itself. These actions are crucial to prevent carcinogenesis, and a loss of functional P53 is identified in over 50% of all cancers. The huge importance of P53 towards protecting the cell from damaging mutations has led to it deservedly being known as 'the guardian of the genome'. The implications of this name are clear – any cell that has a mutation in P53 is at serious risk of developing a potentially dangerous mutation.

Which of the following **CANNOT** be reliably concluded from this passage?
A. P53 is responsible for detecting DNA damage.
B. Most cancers have lost functional P53.
C. P53 deserves its name 'guardian of the genome'.
D. A cell that has a mutation in P53 will develop damaging mutations.
E. None of the above.

Question 60:

Sam is buying a new car, and deciding whether to buy a petrol or a diesel model. He knows he will drive 9,000 miles each year. He calculates that if he drives a petrol car, he will spend £500 per 1,000 miles on fuel, but if he buys a diesel model he will only spend £300 per 1,000 miles on fuel.

He calculates, therefore, that if he purchases a Diesel car, then this year he will make a saving of £1800, compared to if he bought the petrol car.

Which of the following is **NOT** an assumption that Sam has made?
A. The price of diesel will not fluctuate relative to that of petrol.
B. The cars will have the same initial purchase cost.
C. The cars will have the same costs for maintenance and garage expenses.
D. The cars will use the same amount of fuel.
E. All of the above are assumptions.

Question 61:

In the UK, cannabis is classified as a Class B drug, with a maximum penalty of up to 5 years imprisonment for possession, or up to 14 years for possession with intent to supply. The justification for drug laws in the UK is that classified drugs are harmful, addictive, and destructive to people's lives. However, available medical evidence indicates that cannabis is relatively safe, non-addictive and harmless. In particular, it is certainly shown to be less dangerous than alcohol, which is freely sold and advertised in the UK. The fact that alcohol can be freely sold and advertised, but cannabis, a less harmful drug, is banned highlights the gross inconsistencies in UK drugs policy.

Which of the following best illustrates the main conclusion of this passage?
A. Cannabis is a less dangerous drug than alcohol.
B. Alcohol should be banned, so we can ensure consistency in the UK drug policy.
C. Cannabis should not be banned, and should be sold freely, in order to ensure consistency in the UK drug policy.
D. The UK government's policy on drugs is grossly inconsistent.
E. Alcohol should not be advertised in the UK.

Question 62:

Every year in Britain, there are thousands of accidents at people's homes such as burns, broken limbs and severe cuts, which cause a large number of deaths and injuries. Despite this, very few households maintain a sufficient first aid kit equipped with bandages, burn treatments, splints and saline to clean wounds. If more households stocked sufficient first aid supplies, many of these accidents could be avoided.

Which of the following best illustrates a flaw in this argument?
A. It ignores the huge cost associated with maintaining good first aid supplies, which many households cannot afford.
B. It implies that presence of first aid equipment will lead to fewer accidents.
C. It ignores the many accidents that could not be treated even if first aid supplies were readily available.
D. It neglects to consider the need for trained first aid persons in order for first aid supplies to help in reducing the severity of injuries caused by accidents.

Question 63:

Researchers at SmithJones Inc., an international drug firm, are investigating a well-known historic compound, which is thought to reduce levels of DNA replication by inhibiting DNA polymerases. It is proposed that this may be able to be used to combat cancer by reducing the proliferation of cancer cells, allowing the immune system to combat them before they spread too far and become too damaging. Old experiments have demonstrated the effectiveness of the compound via monitoring DNA levels with a dye that stains DNA red, thus monitoring the levels of DNA present in cell clusters. They report that the compound is observed to reduce the rate at which DNA replicates.

However, it is known that if researchers use the wrong solutions when carrying out these experiments, then the amount of red staining will decrease, suggesting DNA replication has been inhibited, even if it is not inhibited. As several researchers previously used this wrong solution, we can conclude that these experiments are flawed, and do not reflect what is actually happening.

Which of the following best illustrates a flaw in this argument?

A. From the fact that the compound inhibits DNA replication, it cannot be concluded that it has potential as an anticancer drug.
B. From the fact that the wrong solutions were used, it cannot be concluded that the experiments may produce misleading results.
C. From the fact that the experiments are old, it cannot be concluded that the wrong solutions were used.
D. From the fact that the compound is old, it cannot be concluded that it is safe.

Question 64:

Rotherham football club are currently top of the league, with 90 points. Their closest competitors are South Shields football club, with 84 points. Next week, the teams will play each other, and after this, they each have 2 games left before the end of the season. Each win is worth 3 points, a draw is worth 1 point, and a loss is worth 0 points. Thus, if Rotherham beat South Shields, they will win the league (as they will then be 9 points clear, and South Shields would only be able to earn 6 more points).

In the match of Rotherham vs. South Shields, Rotherham are winning until the 85th minute, when Alberto Simeone scores an equaliser for South Shields, and South Shields then go on to win the match. Thus, Rotherham will not win the league.

Which of the following best illustrates a flaw in this passage's reasoning?

A. It has assumed that Alberto Simeone scored the winning goal for South Shields.

B. It has assumed that beating South Shields was necessary for Rotherham to win the league, when in fact it was only sufficient.

C. Rotherham may have scored an equaliser later in the game, and not lost the match.

D. It has failed to consider what other teams might win the league.

Question 65:

Oakville Supermarkets is looking to build a new superstore, and a meeting of its directors has been convened to decide where the best place to build the supermarket would be. The Chairperson of the Board suggests that the best place would be Warrington, a town that does not currently have a large supermarket, and would thus give them an excellent share of the shopping market.

However, the CEO notes that the population of Warrington has been steadily declining for several years, whilst Middlesbrough has recently been experiencing high population growth. The CEO therefore argues that they should build the new supermarket in Middlesbrough, as they would then be within range of more people, and so of more potential customers.

Which of the following best illustrates a flaw in the CEO's reasoning?

A. Middlesbrough may already have other supermarkets, so the new superstore may get a lower share of the town's shoppers.
B. Despite the recent population changes, Warrington may still have a larger population than Middlesbrough.
C. Middlesbrough's population is projected to continue growing, whilst Warrington's is projected to keep falling.
D. Many people in Warrington travel to Liverpool or Manchester, 2 nearby major cities, in order to do their shopping.

Question 66:

Global warming is a key challenge facing the world today, and the changes in weather patterns caused by this phenomenon have led to the destruction of many natural habitats, causing many species to become extinct. Recent data has shown that extinctions have been occurring at a faster rate over the last 40 years than at any other point in the earth's history, exceeding the great Permian mass extinction, which wiped out 96% of life on earth. If this rate continues, over 50% of species on earth will be extinct by 2100. It is clear that in the face of this huge challenge, conservation programmes will require significantly increased levels of funding in order to prevent most of the species on earth from becoming extinct.

Which of the following are assumptions in this argument?

1. The rate of extinctions seen in the last 40 years will continue to occur without a step-up in conservation efforts.
2. Conservation programmes cannot prevent further extinctions without increased funding.
3. Global warming has caused many extinction events, directly or indirectly.

A.   1 only
B.   2 only
C.   3 only
D.   1 and 2
E.   1 and 3
F.   2 and 3
G.   1, 2 and 3

Question 67:

After an election in Britain, the new government is debating what policy to adopt on the railway system, and whether it should be entirely privatised, or whether public subsidies should be used to supplement costs and ensure that sufficient services are run. Studies in Austria, which has high public funding for railways, have shown that the rail service is used by many people, and is highly thought of by the population. However, this is clearly down to the fact that Austria has many mountainous and high-altitude areas, which experience significant amounts of snow and ice. This makes many roads impassable, and travelling by road difficult. Thus, rail is often the only way to travel, explaining the high passenger numbers and approval ratings. Thus, the high public subsidies clearly have no effect.

Which of the following, if true, would weaken this argument?

1. France also has high public subsidy of railways, but does not have large areas where travel by road is difficult. The French railway also has high passenger numbers and approval ratings.
2. Italy also has high public subsidy of railways, but the local population dislike using the rail service, and it has poor passenger numbers.
3. There are many reasons affecting the passenger numbers and approval ratings of a given country's rail serviced.

A. 1 only
B. 2 only
C. 3 only
D. 1 and 2
E. 1 and 3
F. 2 and 3

Questions 68 & 69 are based on the passage below:

Tobacco companies sell cigarettes despite being fully aware that cigarettes cause significant harm to the wellbeing of those that smoke them. Diseases caused or aggravated by smoking cost billions of pounds for the NHS to treat each year. This is extremely irresponsible behaviour from the tobacco companies. Tobacco companies should be taxed, and the money raised put towards funding the NHS.

Question 68:

Which of these following arguments best illustrates the principle used in this argument?

A. Many homeless people in the UK cannot afford medical treatment. This is morally outrageous, as many are homeless through no fault of their own. Therefore, we should tax the rich in the UK, and use the money to fund medical treatment for the homeless.

B. Alcohol induced diseases such as liver failure cost significant amounts to treat, and put a large strain on the NHS. Therefore, people who drink heavily and then suffer from alcohol induced diseases should be made to pay for their own medical treatment.

C. Many people are poor due to spending large amounts of money on gambling or other wasteful obsessions. People such as this, who are poor through their own fault, should not receive free medical treatment. Free medical treatment should only go to those who cannot afford it through no fault of their own.

D. People who use private healthcare providers should not be forced to pay taxes that go towards funding the NHS. People should only be forced to contribute money to the NHS if they use the services it provides.

E. Fireworks are responsible for starting large numbers of fires each year, killing many people and putting a significant strain on the fire service. Despite this, companies continue to sell fireworks. Therefore, companies selling fireworks should be taxed to provide extra funding for the fire service.

Question 69:

Which of the following conclusions **CANNOT** be drawn from the above?

A. There is a connection between lung cancer and smoking.

B. There is a connection between liver disease and smoking.

C. There is a connection between oral cancer and smoking.

D. All smokers drink excessively.

E. All of the above.

Question 70:

Investigations in the origins of species suggest that humans and the great apes have the same ancestors. This is suggested by the high degree of genetic similarity between humans and chimpanzees (estimated at 99%). At the same time there is an 84% homology between the human genome and that of pigs. This raises the interesting question of whether it would be possible to use pig or chimpanzee organs for the treatment of human disease.

Which conclusion can be reasonably drawn from the above article?

A. Pigs and chimpanzees have a common ancestor.
B. Pigs and humans have a common ancestor.
C. It can be assumed that chimpanzees will develop into humans if given enough time.
D. There seems to be great genetic homology across a variety of species.
E. Organs from pigs or chimpanzees present a good alternative for human organ donation.

Question 71:

Poor blood supply to a part of the body can cause damage of the affected tissue - i.e. lead to an infarction. There are a variety of known risk factors for vascular disease. Diabetes is a major risk factor. Other risk factors are more dependent on the individual as they represent individual choices such as smoking, poor dietary habits as well as little to no exercise. In some cases infarction of the limbs and in particular the feet can become very bad and extensive with patches of tissue dying. This is known as necrosis and is marked by affected area of the body turning black. Necrotic tissue is usually removed in surgery.

Which of the following statements **CANNOT** be concluded from the information in the above passage?

A. Smoking causes vascular disease.
B. Diabetes causes vascular disease.
C. Vascular disease always leads to infarctions.
D. Necrotic tissue must be removed surgically.
E. Necrotic tissue only occurs following severe infarction.
F. All of the above

Question 72:

People who can afford to pay for private education should not have access to the state school system. This would allow more funding for students from lower income backgrounds. More funding will provide better resources for students from lower income backgrounds, and will help to bridge the gap in educational attainment between students from higher income and lower income backgrounds.

Which of the following statements, if true, would most strengthen the above argument?

A. Educational attainment is a significant factor in determining future prospects.

B. Providing better resources for students has been demonstrated to lead to an increase in educational attainment.

C. Most people who can afford to do so choose to purchase private education for their children.

D. A significant gap exists in educational attainment between students from high income and low-income backgrounds.

E. Most schools currently receive a similar amount of funding relative to the number of students in the school.

Question 73:

Increasing numbers of people are choosing to watch films on DVD in recent years. In the past few years, cinemas have lost customers, causing them to close down. Many cinemas have recently closed, removing an important focal point for many local communities and causing damage to those communities. Therefore, we should ban DVDs in order to help local communities.

Which of the following best states an assumption made in this argument?

A. The cinemas that have recently closed have done so because of reduced profits due to people choosing to watch DVDs instead.

B. Cinemas being forced to close causes damage to local communities.

C. DVDs are improving local communities by allowing people to meet up and watch films together.

D. Sales of DVDs have increased due to economic growth.

E. Local communities have called for DVDs to be banned.

Question 74:

Aeroplanes are the fastest form of transport available. An aeroplane can travel a given distance in less time than a train or a car. John needs to travel from Glasgow to Birmingham. If he wants to arrive as soon as possible, he should travel by aeroplane.

Which of the following best illustrates a flaw in this argument?

A. One day, there could be faster cars built that could travel as fast as aeroplanes.

B. Travelling by air is often more expensive.

C. It ignores the time taken to travel to an airport and check in to a flight, which may mean he will arrive later if travelling by aeroplane.

D. John may not own a car, and thus may not have any option.

E. John may not be legally allowed to make the journey.

Question 75:

During autumn, spiders frequently enter people's homes to escape the cold weather. Many people dislike spiders and seek ways to prevent them from entering properties, leading to spider populations falling as they struggle to cope with the cold weather. Studies have demonstrated that when spider populations fall, the population of flies rises. Higher numbers of flies are associated with an increase in food poisoning cases. Therefore, people must not seek to prevent spiders from entering their homes.

Which of the following best illustrates the main conclusion of this argument?

A. People should not dislike spiders being present in their homes.

B. People should seek methods to prevent flies from entering their homes.

C. People should actively encourage spiders to occupy their homes to increase biodiversity.

D. People should accept the presence of spiders in their homes to reduce the incidence of food poisoning.

E. Spiders should be cultivated and used as a biological pest control to combat flies.

Question 76:

Each year, thousands of people acquire infections during prolonged stays at hospital. Concurrently, bacteria are becoming resistant to antibiotics at an ever-increasing rate. In spite of this, progressively less pharmaceutical companies are investing in research into new antibiotics, and the number of antibiotics coming onto the market is decreasing. As a result, the number of antibiotics that can be used to treat infections is falling. If pharmaceutical companies were pressured into investing in new antibiotic research, many lives could be saved.

Which of the following best illustrates a flaw in this argument?

A. It assumes the infections acquired during stays at hospital are resulting in deaths.
B. It ignores the fact that many people never have to stay in hospital.
C. It does not take into account the fact that antibiotics do not produce much profit for pharmaceutical companies.
D. It ignores the fact that some hospital-acquired infections are caused by organisms that cannot be treated by antibiotics, such as viruses.
E. It assumes that bacterial resistance to antibiotics has not been happening for some time.

Question 77:

Katherine has shaved her armpits most of her adult life, but has now decided to stop. She explains her reasons for this to John, saying she does not like the pressures society puts on women to be shaven in this area. John listens to her reasons, but ultimately responds 'just because you explain why I should find your hairiness attractive, it does not mean I will. I find you unattractive, as I do not like girls with hair on their arm pits.'

What assumption has John made?

A. That just because he finds Katherine unattractive, he would find other girls with unshaven arm pits unattractive.
B. That Katherine is trying to make John find her armpit hair attractive.
C. That Katherine will never conceal her armpit hair.
D. Katherine must be wrong, because she is a woman.
E. That Katherine thinks women should stop shaving.

Question 78:

Medicine has improved significantly over the last century. Better medicine causes a reduction in the death rate from all causes. However, as people get older, they suffer from infectious disease more readily.

Many third world countries have a high rate of deaths from infectious disease. Sunita argues that this high death rate is caused by better medicine, which has given an ageing population, thus giving a high rate of deaths from infectious disease as elderly people suffer from infectious disease more readily. Sunita believes that better medicine is thus indirectly responsible for this high death rate from infectious disease.

However, this cannot be the case. In third world countries, most people do not live to old age, often dying from infectious disease at a young age. Therefore, an ageing population cannot be the reason behind the high rate of death from infectious disease. As better medicine causes a reduction in the death rate from all causes, it is clear that better medicine will lead to a reduction in the death rate from infectious disease in third world countries.

Which of the following best states the main conclusion of this argument?

A. We can expect that improvements in medicine seen over the last century will improve.
B. Better medicine is not responsible for the increased prevalence of infectious disease in third world countries.
C. Better medicine has caused the overall death rate of third world countries to increase.
D. Better medicine will cause a decrease in the rate of death from infectious disease in third world countries.
E. As people get older, they suffer from infectious disease more readily.

Question 79:

Bristol and Cardiff are 2 cities with similar demographics, and located in a roughly similar area of the country. Bristol has higher demand for housing than Cardiff. Therefore, a house in Bristol will cost more than a similar house in Cardiff.

Which of the following best illustrates an assumption in the statement above?
A. House prices will be higher if demand for housing is higher.
B. People can commute from Cardiff to Bristol.
C. Supply of housing in Cardiff will not be lower than in Bristol.
D. Bristol is a better place to live.
E. Cardiff has sufficient housing to provide for the needs of its communities.

Question 80:

Jellicoe Motors is a small motor company in Sheffield, employing 3 people. The company is hiring a new mechanic and interviews several candidates. New research into production lines has indicated that having employees with a good ability to work as part of a team boosts a company's productivity and profits. Therefore, Jellicoe motors should hire a candidate with good team-working skills.

Which of the following best illustrates the main conclusion of this argument?
A. Jellicoe Motors should not hire a new mechanic.
B. Jellicoe motors should hire a candidate with good team-working skills in order to boost their productivity and profits.
C. Jellicoe motors should hire several new candidates in order to form a good team, and boost their productivity.
D. If Jellicoe motors does not hire a candidate with good team-working skills, they may struggle to be profitable.
E. Jellicoe motors should not listen to the new research.

Question 81:

Research into new antibiotics does not normally hold much profit for pharmaceutical firms. As a consequence many firms are not investing in antibiotic research, and very few new antibiotics are being produced. However, with bacteria becoming increasingly resistant to current antibiotics, new ones are desperately needed to avoid running the risk of thousands of deaths from bacterial infections. Therefore, the UK government must provide financial incentives for pharmaceutical companies to invest in research into new antibiotics.

Which of the following best expresses the main conclusion of this argument?

A. If bacteria continue to become resistant to antibiotics, there could be thousands of deaths from bacterial infections.
B. Pharmaceutical firms are not investing in new antibiotic research due to a lack of potential profit.
C. If the UK government invests in research into new antibiotics, thousands of lives will be saved.
D. The pharmaceutical firms should invest in areas of research that are profitable, and ignore antibiotic research.
E. The UK government must provide financial incentives for pharmaceutical firms to invest into antibiotic research if it wishes to avoid risking thousands of deaths from bacterial infections.

Question 82:

People in developing countries use far less water per person than those in developed countries. It is estimated that at present, people in the developing world use an average of 30 litres of water per person per day, whilst those in developed countries use on average 70 litres of water per person per day. It is estimated that for the current world population, an average water usage of 60 litres per person per day would be sustainable, but any higher than this would be unsustainable.

The UN has set development targets such that in 20 years, people living in developing countries will be using the same amount of water per person per day as those living in developed countries. Assuming the world population stays constant for the next 20 years, if these targets are met the world's population will be using water at an unsustainable rate.

Which of the following, if true, would most weaken the argument above?

A. The prices of water bills are dropping in developed countries like the UK.
B. The level of water usage in developed countries is falling, and may be below 60 litres per person per day in 20 years.
C. The population of all developing countries is less than the population of all developed countries.
D. Climate change is likely to decrease the amount of water available for human use over the next 20 years.
E. The UN's development targets are unlikely to be met.

Question 83:

In this Senior Management post we need someone who can keep a cool head in a crisis and react quickly to events. The applicant says he suffers from a phobia about flying, and panics especially when an aircraft is landing and that therefore he would prefer not to travel abroad on business if it could be avoided. He is obviously a very nervous type of person who would clearly go to pieces and panic in an emergency and fail to provide the leadership qualities necessary for the job. Therefore this person is not a suitable candidate for the post.

Which of the following highlights the biggest flaw in the argument above?

A. It falsely assumes phobias are not treatable or capable of being eliminated.
B. It falsely assumes that the person appointed to the job will need to travel abroad.
C. It falsely assumes that a specific phobia indicates a general tendency to panic.
D. It falsely assumes that people who stay cool in a crisis will be good leaders.
E. It fails to take into account other qualities the person might have for the post.

Question 84:

There are significant numbers of people attending university every year, as many as 45% of 18 year olds. As a result, there are many more graduates entering the workforce with better skills and better earning potential. Going to university makes economic sense and we should encourage as many people to go there as possible.

Which of the following highlights the biggest flaw in the argument above?

A. There are no more university places left.
B. Students can succeed without going to university.
C. Not all degrees equip students with the skills needed to earn higher salaries.
D. Some universities are better than others.

Question 85:

Young people spend too much time watching television, which is bad for them. Watching excessive amounts of TV is linked to obesity, social exclusion and can cause eye damage. If young people were to spend just one evening a week playing sport or going for a walk the benefits would be manifold. They would lose weight, feel better about themselves and it would be a sociable activity. Exercise is also linked to strong performance at school and so young people would be more likely to perform well in their exams.

Which of the following highlights the biggest flaw in the argument above?

A. Young people can watch sport on television.
B. There are many factors that affect exam performance.
C. Television does not necessarily have any damaging effect.
D. Television and sport are not linked.

Question 86:

Campaigners pushing for legalisation of cannabis have many arguments for their cause. Most claim there is little evidence of any adverse effects to health caused by cannabis usage, that many otherwise law-abiding people are users of cannabis and that in any case, prohibition of drugs does not reduce their usage. Legalising cannabis would also reduce crime associated with drug trafficking and would provide an additional revenue stream for the government.

Which of the following best represents the conclusion of the passage?

A. Regular cannabis users are unlikely to have health problems.
B. Legalising cannabis would be good for cannabis users.
C. There are multiple reasons to legalise cannabis.
D. Prohibition is an effective measure to reduce drugs usage.
E. Drug associated crime would reduce if cannabis was legal.

Question 87:

Mohan has been offered a new job in Birmingham, starting in several months with a fixed salary. In order to ensure he can afford to live in Birmingham on his new salary, Mohan compares the prices of some houses in Birmingham. He finds that a 2 bedroomed house will cost £200,000. A 3 bedroomed house will cost £250,000. A 4 bedroomed house with a garden will cost £300,000.

Mohan's bank tells him that if he is earning the salary of the job he has been offered, they will grant him a mortgage for a house costing up to £275,000. After a month of deliberation, Mohan accepts the job and decides to move to Wolverhampton. He begins searching for a house to buy. He reasons that he will not be able to purchase a 4-bedroomed house.

Which of the following is **NOT** an assumption that Mohan has made?

A. A house in Wolverhampton will cost the same as a similar house in Birmingham.
B. A different bank will not offer him a mortgage for a more expensive house on the same salary.
C. The salary for the job could increase, allowing him to purchase a more expensive house.
D. A 4-bedroomed house without a garden will not cost less than a 4-bedroomed house with a garden.
E. House prices in Birmingham will not have fall in the time between now and Mohan purchasing a house.

Question 88:

We should teach the Holocaust in schools. It is important that young people see what it was like for Jewish people under Nazi rule. If we expose the harsh realities to impressionable people then this will help improve tolerance of other races. It will also prevent other such terrible events happening again.

Which is the best conclusion?
A. We should teach about the Holocaust in schools.
B. The Holocaust was a tragedy.
C. The Nazis were evil.
D. We should not let terrible events happen again.
E. Educating people is the best solution to the world's problems.

Question 89:

The popular series 'Game of Thrones' should not be allowed on television because it shows scenes of a disturbing nature, in particular scenes of rape. Children may find themselves watching the programme on TV, and then going on to commit the terrible crime of rape, mimicking what they have watched.

Which of the following best illustrates a flaw in this argument?

A. Children may also watch the show on DVD.
B. Adults may watch the show on television.
C. Watching an action does not necessarily lead to recreating the action yourself.
D. There are lots of non-violent scenes in the show.

Question 90:

The TV series 'House of Cards' teaches us all a valuable lesson: the world is not a place that rewards kind behaviour. The protagonist of the series, Frank Underwood, uses intrigue and guile to achieve his goals, and through clever political tactics he is able to climb in rank. If he were to be kinder to people, he would not be able to be so successful. Success is predicated on his refusal to conform to conventional morality. The TV series should be shown to small children in schools, as it could teach them how to achieve their dreams.

Which of the following is an assumption made in the argument?

A. Children pay attention to school lessons.
B. The TV series is sufficiently entertaining.
C. One cannot both obey a moral code and succeed.
D. Frank Underwood is a likable character.

Question 91:

Freddy makes lewd comments on a female passer-by's body to his friend, Neil, loud enough for the woman in question to hear. Neil is uncomfortable with this, and states that it is inappropriate for Freddy to do so, and that Freddy is being sexist. Freddy refutes this, and Neil retorts that Freddy would not make these comments about a man's body. Freddy replies by saying 'it is not sexist, I am a feminist, I believe in equality for men and women.'

Which of the following describes a flaw made in Freddy's logic?
A. A self-proclaimed feminist could still say a sexist thing.
B. The female passer-by in question felt uncomfortable.
C. Neil, too, considers himself a feminist.
D. It would still not be okay to make lewd comments at male passers-by.
E. Lewd comments are always inappropriate.

Question 92:

The release of CO_2 from consumption of fossil fuels is the main reason behind global warming, which is causing significant damage to many natural environments throughout the world. One significant source of CO_2 emissions is cars, which release CO_2 as they use up petrol. In order to tackle this problem, many car companies have begun to design cars with engines that do not use as much petrol. However, engines which use less petrol are not as powerful, and less powerful cars are not attractive to the public. If a car company produces cars which are not attractive to the public, they will not be profitable.

Which of the following best illustrates the main conclusion of this argument?
A. Car companies which produce cars that use less petrol will not be profitable.
B. The public prefer more powerful cars.
C. Car companies should prioritise profits over helping the environment.
D. Car companies should seek to produce engines that use less petrol but are still just as powerful.
E. The public are not interested in helping the environment.

SECTION 1: Problem Solving

Section 1 problem solving questions are arguably the hardest to prepare for. However, there are some useful techniques you can employ to solve some types of questions much more quickly:

Constructing Equations

Some of the problems in Section 1 are quite complex and you'll need to be comfortable with turning prose into equations and manipulating them. For example, when you read "Mark is twice as old as Jon" – this should immediately register as $M = 2J$. Once you get comfortable forming equations, you can start to approach some of the harder questions in this book (and past papers) which may require you to form and solve simultaneous equations. Consider the example:

$$H + C = 44$$
$$4H + 2C = 132$$
$$2H = 44$$
$$H = 22$$
$$C = 22$$

Nick has a sleigh that contains toy horses and clowns and counts 44 heads and 132 legs in his sleigh. Given that horses have one head and four legs, and clowns have one head and two legs, calculate the difference between the number of horses and clowns.

A. 0   B. 5   C. 22   D. 28   E. 132

To start with, let C = Clowns and H = Horses.
For Heads: $C + H = 44$; For Legs: $2C + 4H = 132$
This now sets up your two equations that you can solve simultaneously.
$C = 44 - H$ so $2(44 - H) + 4H = 132$
Thus, $88 - 2H + 4H = 132$;
Therefore, $2H = 44$; $H = 22$
Substitute back in to give $C = 44 - H = 44 - 22 = 22$
Thus the difference between horses and clowns $= C - H = 22 - 22 = 0$

It is important you are able to do these types of questions quickly (and without resorting to trial & error as they are commonplace in section 1.

Diagrams

When a question asks about timetables, orders or sequences, draw out diagrams. By doing this, you can organise your thoughts and help make sense of the question.

"Mordor is West of Gondor but East of Rivendale. Lorien is midway between Gondor and Mordor. Erebus is West of Mordor. Eden is not East of Gondor."

*Which of the following **cannot** be concluded?*

A. Lorien is East of Erebus and Mordor.
B. Mordor is West of Gondor and East of Erebus.
C. Rivendale is west of Lorien and Gondor.
D. Gondor is East of Mordor and East of Lorien
E. Erebus is West of Mordor and West of Rivendale.

Whilst it is possible to solve this in your head, it becomes much more manageable if you draw a quick diagram and plot the positions of each town:

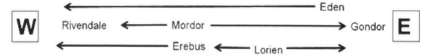

Now, it's a simple case of going through each option and seeing if it is correct according to the diagram. You can now easily see that Option E- Erebus cannot be west of Rivendale.

Don't feel that you have to restrict yourself to linear diagrams like this either – for some questions you may need to draw tables or even Venn diagrams.

Consider the example:

Slifers and Osiris are not legendary. Krakens and Minotaurs are legendary. Minotaurs and Lords are both divine. Humans are neither legendary nor divine.

A. Krakens may be only legendary or legendary and divine.
B. Humans are not divine
C. Slifers are only divine.
D. Osiris may be divine.
E. Humans and Slifers are the same in terms of both qualities.

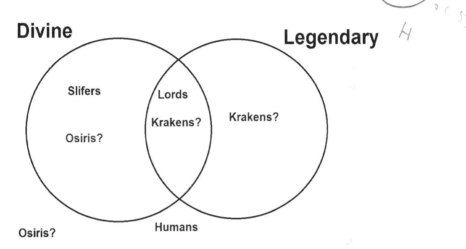

Constructing a Venn diagram allows us to quickly see that the position of Osiris and Krakens aren't certain. Thus, A and D must be true. Humans are neither so B is true. Krakens may be divine so A is true. E cannot be concluded as Slifers are divine but are humans are not. Thus, E is False.

Spatial Reasoning

There are usually 1-2 spatial reasoning questions every year. They usually give nets for a shape or a patterned cuboid and ask which options are possible rotations. Unfortunately, they are extremely difficult to prepare for because the skills necessary to solve these types of questions can take a very long time to improve.

The best thing you can do to prepare is to familiarise yourself with the basics of how cube nets work and what the effect of transformations are e.g. what happens if a shape is reflected in a mirror etc. It is also a good idea to try to learn to draw basic shapes like cubes from multiple angles if you can't do so already.

Options First

Despite the fact that you may have lots of data to contend with, the rule about looking at the options first still stands in this section. This will allow you to register what type of calculation you are required to make and what data you might need to look at for this. Remember, Options → Question → Data/Passage.

Working with Numbers

Percentages frequently make an appearance in this section and it's vital that you're able to work comfortably with them. For example, you should be able to comfortable increasing and decreasing by percentages, and working out inverse percentages too. When dealing with complex percentages, break them down into their components. E.g. $17.5\% = 10\% + 5\% + 2.5\%$

Problem Solving Questions

Question 93:

Pilbury is south of Westside, which is south of Harrington. Twotown is north of Pilbury and Crewville but not further north than Westside. Crewville is:

A. South of Westside, Pilbury and Harrington but not necessarily Twotown.
B. North of Pilbury, and Westside.
C. South of Westside and Twotown, but north of Pilbury.
D. South of Westside, Harrington and Twotown but not necessarily Pilbury.
E. South of Harrington, Westside, Twotown and Pilbury.

Question 94:

The hospital coordinator is making the rota for the ward for next week; two of Drs Evans, James and Luca must be working on weekdays, none of them on Sundays and all of them on Saturdays. Dr Evans works 4 days a week including Mondays and Fridays. Dr Luca cannot work Monday or Thursday Only Dr James can work 4 days consecutively, but he cannot do 5.

What days does Dr James work?

A. Saturday, Sunday and Monday.
B. Monday, Tuesday, Wednesday, Thursday and Saturday.
C. Monday, Thursday Friday and Saturday.
D. Tuesday, Wednesday, Friday and Saturday.
E. Monday, Tuesday, Wednesday, Thursday and Friday.

Question 95:

Michael, a taxi driver, charges a call out rate and a rate per mile for taxi rides. For a 4 mile ride he charges £11, and for a 5 mile ride, £13.
How much does he charge for a 9-mile ride?

A. £15   B. £17   C. £19   D. £20   E. £21

Question 96:

Goblins and trolls are not magical. Fairies and goblins are both mythical. Elves and fairies are magical. Gnomes are neither mythical nor magical.

Which of the following is not true?

A. Elves may be only magical or magical and mythical.
B. Gnomes are not mythical.
C. Goblins are only mythical.
D. Trolls may be mythical.
E. Gnomes and goblins are the same in terms of both qualities.

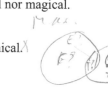

Question 97:

Jessica runs a small business making bespoke wall tiles. She has just had a rush order for 100 tiles placed that must be ready for today at 7 PM. The client wants the tiles packed all together, a process which will take 15 minutes. Only 50 tiles can go in the kiln at any point and they must be put in the kiln to heat for 45 minutes. The tiles then sit in the kiln to cool before they can be packed, a process which takes 20 minutes. While tiles are in the kiln Jessica is able to decorate more tiles at a rate of 1 tile per minute.

What is the latest time Jessica can start making the tiles?

A. 2:55pm B. 3:15pm C. 3:30pm D. 3:45pm

Question 98:

Pain nerve impulses are twice as fast as normal touch impulses. If Yun touches a boiling hot pan this message reaches her brain, 1 metre away, in 1 millisecond. What is the speed of a normal touch impulse?

A. 5 m/s C. 50 m/s E. 500 m/s
B. 20 m/s D. 200m/s

Question 99:

A woman has two children Melissa and Jack, yearly, their birthdays are 3 months apart, both being on the 22nd. The woman wishes to continue the trend of her children's names beginning with the same letter as the month they were born. If her next child, Alina is born on the 22nd 2 months after Jack's birthday, how many months after Alina is born will Melissa have her next birthday?

A. 2 months C. 5 months E. 7 months
B. 4 months D. 6 months

Question 100:

Policemen work in pairs. PC Carter, PC Dirk, PC Adams and PC Bryan must work together but not for more than seven days in a row, which PC Adams and PC Bryan now have. PC Dirk has worked with PC Carter for 3 days in a row. PC Carter does not want to work with PC Adams if it can be avoided.

Who should work with PC Bryan?

A. PC Carter
B. PC Dirk
C. PC Adams
D. Nobody is available under the guidelines above.

7 Adams Bryan
3 Dirk Carter
Carter × Adams

Question 101:

My hair-dressers charges £30 for a haircut, £50 for a cut and blow-dry, and £60 for a full hair dye. They also do manicures, of which the first costs £15, and includes a bottle of nail polish, but are subsequently reduced by £5 if I bring my bottle of polish. The price is reduced by 10% if I book and pay for the next 5 appointments in advance and by 15% if I book at least the next 10.

I want to pay for my next 5 cut and blow-dry appointments, as well as for my next 3 manicures. How much will it cost?

50 × 5 = 250
(−) 225

A. £170
B. £255
C. £260
D. £285

15 + 10 + 10
= 35

E. £305

Question 102:

Alex, Bertha, David, Gemma, Charlie, Elena and Frankie are all members of the same family consisting of three children, two of whom, Frankie and Gemma are girls. No other assumption of gender based on name can be established. There are also four adults. Alex is a doctor and is David's brother. One of them is married to Elena, and they have two children. Bertha is married to David; Gemma is their child.

Girls: Frankie, Gemma

Who is Charlie?

A. Alex's daughter
B. Frankie's father
C. Gemma's brother

D. Elena's son
E. Gemma's sister

Bertha Alex David Elena

Question 103:

At 14:30 three medical students were asked to examine a patient's heart. Having already watched their colleague, the second two students were twice as fast as the first to examine. During the 8 minutes break after the final student had finished, they were told by their consultant that they had taken too long and so should go back and do the examinations again. The second time all the students took half as long as they had taken the first time with the exception of the first student who, instead took the same time as his two colleagues' second attempt. Assuming there was a one minute change over time between each student and they were finished by 15:15, how long did the second student take to examine the first time?

A. 3 minutes
B. 4 minutes
C. 6 minutes
D. 7 minutes
E. 8 minutes

Question 104:

I pay for 2 chocolate bars that cost £1.65 each with a £5 note. I receive 8 coins change, only 3 of which are the same.
Which **TWO** coins do I not receive in my change?
A. 1p
B. 2p
C. 5p
D. 10p
E. 20p
F. £2

Question 105:

Two 140m long trains are running at the same speed in opposite directions. If they cross each other in 14 seconds then what is speed of each train?

A. 10 kmph
B. 18 kmph
C. 32 kmph
D. 36 kmph
E. 42 kmph

Question 106:

After cleaning, the gym centre had to refill its swimming pool. It has four hoses which all run at different speeds. Alone, the first would completely fill the pool with water in 6 hours, the second in two days, the third in three days and the fourth in four days.

Using all the hoses together, how long will it take to fill the pool to the nearest quarter of an hour?

A. 4 hours 15 minutes
B. 4 hours 30 minutes
C. 4 hours 45 minutes
D. 5 hours
E. 5 hours 15 minutes

Question 107:

An ant is stuck in a 30cm deep ditch. When the ant reaches the top of the ditch he will be able to climb out straight away. The ant is able to climb 3 cm upwards during the day, but falls back 2cm at night.

How many days does it take for the ant to climb out of the ditch?

A. 27　　　　B. 28　　　　C. 29　　　　D. 30　　　　E. 31

Question 108:

When buying his ingredients a chef gets a discount of 10% when he buys 10 or more of each item, and 20% discount when he buys 20 or more. On one order he bought 5 sausages and 10 Oranges and paid £8.50. On another, he bought 10 sausages and 10 apples and paid £9, on a third he bought 30 oranges and paid £12.

How much would an order of 2 oranges, 13 sausages and 12 apples cost?

A. £12.52
B. £12.76
C. £13.52
D. £13.76
E. £13.80

Question 109:

My hairdressers encourage all of its clients to become members. By paying an annual member fee, the cost of haircuts decreases. VIP membership costs £125 annually with a £10 reduction on haircuts. Executive VIP membership costs £200 for the year with a £15 reduction per haircut. At the moment I am not a member and pay £60 per haircut. I know how many haircuts I have a year, and I work out that by becoming a member on either programme it would work out cheaper, and I would save the same amount of money per year on either programme.

$$125 + 50x = 200 + 45x$$
$$5x = 75$$
$$x = 15$$

How much will I save this year by buying membership?
A. £10   B. £15   C. £25   D. £30   E. £50

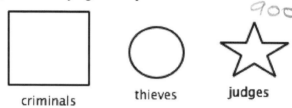

Question 110:

If criminals, thieves and judges are represented below:

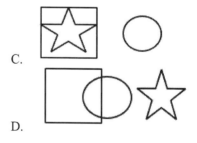

criminals   thieves   judges

Assuming that judges must have clean record, all thieves are criminals and all those who are guilty are convicted of their crimes, which of one of the following best represents their interaction?

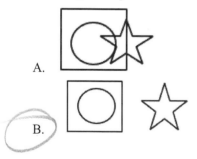

A.

B.

C.

D.

Question 111:

The months of the year have been made into number codes. The code is comprised of three factors, including two of these being related the letters that make up the name of the month. No two months would have the same first number. But some such as March, which has the code 3513, have the same last number as others, such as May, which has the code 5313. October would be coded as 10715 while February is 286.

What would be the code for April?

A. ~~154~~   B. 441   C. 451   D. ~~514~~   E. ~~541~~

Question 112:

A mother gives yearly birthday presents of money to her children based on the age and their exam results. She gives them £5 each plus £3 for every year they are older than 5, and a further £10 for every A* they achieved in their results. Josie is 16 and gained 9 A*s in her results. Although Josie's brother Carson is 2 years older he receives £44 less a year for his birthday.

$5 + 33 + 90 - 44 = 5 +$
$39 +$
$10 A$

How many more A*s did Josie get than Carson?

A. 2   B. 3   C. 4   D. 5   E. 10

$10 A = 33 + 90 - 44$
-29

Question 113:

Apples are more expensive than pears, which are more expensive than oranges. Peaches are more expensive than oranges. Apples are less expensive than grapes.

O   Pears   A   Grapes

$10 A = 46 - 6$

$10 A = 40$

$(A) = 4$

Which two of the following must be true?

A. Grapes are less expensive than oranges. ✗
B. Peaches may be less expensive than pears. ~
C. Grapes are more expensive than pears.
D. Pears and peaches are the same price. ✗
E. Apples and peaches are the same price. ✗

Question 114:

What is the minimum number of straight cutting motions needed to slice a cylindrical cake into 8 equally sized pieces?

A. 2   B. 3   C. 4   D. 5   E. 6   F. 8

Question 115

Three friends, Mark, Russell and Tom had agreed to meet for lunch at 12 PM on Sunday. Daylight saving time (GMT+1) had started at 2 AM the same day, where clocks should be put forward by one hour. Mark's phone automatically changes the time but he does not realise this so when he wakes up he puts his phone forward an hour and uses his phone to time his arrival to lunch. Tom puts all of his clocks forward one hour at 7 AM. Russell forgets that the clocks should go forward, wakes at 10 AM doesn't change his clocks. All of the friends arrive on time as far as they are concerned.

Assuming that none of the friends realise any errors before arriving, which **TWO** of the following statements are **FALSE**?

A.   Tom arrives at 12 PM (GMT +1).
B.   All three friends arrive at the same time.
C.   There is a 2 hour difference between when the first and last friend arrive.
D.   Mark arrives late.
E.   Mark arrives at 1 PM (GMT+3).
F.   Russell arrives at 12 PM (GMT+0).

Question 116:

A class of young students has a pet spider. Deciding to play a practical joke on their teacher, one day during morning break one of the students put the spider in their teachers' desk. When first questioned by the head teacher, Mr Jones, the five students who were in the classroom during morning break all lied about what they saw. Realising that the students were all lying, Mr Jones called all 5 students back individually and, threatened with suspension, all the students told the truth. Unfortunately Mr Jones only wrote down the student's statements not whether they had been told in the truthful or lying questioning.

The students' two statements appear below:

Archie: "It wasn't Edward. "
        "It was Bella."   **Charlotte**: "It was Edward."
                                                      "It wasn't Archie"

Darcy: "It was Charlotte"
        "It was Bella"   **Bella**: "It wasn't Charlotte."
                                                      "It wasn't Edward."

Edward: "It was Darcy"
        "It wasn't Archie"   *Charlotte or Bella*

Who put the spider in the teacher's desk?

A.   Edward   D.   Charlotte
B.   Bella   E.   More information needed
C.   Darcy

Question 117:   *100ml*

A scientist wants to measure out 0.1litres of solution. Unfortunately the lab assistant dropped the 200 ml measuring cylinder, and so the scientist only has a 300ml and a half litre-measuring beaker. Assuming he cannot accurately use the beakers to measure anything less than their full capacity, what is the minimum volume he will have to use to be able to ensure he measures the right amount?   *300   500*

A.   100 ml   C.   300 ml   E.   500 ml
B.   200 ml   D.   400 ml   F.   600 ml

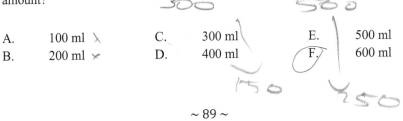

~ 89 ~

Question 118:

Francis lives on a street with houses all consecutively numbered evenly. When one adds up the value of all the house numbers it totals 870.

In order to determine Francis' house number:

1. The relative position of Francis' house must be known.
2. The number of houses in the street must be known.
3. At least three of the house numbers must be known.

A. 1 only
B. 2 only
C. 3 only
D. 1 and 2
E. 2 and 3

Question 119:

There were 20 people exercising in the cardio room of a gym. Four people were about to leave when suddenly a man collapsed on one of the machines. Fortunately a doctor was on the machine beside him. Emerging from his office, one of the personal trainers called an ambulance. In the 5 minutes that followed before the two paramedics arrived, half of the people who were leaving, left upon hearing the commotion, and eight people came in from the changing rooms to hear the paramedics pronouncing the man dead.

How many living people were left in the room?

A. 25   B. 26   C. 27   D. 28   E. 29   F. 30

-2
$+8$

Question 120:

A man and woman are in an accident. They both suffer the same trauma, which causes both of them to lose blood at a rate of 0.2 Litres/minute. At normal blood volume the man has 8 litres and the woman 7 litres, and people collapse when they lose 40% of their normal blood volume.

$$\frac{2}{5} \times 8 = \frac{16}{5}$$

Which **TWO** of the following are true?

A. The man will collapse 2 minutes before the woman.
B. The woman collapses 2 minutes before the man.
C. The total blood loss is 5 litres.
D. The woman has 4.2 litres of blood in her body when she collapses.
E. The man's blood loss is 4.8 litres when he collapses.
F. Blood loss is at a rate of 2 litres every 12 minutes.

Question 121:

Jenny, Helen and Rachel have to run a distance of 13 km. Jenny runs at a pace of 8 km/h, Helen at a pace of 10 km/h, and Rachel 11 km/h.

If Jenny sets off 15 minutes before Helen, and 25minutes before Rachel, what order will they arrive at the destination?

A. Jenny, Helen, Rachel.
B. Helen, Rachel, Jenny.
C. Helen, Jenny, Rachel.
D. Rachel, Helen, Jenny.
E. Jenny, Rachel, Helen.
F. None of the above.

Question 122:

On a specific day at a GP surgery 150 people visited the surgery and common complaints were recorded as a percentage of total patients. Each patient could use their appointment to discuss up to 2 complaints. 56% flu-like symptoms, 48% pain, 20% diabetes, 40% asthma or COPD, 30% high blood pressure.

Which statement must be true?

A. A minimum of 8 patients complained of pain and flu-like symptoms.
B. No more than 45 patients complained of high blood pressure and diabetes.
C. There were a minimum of 21 patients who did not complain about flu-like symptoms or high blood pressure.
D. There were actually 291 patients who visited the surgery.
E. None of the above.

Question 123:

All products in a store were marked up by 15%. They were subsequently reduced in a sale with quoted saving of 25% from the higher price.

What is the true reduction from the original price?

A. 5%
B. 10%
C. 13.75%
D. 18.25%
E. 20%
F. 25%

~ 91 ~

Question 124:

A recipe states it makes 12 pancakes and requires the following ingredients: 2 eggs, 100g plain flour, and 300 ml milk. Steve is cooking pancakes for 15 people and wants to have sufficient mixture for 3 pancakes each.

15 × 3 = 45

What quantities should Steve use to ensure this whilst using whole eggs?

A. 2½ eggs, 125g plain flour, 375 ml milk ✗   *2 eggs*
B. 3 eggs , 150g plain flour, 450 ml milk
C. 7½ eggs, 375g plain flour, 1125 ml milk, ✓   *400g*
D. 8 eggs, 400g plain flour, 1200 ml milk
E. 12 eggs, 600g plain flour, 1800 ml milk ✗

Question 125:

Spring Cleaning cleaners buy industrial bleach from a warehouse and dilute it twice before using it domestically. The first dilution is by 9:1 and then the second, 4:1. If the cleaners require 6 litres of diluted bleach, how much warehouse bleach do they require?

$\frac{1}{10} \rightarrow \frac{1}{50}$

A. 30 ml   *$\frac{6}{50} = \frac{12}{100}$*   D. 666 ml
B. 120 ml   E. 1,200 ml
C. 166 ml

⤷ = 0.120

Question 126:

During a GP consultation in 2015, Ms Smith tells the GP about her grandchildren. Ms Smith states that Charles is the middle grandchild and was born in 2002. In 2010, Bertie was twice the age of Adam and that in 2015 there are 5 years between Bertie and Adam. Charles and Adam are separated by 3 years.

How old are the 3 grandchildren in 2015?

$B - 5 = 2(A - 5)$

A. Adam = 16, Bertie = 11, Charles = 13 ✓   *$B = A + 5$*
B. Adam = 5, Bertie = 10, Charles = 8, ✗
C. Adam = 10, Bertie = 15, Charles = 13   *$B = 2A - 5$*
D. Adam = 10, Bertie = 20, Charles = 13
E. Adam = 11, Bertie = 10, Charles = 8 ✗
F. More information needed.

↓

$2A - 5 = A + 5$

$A = 10$

Question 127:
Kayak Hire charges a fixed flat rate and then an additional half-hourly rate. Peter hires the kayak for 3 hours and pays £14.50, and his friend Kevin hires 2 kayaks for 4hrs30mins each and pays £41. How much would Tom pay to hire one kayak for 2 hours? $x + 6y = 14.50$

A. £8   D. £33.20
B. £10.50 $x + 9y = 20.50$ E. £35.70
C. £15   F. None of the above

$2.5 + 8 \cdot 10.6$ $\rightarrow 3y = 6 \rightarrow y = 2$
$x = 7.5$

Question 128:
A ticketing system uses a common digital display of numbers 0 – 9. The number 7 is showing. However, a number of the light elements are not currently working.

Which set of the following digits is possible?

A. 3, 4, 7   C. 2, 7, 8   E. 3, 8, 9
B. 0, 1, 9   D. 0, 5, 9   F. 3, 4, 9

Question 129:
A team of 4 builders take 12 days of 7 hours work to complete a house. The company decides to recruit 3 extra builders.   1 builder = 48 days

How many 8 hour days will it take the new workforce to build a house? $\frac{48}{7} \times 7 = 48$

A. 2 days   C. 7 days   E. 11 days
B. 6 days   D. 10 days   F. 12 days

Question 130:
All astragalus are fabacaea as are all gummifer. Acacia are not astragalus.

Which of the following statements is true?
A. Acacia are not fabacaea
B. No astragalus are also gummifer.
C. All fabacae are astragalus or gummifer.
D. Some acacia may be fabacaea.
E. Gummifer are all acacia.
F. None of the above.

Question 131:

The Smiths want to reupholster both sides of their seating cushions (dimensions shown on diagram). The fabric they are using costs £10/m, can only be bought in whole metre lengths and has a standard width of 1m. Each side of a cushion must be made from a single piece of fabric. The seamstress changes a flat rate of £25 per cushion. How much will it cost them to reupholster 4 cushions?

$4 \times £10 = 40$

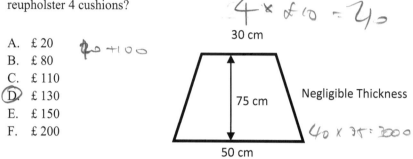

A. £ 20

$40 + 100$

B. £ 80

C. £ 110

D. £ 130

E. £ 150

F. £ 200

30 cm

75 cm   Negligible Thickness

$40 \times 75 = 3000$

50 cm

Question 132:

Lisa buys a cappuccino from either Milk or Beans Coffee shops each day. The quality of the coffee is the same but she wishes to work out the relative costs once the loyalty scheme has been taken into account. In Milk, a regular cappuccino is £2.40, and in Beans, £2.15. However, the loyalty scheme in Milk gives Lisa a free cappuccino for every 9 she buys, whereas Beans use a points system of 10 points per full pound spent (each point is worth 1p) which can be used to cover the cost of a full cappuccino.

If Lisa buys a cappuccino each day of September, which coffee shop would work out cheaper, and by how much?

A. Milk, by £4.60   C. Beans, by £4.60   E. Milk, by £2.45

B. Beans by £6.30   D. Beans, by £2.45   F. Milk, by £6.25

$2.16 \times 3 = 64.80$

$B = 21.50 \times 3 = 64.50 - 6.6$

$= 58.1$

$2.55 \times 3 = 6 + 1.75$

$= 7.75$

$2.2 \times 3 = 6.60$

M   2.40

B   2.15

$\frac{10}{21.60}$

$21.15 - 0.1 \times 21$

$= 21.50 - 2.1$

$= 19.40$

Question 133:

Paula needs to be at a meeting in Notting Hill at 11am. The route requires her to walk 5 minutes to the 283 bus which takes 25 minutes, and then change to the 220 bus which takes 14 minutes. Finally she walks for 3 minutes to her meeting. If the 283 bus comes every 10 minutes, and the 220 bus at 0 minutes, 20 minutes and 40 minutes past the hour, what is the latest time she can leave and still be at her meeting on time?

A. 9.45   C. 10.01   E. 10.10
B. 9.58   D. 10.05   F. 10.15

Question 134:

Two trains, a high speed train A and a slower local train B, travel from Manchester to London. Train A travels the first 20 km at 100 km/hr and then at an average speed of 150 km/hr. Train B travels at a constant average speed of 90 km/hr.

If train B leaves 20 minutes before train A, at what distance will train A pass train B?

A. 75km   B. 90km   C. 100km   D. 120km

Question 135:

The university gym has an upfront cost of £35 with no contract fee, but classes are charged at £3 each. The local gym has no joining fee and is £15 per month.

What is the minimum number of classes I need to attend in a 12 month period to make the local gym cheaper than the university gym?

A. 40   C. 49   E. 55
B. 48   D. 50   F. 60

Question 136:

"All medicines are drugs, but not all drugs are medicines", goes a well-known saying. If we accept this statement as true, and consider that all antibiotics are medicines, but no herbal drugs are medicines, then which of the following is definitely **FALSE**?

A. Some herbal drugs are not medicines.
B. All antibiotics are drugs.
C. Some herbal drugs are antibiotics.
D. Some medicines are antibiotics

Question 137:

Sonia has been studying the paths taken by various trains travelling between London and Edinburgh on the East coast. Trains can stop at the following stations: Newark, Peterborough, Doncaster, York, Northallerton, Darlington, Durham and Newcastle. She notes the following:

-   All trains stop at Peterborough, York, Darlington and Newcastle.
-   All trains which stop at Northallerton also stop at Durham.
-   Each day, 50% of the trains stop at both Newark *and* Northallerton.
-   All designated "Fast" trains make less than 5 stops. All other trains make 5 stops or more.
-   On average, 16 trains run each day.

Which of the following can be reliably concluded from these observations?

A. All trains, which are not designated "fast" trains, must stop at Durham.
B. No more than 8 trains on any 1 day will stop at Northallerton.
C. No designated "Fast" trains will stop at Durham.
D. It is possible for a train to make 5 stops, including Northallerton.
E. A train which stops at Newark will also stop at Durham.

Question 138:

Rakton is 5 miles directly north of Blueville. Gallford is 8 miles directly south of Haston. Lepstone is situated 5 miles directly east of Blueville, and 5 miles directly west of Gallford.

Which of the following **CANNOT** be reliably concluded from this information?
A. Lepstone is South of Rakton
B. Haston is North of Rakton
C. Gallford is East of Rakton
D. Blueville is East of Haston
E. Haston is North of Lepstone

Question 139

The Eastminster Parliament is undergoing a new set of elections. There are 600 seats up for election, each of which will be elected separately by the people living in that constituency. 6 parties win at least 1 seat in the election, the Blue Party, the Red party, the Orange party, the Yellow party, the Green party and the Purple party. In order to form a government, a party (or coalition) must hold *over* 50% of the seats. After the election, a political analysis committee produces the following report:

- No party has gained more than 45% of the seats, so nobody is able to form a government by themselves.
- The red and the blue party each gained over 40% of the seats.
- No other party gained more than 4% of the seats.
- The green party gained the 4th highest number of seats.

The red party work out that if they collaborate with the green party and the orange party, between the 3 of them, they will have enough seats to form a coalition government.

What is the minimum number of seats that the green party could have?
A. 5   B. 6   C. 13   D. 14   E. 23   F. 24

Questions 140-144 are based on the following information:

A grandmother wants to give her 5 grandchildren £100 between them for Christmas this year. She wants to grade the money she gives to each grandchild exactly so that the older children receive more than the younger ones. She wants share the money such that she will give the 2nd youngest child as much more than the youngest, as the 3rd youngest gets than the 2nd youngest, as the 4th youngest gets from the 3rd youngest and so on. The result will be that the two youngest children together will get seven times as less money than the three oldest.

M is the amount of money the youngest child receives, and D the difference between the amount the youngest and 2nd youngest children receive.

Question 140:

What is the expression for the amount the oldest child receives?

A. M

B. $M + D$

C. $2M$

D. $4M^2$

E. $M + 4D$

Question 141:

What is the correct expression for the total money received?

A. $5M = £100$

B. $5D + 10M = £100$

C. $D = \dfrac{M}{100}$

D. $5M + 10D = £100$

E. $M = \dfrac{2D}{11}$

Question 142:

"*The two youngest children together will get seven times less money than the three oldest.*" Which one of the following best expresses the above statement?

A. $7(3M + 9D) = 2M + D$

B. $7D = M$

C. $7(2M + D) = 3M + 9D$

D. $2(7M + D) = 3M + 9D$

Question 143:

Using the statement in the previous question, what is the expression for M?

A. $\dfrac{2D}{11}$ B. $\dfrac{2}{11}$ C. $\dfrac{10D}{11}$ D. $\dfrac{120}{11}$

Question 144:

Express £100 in terms of D.

A. $£100 = \dfrac{120D}{11}$

B. $£100 = \dfrac{120D}{10}$

C. $£100 = \dfrac{120}{11D}$

D. $£100 = 21D$

Question 145:

Four young girls entered a local baking competition. Though a bit burnt, Ellen's carrot cake did not come last. The girl who baked a Madeira sponge had practiced a lot, and so came first, while Jaya came third with her entry. Aleena did better than the girl who made the Tiramisu, and the girl who made the Victoria sponge did better than Veronica.

Which **TWO** of the following were **NOT** results of the competition?

A. Veronica made a tiramisu.
B. Ellen came second.
C. Aleena made a Victoria sponge.
D. The Victoria sponge came in 3rd place.
E. The carrot cake came 3rd.

Question 146:

In a young children's football league of 5 teams were; Celtic Changers, Eire Lions, Nordic Nesters, Sorten Swipers and the Whistling Winners. One of the boys playing in the league, after being asked by his parents, said that while he could remember the other teams' total points he could not remember his own, the Eire Lions, score. He said that all the teams played each other and when teams lost they were given 0 points, when they drew, 1 point, and 3 for a win. He remembered that the Celtic Changers had a total of 2 points; the Sorten Swipers had 5; the Nordic Nesters had 8, and the Whistling Winners 1.

How many did the boy's team score?

A. 1   B. 4   C. 8   D. 10   E. 11

Question 147:

T is the son of Z, Z and J are sisters, R is the mother of J and S is the son of R. Which one of the following statements is correct?

A. T and J are cousins.
B. S and J are sisters.
C. J is the maternal uncle of T
D. S is the maternal uncle of T
E. R is the grandmother of Z.

Question 148:

John likes to shoot bottles off a shelf. In the first round he places 16 bottles on the shelf and knocks off 8 bottles. 3 of the knocked off bottles are damaged and can no longer be used, whilst 1 bottle is lost. He puts the undamaged bottles back on the shelf before continuing. In the second round he shoots six times and misses 50% of these shots. He damages two bottles with every shot which does not miss. 2 bottles also fall off the shelf at the end. He puts up 2 new bottles before continuing. In the final round, John misses all his shots and in frustration, knocks over gets angry and knocks over 50% of the remaining bottles.

How many bottles were left on the wall after the final round?

A. 2
B. 3
C. 4
D. 5
E. 6
F. More information needed

Questions 149-155 are based on the information below:

All lines are named after a station they serve, apart from the Oval and Rectangle lines, which are named for their recognisable shapes. Trains run in both directions.

➢ There are express trains that run from end to end of the St Mark's and Straightly lines in 5 and 6 minutes respectively.

➢ It takes 2 minutes to change between St Mark's and both Oval and Rectangle lines, 1 minute between Rectangle and Oval.

➢ It takes 3 minutes to change between the Straightly and all other lines, except with the St Mark's line which only takes 30 seconds

➢ The Straightly line is a fast line and takes only 2 minutes between stops apart from to and from Keyton, which only takes 1 minute, and to and from Lime St which takes 3 minutes.

➢ The Oval line is much slower and takes 4 minutes between stops, apart from between Baxton and Marven, and also Archite and West Quays, which takes 5 minutes.

➢ The Rectangle line a reliable line; never running late but as a consequence is much slower taking 6 minutes between stops.

➢ The St Mark's line is fast and takes 2 and half minutes between stations.

➢ If a passenger reaches the end of the line, it takes three minutes to change onto a train travelling back in the opposite direction.

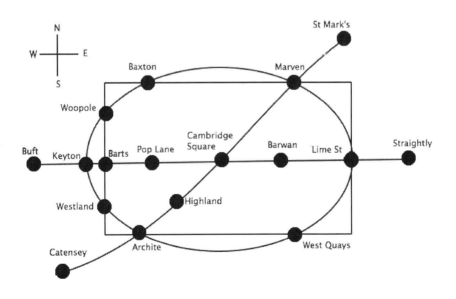

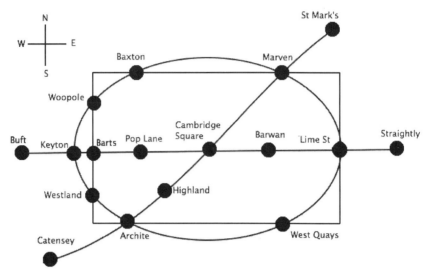

Question 149:

Assuming all lines are running on time, how long does it take to go from St Mark's to Archite on the St Mark's line?

A. 5 minutes   C. 7.5 minutes

B. 6 minutes   D. 10 minutes

Question 150:

Assuming all lines are running on time, what's the shortest time it will take to go from Buft to Straightly?

A. 6 minutes   C. 12 minutes

B. 10 minutes   D. 14 minutes

Question 151:

What is the shortest time it will take to go from Baxton to Pop Lane?

A. 11 minutes   C. 13 minutes

B. 12 minutes   D. 14 minutes

Question 152:

Which station, even at the quickest journey time, is furthest in terms of time from Cambridge Square?

A. Catensey   C. Woopole

B. Buft   D. Westland

Questions 153-155 use this additional information:

On a difficult day there are signal problems whereby all lines except the reliable line are delayed, such that train travel times between stations are doubled. These delays have caused overcrowding at the platforms which means that while changeover times between lines are still the same, passengers always have to wait an extra 5 minutes on all of the platforms before catching the next train.

Question 153

At best, how long will it now take to go from Westland to Marven?

A. 25 minutes   C. 31.5 minutes
B. 30 minutes   D. 33 minutes

Question 154:

There is a bus that goes from Baxton to Archite and takes 27-31 minutes. Susan lives in Baxton and needs to get to her office in Archite as quickly as possible. With all the delays and lines out of service,

How should you advise Susan best to get to work?

A. Baxton to Archite via Barts using the Rectangle line.
B. Baxton to Woopole on the Rectangle line, then Oval to Archite via Keyton.
C. It is not possible to tell between the fastest two options.
D. Baxton to Woopole on the Rectangle line, then Oval to Archite via Keyton.
E. Baxton to Archite on the Oval line.
F. Baxton to Archite using the bus.

Question 155:

In addition to the delays the Oval line signals fail completely, so the line falls out of service. How long will it now take to go from St Mark's to West Quays as quickly as possible in minutes?

A. 35   B. 33   C. 30   D. 29

Question 156:

In an unusual horserace, only 4 horses, each with different racing colours and numbers competed. Simon's horse wore number 1. Lila's horse wasn't painted yellow nor blue, and the horse that wore 3, which was wearing red, beat the horse that came in third. Only one horse wore the same number as the position it finished in. Arthur's horse beat Simon's horse, whereas Celia's horse beat the horse that wore number 1. The horse wearing green, Celia's, came second, and the horse wearing blue wore number 4.

Which one of the following must be true?

A. Simon's horse was yellow and placed 3rd.
B. Celia's horse was red.
C. Celia's horse was in third place.
D. Arthur's horse was blue.
E. Lila's horse wore number 4.

Question 157:

Fred plants a tree with a height of 40cm. The information leaflet states that the plant should grow by 20% each year for the first 2 years, and then 10% each year thereafter.

What is the expected height at 4 years?

A. 58.08 cm
B. 64.89 cm
C. 69.696 cm
D. 89.696 cm
E. 82.944 cm
F. None of the above

Question 158:

A company is required to pay each employee 10% of their wage into a pension fund if their annual total wage bill is above £200,000. However, there is a legal loophole that if the company splits over two sites, the £200,000 bill is per site. The company therefore decides to have an east site, and a west site.

Name	Annual Salary (£)
Luke	47,000
John	78,400
Emma	68,250
Nicola	88,500
Victoria	52,500
Daniel	63,000

Which employees should be grouped at the same site to minimise the cost to the company?

A. John, Nicola, Luke
B. Nicola, Victoria, Daniel
C. Nicola, Daniel, Luke

D. John, Daniel, Emma
E. Luke, Victoria, Emma

Question 159:

A bus takes 24 minutes to travel from White City to Hammersmith with no stops. Each time the bus stops to pick up and/or drop off passengers, it takes approximately 90 seconds. This morning, the bus picked up passengers from 5 stops, and dropped off passengers at 7 stops.

What is the minimum journey time from White City to Hammersmith this morning?

A. 28 minutes
B. 34 minutes

C. 34.5 minutes
D. 36 minutes

E. 37.5 minutes
F. 42 minutes

Question 160:

Sally is making a Sunday roast for her family and is planning her schedule regarding cooking times. The chicken takes 15 minutes to prepare, 75 minutes to cook, and needs to stand for exactly 5 minutes after cooking. The potatoes take 18 minutes to prepare, 5 minutes to boil, then 50 minutes to roast, and must be roasted immediately after boiling, and then served immediately. The vegetables require only 5 minutes preparation time and 8 minutes boiling time before serving, and can be kept warm to be served at any time after cooking.

Given that the cooker can only be cooking two items at any given time and Sally can prepare only one item at a time, what should Sally's schedule be if she wishes to serve dinner at 4pm and wants to start cooking each item as late as possible?

A. Chicken 2.25, potatoes 2.47, vegetables 2.42
B. Chicken 2.25, potatoes 2.47, vegetables 3.47
C. Chicken 2.35, potatoes 3.47, vegetables 2.47
D. Chicken 2.35, potatoes 2.47, vegetables 3.47
E. Chicken 2.45, potatoes 3.47, vegetables 2.47
F. Chicken 2.45, potatoes 2.47, vegetables 3.47

Question 161:

The Smiths have 4 children whose total age is 80. Paul is double the age of Jeremy. Annie is exactly half way between the ages of Jeremy and Paul, and Rebecca is 2 years older than Paul. How old are each of the children?

A. Paul 23, Jeremy 12, Rebecca 26, Annie 19
B. Paul 22, Jeremy, 11, Rebecca 24, Annie 16
C. Paul 24, Jeremy 12, Rebecca 26, Annie 18
D. Paul 28, Jeremy 14, Rebecca 30, Annie 21
E. More information needed

Question 162:

Sarah has a jar of spare buttons that are a mix of colours and sizes. The jar contains the following assortment of buttons:

	10mm	25mm	40mm
Cream	15	22	13
Red	6	15	7
Green	9	19	8
Blue	20	6	15
Yellow	4	8	26
Black	17	16	14
Total	**71**	**86**	**83**

Sarah wants to use a 25mm diameter button, but doesn't mind if it is cream or yellow. What is the maximum number of buttons she will have to remove in order to guarantee to pick a suitable button on the next attempt?

A. 210

B. 218

C. 219

D. 239

E. None of the above.

Question 163:

Ben wants to optimise his score with one throw of a dart. 50% of the time he hits a segment to either side of the one he is aiming at. With this in mind, which segment should he aim for?

[Ignore all double/triple modifiers]

A. 15

B. 16

C. 17

D. 18

E. 19

F. 20

Question 164:

Victoria is completing her weekly shop, and the total cost of the items is £8.65. She looks in her purse and sees that she has a £5 note, and a large amount of change, including all types of coins. She uses the £5 note, and pays the remainder using the maximum number of coins possible in order to remove some weight from the purse.

However, the store has certain rules she has to follow when paying:
- No more than 20p can be paid in "bronze" change (the name given to any combination of 1p pieces and 2p pieces)
- No more than 50p can be paid using any combination of 5p pieces and 10p pieces.
- No more than £1.50 can be paid using any combination of 20p pieces and 50p pieces.

Victoria pays the exact amount, and does not receive any change. Under these rules, what is the *maximum* number of coins that Victoria can have paid with?

A. 30   B. 31   C. 36   D. 41   E. 46

Question 165:

I look at the clock on my bedside table, and I see the following digits:

However, I also see that there is a glass of water between me and the clock, which is in front of 2 adjacent figures. I know that this means these 2 figures will appear reversed. For example, 10 would appear as 01, and 20 would appear as 05 (as 5 on a digital clock is a reversed image of a 2). Some numbers, such as 3, cannot appear reversed because there are no numbers which look like the reverse of 3.

Which of the following could be the actual time?

A. 15:52   C. 12:55   E. 21:52
B. 21:25   D. 12:22

Question 166:

Slavica has invaded Worsid, whilst Nordic has invaded Lorkdon. Worsid, spotting an opportunity to bolster its amount of land and natural resources, invades Nordic. Each of these countries is either a dictatorship or a democracy. Slavica is a dictatorship, but Lorkdon is a democracy. 10 years ago, a treaty was signed which guaranteed that no democracy would invade another democracy. No dictatorship has both invaded another dictatorship *and* been invaded by another dictatorship.

Assuming the aforementioned treaty has been upheld, what style of government is practiced in Worsid?

A. Worsid is a Dictatorship.
B. Worsid is a Democracy.
C. Worsid does not practice either of these forms of government.
D. It is impossible to tell.

Question 167:

Pixie is on a shift at the local supermarket. Unfortunately, the till has developed a fault, meaning it cannot tell her how much change to give each customer. A customer is purchasing the following items, at the following costs:
- A packet of grated cheese priced at £3.25
- A whole cucumber, priced at 75p
- A fish pie mix, priced at £4.00
- 3 DVDs, each priced at £3.00

Sheila knows there is an offer on DVDs in the store at present, in which 3 DVDs bought together will only cost £8.00. The customer pays with a £50 note.

How much change will Sheila need to give the customer?
A. £4   B. £33   C. £34   D. £36   E. £38

Question 168:

Mr Salt is cooking breakfast for several guests at his hotel. He is frying most of the items using the same large frying pan, to get as much food prepared in as little time as possible. Mr Salt is cooking Bacon, Sausages, and eggs in this pan. He calculates how much room is taken up in the pan by each item.

He calculates the following:
- Each rasher of bacon takes up 7% of the available space in the pan
- Each sausage takes up 3% of the available space in the pan.
- Each egg takes up 12% of the available space in the pan.

Mr Salt is cooking 2 rashers of bacon, 4 sausages and 1 egg for each guest. He decides to cook all the food for each guest at the same time, rather than cooking all of each item at once.

How many guests can he cook for at once?

A. 1   B. 2   C. 3   D. 4   E. 5

Question 169:

SafeEat Inc. is a national food development testing agency. The Manchester-based laboratory has a system for recording all the laboratory employees' birthdays, and presenting them with cake on their birthday, in order to keep staff morale high. Certain amounts of petty cash are set aside each month in order to fund this.40% of the staff have their birthday in March, and the secretary works out that £60 is required to fund the birthday cake scheme during this month.

If all birthdays cost £2 to provide a cake for, how many people work at the laboratory?

A. 45   C. 75   E. 150
B. 60   D. 100   F. 200

Question 170:

Many diseases, such as cancer, require specialist treatment, and thus cannot be treated by a general practitioner. Instead, these diseases must be *referred* to a specialist after an initial, more generalised, medical assessment. Bob has had a biopsy on the 1st of August on a lump found in his abdomen. The results show that it is a tumour, with a slight chance of becoming metastatic, so he is referred to a waiting list for specialist radiotherapy and chemotherapy.

The average waiting time in the UK for such treatment is 3 weeks, but in Bob's local district, high demand means that it takes 50% longer for each patient to receive treatment. As he is a lower risk case, with a low risk of metastasis, his waiting time is extended by another 20%.

How many weeks will it be before Bob receives specialist treatment?

A. 4.5	C. 5.0	E. 5.4
B. 4.6	D. 5.1	F. 5.6

Question 171:

In a class of 30 seventeen year old students, 40% drink alcohol at least once a month. Of those who drink alcohol at least once a month, 75% drink alcohol at least once a week. 1 in 3 of the students who drink alcohol at least once a week also smoke marijuana. 1 in 3 of the students who drink alcohol less than once a month also smoke marijuana.

How many of the students in total smoke marijuana?

A. 3	C. 6	E. 10
B. 4	D. 9	F. 15

Question 172:

Complete the following sequence of numbers: 1, 4, 10, 22, 46, ...

A. 84   B. 92   C. 94   D. 96   E. 100

Question 173:

If the mean of 5 numbers is 7, the median is 8 and the mode is 3, what must the two largest numbers in the set of numbers add up to?

A. 14   B. 21   C. 24   D. 26   E. 35

Question 174:

Ahmed buys 1kg bags of potatoes from the supermarket. 1kg bags have to weigh between 900 and 1100 grams. In the first week, there are 10 potatoes in the bag. The next week, there are only 5.

Assuming that the potatoes in the bag in week 1 are all the same weight as each other, and the potatoes in the bag in week 2 are all the same weight as each other, what is the maximum possible difference between the heaviest and lightest potato in the two bags?

A. 50g

B. 70g

C. 90g

D. 110g

E. 130g

Question 175:

A football tournament involves a group stage, then a knockout stage. In the group stage, groups of four teams play in a round robin format (i.e. each team plays every other team once) and the team that wins the most matches in each group, as well as the "best" second place team, proceed through to a knockout stage. In the knockout stage, sets of two teams play each other and the one that wins proceeds to the next round until there are two teams left, who play the final.

If we start with 60 teams, how many matches are played altogether?

A. 75   B. 90   C. 100   D. 105   E. 165

Question 176:

The last 4 digits of my card number are 2 times my PIN number, plus 200. The last 4 digits of my husband's card number are the last four digits of my card number doubled, plus 200. My husband's PIN number is 2 times the last 4 digits of his card number, plus 200.

Given that all these numbers are 4 digits long, whole numbers, and cannot begin with 0, what is the largest number my PIN number can be?

A. 1,074

B. 1,174

C. 2,348

D. 4,096

E. 9,999

Question 177:

All women between 50 and 70 in the UK are invited for breast cancer screening every 3 years. Patients at Doddinghurst Surgery are invited for screening for the first time at any point between their 50th and 53rd birthday. If they ignore an invitation, they are sent reminders every 5 months. We can assume that a woman is screened exactly 1 month after she is sent the invitation or reminder that she accepts. The next invitation for screening is sent exactly 3 years after the previous screening.

If a woman accepts the screening on the second reminder each time, what is the youngest she can be when she has her 4th screening?

A. 60   B. 61   C. 62   D. 63   E. 64   F. 65

Question 178:

Ellie gets a pay rise of k thousand pounds on every anniversary of joining the company, where k is the number of years she has been at the company. She currently earns £40,000, and she has been at the company for 5.5 years.
What was her salary when she started at the company?

A. £ 25,000   D. £ 30,000
B. £ 27,000   E. £ 31,000
C. £ 28,000   F. £ 32,000

Question 179:

Northern Line trains arrive into Kings Cross station every 8 minutes, Piccadilly Line trains every 5 minutes and Victoria Line trains every 2 minutes. If trains from all 3 lines arrived into the station exactly 15 minutes ago, how long will it be before they do so again?

A. 24 minutes   D. 60 minutes
B. 25 minutes   E. 65 minutes
C. 40 minutes   F. 80 minutes

Question 180:

If you do not smoke or drink alcohol, your risk of getting Disease X is 1 in 12. If you smoke, you are half as likely to get Disease X as someone who does not smoke. If you drink alcohol, you are twice as likely to get Disease X. A new drug is released that halves anyone's total risk of getting Disease X for each tablet taken.

How many tablets of the drug would someone who drinks alcohol have to take to reduce their risk to the same level as someone who smoked but did not take the drug?

A. 0   B. 1   C. 2   D. 3   E. 4   F. 5

Questions 181 – 183 refer to the following information:

There are 20 balls in a bag. 1/2 are red. 1/10 of those that are not red are yellow. The rest are green except 1, which is blue.

Question 181:

If I draw 2 balls from the bag (without replacement), what is the most likely combination to draw?

A. Red and green
B. Red and yellow
C. Red and red
D. Blue and yellow

Question 182:

If I draw 2 balls from the bag (without replacement), what is the least likely (without being impossible) combination to draw?

A. Blue and green
B. Blue and yellow
C. Yellow and yellow
D. Yellow and green

Question 183:

How many balls do you have to draw (without replacement) to guarantee getting at least one of at least three different colours?

A. 5   C. 13   E. 18
B. 12   D. 17   F. 19

Question 184:

A general election in the UK resulted in a hung parliament, with no single party gaining more than 50% of the seats. Thus, the main political parties are engaged in discussion over the formation of a coalition government. The results of this election are shown below:

Political Party	Seats won
Conservatives	260
Labour	270
Liberal Democrats	50
UKIP	35
Green Party	20
Scottish National Party	17
Plaid Cymru	13
Sinn Fein	9
Democratic Unionist Party (DUP)	11
Other	14 (14 other parties won 1 seat each)

There are a total of 699 seats, meaning that in order to form a government, any coalition must have at least 350 seats between them. Several of the party leaders have released statements about who they are and are not willing to form a coalition with, which are summarised as follows:

–   The Conservative party and Labour are not willing to take part in a coalition together.
–   The Liberal Democrats refuse to take part in any coalition which also involves UKIP.
–   The Labour party will only form a coalition with UKIP if the Green party are also part of this coalition.
–   The Conservative party are not willing to take part in any coalition with UKIP unless the Liberal Democrats are also involved.

Considering this information, what is the minimum number of parties required to form a coalition government?

A) 2   B) 3   C) 4   D) 5   E) 6

Question 185:

On Tuesday, 360 patients attend appointments at Doddinghurst Surgery. Of the appointments that are booked in, only 90% are attended. Of the appointments that are booked in, 1 in 2 are for male patients, the remaining appointments are for female patients. Male patients are three times as likely to miss their booked appointment as female patients.

How many male patients attend appointments at Doddinghurst Surgery on Tuesday?

A.　30　　　　B.　60　　　　C.　130　　　　D.　150　　　　E.　170

Question 186:

Every A Level student at Greentown Sixth Form studies Maths. Additionally, 60% study Biology, 50% study Economics and 50% study Chemistry. The other subject on offer at Greentown Sixth Form is Physics.

Assuming every student studies 3 subjects and that there are 60 students altogether, how many students study Physics?

A.　15　　　　B.　24　　　　C.　30　　　　D.　40　　　　E.　60

Question 187:

100,000 people are diagnosed with chlamydia each year in the UK. An average of 0.6 sexual partners are informed per diagnosis. Of these, 80% have tests for chlamydia themselves. Half of these tests come back positive.

Assuming that each of the people diagnosed has had an average of 3 sexual partners (none of them share sexual partners or have sex with each other) and that the likelihood of having chlamydia is the same for those partners who are tested and those who are not, how many of the sexual partners who were not tested (whether they were informed or not) have chlamydia?

A.　120,000　　　　C.　136,000　　　　E.　240,000
B.　126,000　　　　D.　150,000　　　　F.　252,000

Question 188:

In how many different positions can you place an additional tile to make a straight line of 3 tiles?

A. 6
B. 7
C. 8
D. 9
E. 10
F. 11
G. 12

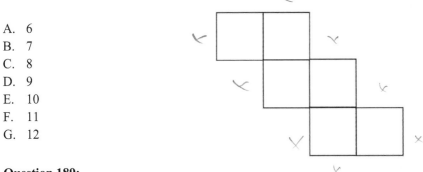

Question 189:

Harry is making orange squash for his daughter's birthday party. He wants to have a 200 ml glass of squash for each of the 20 children attending and a 300 ml glass of squash for him and each of 3 parents who are helping him out. He has 1,040 ml of the concentrated squash. What ratio of water:concentrated squash should he use in the dilution to ensure he has the right amount to go around?

A. 2:1   B. 3:1   C. 4:1   D. 5:1   E. 6:1   F. 5:2

Question 190:

4 children, Alex, Beth, Cathy and Daniel are each sitting on one of the 4 swings in the park. The swings are in a straight line. One possible arrangement of the children is, left to right, Alex, Beth, Cathy, Daniel. How many other possible arrangements are there?

A. 5   B. 12   C. 23   D. 24   E. 64   F. 256

Question 191:

A delivery driver is looking to make deliveries in several towns. He is given the following map of the various towns in the area. The lines indicate roads between the towns, along with the lengths of these roads.

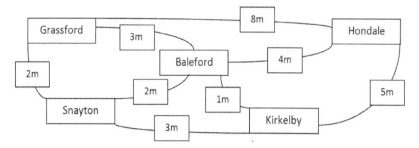

The delivery driver's vehicle has a black box which records the distance travelled and locations visited. At the end of the day, the black box recording shows that he has travelled a total of 14 miles. It also shows that he has visited one town twice, but has not visited any other town more than once.

Which of the following is a possible route the driver could have taken?

A.   Snayton → Baleford → Grassford → Snayton → Kirkelby
B.   Baleford → Kirkelby → Hondale → Grassford → Baleford → Snayton
C.   Kirkelby → Hondale → Baleford → Grassford → Snayton
D.   Baleford → Hondale → Grassford → Baleford → Hondale → Kirkelby
E.   Snayton → Baleford → Kirkelby → Hondale → Grassford
F.   None of the above

Question 192:

Ellie, her brother Tom, her sister Georgia, her mum and her dad line up in height order from shortest to tallest for a family photograph. Ellie is shorter than her dad but taller than her mum. Georgia is shorter than both her parents. Tom is taller than both his parents.

If 1 is shortest and 5 is tallest, what position is Ellie in the line?
A.   1   B.   2   C.   3   D.   4   E.   5

Question 193:

Miss Briggs is trying to arrange the 5 students in her class into a seating plan. Ashley must sit on the front row because she has poor eyesight. Danielle disrupts anyone she sits next to apart from Caitlin, so she must sit next to Caitlin and no-one else. Bella needs to have a teaching assistant sat next to her. The teaching assistant must be sat on the left hand side of the row, near to the teacher. Emily does not get on with Bella, so they need to be sat apart from one another. The teacher has 2 tables which each sit 3 people, which are arranged 1 behind the other.

Who is sitting in the front right seat?

A. Ashley   D. Danielle
B. Bella   E. Emily
C. Caitlin

Question 194:

My aunt runs the dishwasher twice a week, plus an extra time for each person who is living in the house that week. When her son is away at university, she buys a new pack of dishwasher tablets every 6 weeks, but when her son is home she has to buy a new one every 5 weeks.

How many people are living in the house when her son is home?

A. 2   C. 4   E. 6
B. 3   D. 5   F. 7

Question 195:

Dates can be written in an 8 digit form, for example 26-12-2014. How many days after 26-12-2014 would be the next time that the 8 digits were made up of exactly 4 different integers?

A. 6   B. 8   C. 10   D. 16   E. 24   F. 30

Question 196:

Redtown is 4 miles east of Greentown. Bluetown is 5 miles north of Greentown. If every town is due North, South, East or West of at least two other towns, and the only other town is Yellowtown, how many miles away from Yellowtown is Redtown, and in what direction?

A. 4 miles east of Yellowtown.   D. 4 miles west of Yellowtown.
B. 5 miles south of Yellowtown.   E. 5 miles west of Yellowtown.
C. 5 miles north of Yellowtown.

Question 197:

Jessie pours wine from two 750ml bottles into glasses. The glasses hold 250ml, but she only fills them to 4/5 of capacity, except the last glass, where she puts whatever she has left. How full is the last glass compared to its capacity?

A. $\frac{1}{5}$ B. $\frac{2}{5}$ C. $\frac{3}{5}$ D. $\frac{4}{5}$ E. $\frac{5}{5}$

Question 198:

There are 30 children in Miss Ellis's class. Two thirds of the girls in Miss Ellis's class have brown eyes, and two thirds of the class as a whole have brown hair. Given that the class is half boys and half girls, what is the difference between the minimum and maximum number of girls that could have brown eyes and brown hair?

A. 0   B. 2   C. 5   D. 7   E. 10

Question 199:

A biased die with the numbers 1 to 6 on it is rolled twice. The resulting numbers are multiplied together, and then their sum subtracted from this result to get the 'score' of the dice roll. If the probability of getting a negative (non-zero) score is 0.75, what is the probability of rolling a 1 on a third throw of the die?

A. 0.1   B. 0.2   C. 0.3   D. 0.4   E. 0.5

Questions 200 - 202 are based on the following information:

Fares on the number 11 bus are charged at a number of pence per stop that you travel, plus a flat rate. Emma, who is 21, travels 15 stops and pays £1.70. Charlie, who is 43, travels 8 stops and pays £1.14. Children (under 16) pay half the adult flat rate plus a quarter of the adult charge "per stop".

Question 200:

How much does 17 year old Megan pay to travel 30 stops to college?

A. £0.85   B. £2.40   C. £2.90   D. £3.40

Question 201:

How much does 14 year old Alice pay to travel 25 stops to school?

A. £0.50   B. £0.75   C. £1.25   D. £2.50

Question 202:

James, who is 24, wants to get the bus into town. The town stop is the 25th stop along a straight road from his house, but he only has £2.

Assuming he has to walk past the stop nearest his house, how many stops will he need to walk past before he gets to the stop he can afford to catch the bus from?

A. 4   B. 6   C. 7   D. 8   E. 9   F. 10

Questions 203 -205 are based on the following information

Emma mounts and frames paintings. Each painting needs a mount which is 2 inches bigger in each dimension than the painting, and a wooden frame which is 1 inch bigger in each dimension than the mount. Mounts are priced by multiplying 50p by the largest dimension of the mount, so a mount which is 8 inches in one direction and 6 in the other would be £4. Frames are priced by multiplying £2 by the smallest dimension of the frame, so a frame which is 8 inches in one direction and 6 in the other would be £12.

Question 203:

How much would mounting and framing a 10 x 14 inch painting cost?
A. £8   B. £26   C. £27   D. £34   E. £42

Question 204:

How much more would mounting and framing a 10 x 10 inch painting cost than mounting and framing an 8 x 8 inch painting?
A. £3   B. £4   C. £5   D. £6   E. £7

Question 205:

What is the largest square painting that can be framed for £40?
A. 12 inch   D. 15 inch
B. 13 inch   E. 16 inch
C. 14 inch

Question 206:

If the word 'CREATURES' is coded as 'FTEAWUTEV', which itself would be coded as 'HWEAYUWEX'. What would be the second coding of the word 'MAGICAL'?

A. QCKIGAN
B. OCIIEAN
C. PAJIFAN

D. RALIHAQ
E. RCIMGEP

Question 207:

Jane's mum has asked Jane to go to the shops to get some items that they need. She tells Jane that she will pay her per kilometre that she cycles on her bike to get to the shop, plus a flat rate payment for each place she goes to. Jane receives £6 to go to the grocers, a distance of 5km, and £4.20 to go the supermarket, a distance of 3km.

How much would she earn if she then cycles to the library to change some books, a distance of 7km?

A. £7.50
B. £7.70

C. £7.80
D. £8.00

E. £8.10
F. £8.20

Question 208:

In 2001-2002, 1,019 patients were admitted to hospital due to obesity. This figure was more than 11 times higher by 2011-12 when there were 11,736 patients admitted to hospital with the primary reason for admission being obesity.

If the rate of admissions due to obesity continues to increase at the same linear rate as it has from 2001/2 to 2011/12, how many admissions would you expect in 2031/32?

A. 22,453
B. 23,437

C. 33,170
D. 134,964

E. 269,928
F. 300,000

Question 209:

A shop puts its dresses on sale at 20% off the normal selling price. During the sale, the shop makes a 25% profit over the price at which they bought the dresses. What is the percentage profit when the dresses are sold at full price?

A. 36%   C. 56.25%   E. 7.7%

B. 42.5%   D. 64%   F. 80%

Question 210:

The MedSoc committee is made up of 20 students from each of the 6 years at the university. However, the president and vice-president are sabbatical roles (students take a year out from studying). There must be at least two general committee students from each year, as well as the specialist roles. Additionally, the social and welfare officers must be pre-clinical students (years 1-3) but not first years, and the treasurer must be a clinical student (years 4-6).

Which **TWO** of the following statements must be true?

1. There can be a maximum of 13 preclinical (years 1-3) students on the committee.
2. There must be a minimum of 6 2nd and 3rd years.
3. There is an unequal distribution of committee members over the different year groups.
4. There can be a maximum of 10 clinical (years 4-6) students on the committee.
5. There can be a maximum of 2 first year students on the committee.
6. General committee members are equally spread across the 6 years.

A. 1 and 4   C. 2 and 4   E. 4 and 5

B. 2 and 3   D. 3 and 6   F. 4 and 6

Question 211:

Friday the 13th is superstitiously considered an 'unlucky' day. If 13th January 2012 was a Friday, when would the next Friday the 13th be?

A. March 2012
B. April 2012
C. May 2012
D. June 2012
E. July 2012

F. August 2012
G. September 2012
H. January has the only Friday 13th in 2012.

Question 212:

A farmer has 18 sheep, 8 of which are male. Unfortunately, 9 sheep die, of which 5 were female. The farmer decides to breed his remaining sheep in order to increase the size of his herd.

Assuming every female gives birth to two lambs, how many sheep does the farmer have after all the females have given birth once?

A. 10   B. 14   C. 15   D. 16   E. 19

Question 213:

Isobel writes a coded message whereby each letter of the original message is coded as a letter a specific number of characters further on in the alphabet (the specific number is the same for all letters). Isobel's coded message includes the word "PJVN". What could the original word say?

A. CAME
B. DAME
C. FAME

D. GAME
E. LAME

Question 214:

A number of people get on the bus at the station, which is considered the first stop. At each subsequent stop, 1/2 of the people on the bus get off and then 2 people get on. Between the 4th and 5th stop after the station, there are 5 people on the bus.

How many people got on at the station?

A. 4   B. 6   C. 20   D. 24   E. 30

Question 215:

I have recently moved into a new house, and I am looking to repaint my new living room. The price of several different colours of paint is displayed in the table below. A small can contains enough to paint 10 m² of wall. A large can contains enough to paint 25 m² of wall.

Colour	Cost for a Small Can	Cost for a Large Can
Red	£4	£12
Blue	£8	£15
Black	£3	£9
White	£2	£13
Green	£7	£15
Orange	£5	£20
Yellow	£10	£12

I decide to paint my room a mixture of blue and white, and I purchase some small cans of blue paint and white paint. The cost of blue paint accounts for 50% of the total cost. I paint a total of 100m² of wall space.

I use up all the paint. How many m² of wall space have I painted blue?

A. 10m²   B. 20m²   C. 40m²   D. 50m²   E. 80m²

Question 216:

Cakes usually cost 42p at the bakers. The bakers want to introduce a new offer where the amount in pence you pay for each cake is discounted by the square of the number of cakes you buy. For example, buying 3 cakes would mean each cake costs 33p. Isobel says that this is not a good offer from the baker's perspective as it would be cheaper to buy several cakes than just 1.

How many cakes would you have to buy for the total cost to fall below 40p?

A. 2   B. 3   C. 4   D. 5   E. 6

Question 217:

The chart below shows the percentages of students in two different universities who take various courses. There are 800 students in University A and 1200 students in University B. Biology, Chemistry and Physics are counted as "Sciences". Assuming each student only takes one course, how many more students in University A than University B study a "Science"?

	University A	University B
Biology	23.50	13.25
Economics	10.25	14.5
Physics	6.25	14.75
Mathematics	11.50	17.25
Chemistry	30.25	7.00
Psychology	18.25	33.25

A. 10   B. 25   C. 60   D. 250   E. 600

Question 218:

Traveleasy Coaches charge passengers at a rate of 50p per mile travelled, plus an additional charge of £5.00 for each international border crossed during the journey. Europremier Coaches charge £15 for every journey, plus 10p per mile travelled, with no charge for crossing international borders. Sonia is travelling from France to Germany, crossing 1 international border. She finds that both companies will charge the same price for this journey.

How many miles is Sonia travelling?

A. 10   B. 20   C. 25   D. 35   E. 40

Question 219:

Lauren, Amy and Chloe live in different cities across England. They decide to meet up together in London and have a meal together. Lauren departs from Southampton at 2:30pm, and arrives in London at 4pm. Amy's journey lasts twice as long as Lauren's journey, and she arrives in London at 4:15pm. Chloe departs from Sheffield at 1:30pm, and her journey lasts an hour longer than Lauren's journey.

Which of the following statements is definitely true?
A. Chloe's journey took the longest time
B. Amy departed after Lauren
C. Chloe arrived last
D. Everybody travelled by train
E. Amy departed before Chloe

Question 220:

Emma is packing to go on holiday by aeroplane. On the aeroplane, she can take a case of dimension 50cm by 50cm by 20cm, which, when fully packed, can weigh up to 20kg. The empty suitcase weighs 2kg. In her suitcase, she needs to take 3 books, each of which is 0.2m by 0.1m by 0.05m in size, and weighs 1000g. She would also like to take as many items of clothing as possible. Each item of clothing has volume 1500cm^3 and weighs 400 g.

Assuming each item of clothing can be squashed so as to fill any shape gap, how many items of clothing can she take in her case?

A. 28   B. 31   C. 34   D. 37   E. 40

Question 221:

Alex is buying a new bed and mattress. There are 5 bed shops Alex can buy the bed and mattress he wants from, each of which sells the bed and mattress for a different price as follows:

➢ **Bed Shop A:** Bed £120, Mattress £70
➢ **Bed Shop B:** All beds and mattresses £90 each
➢ **Bed Shop C:** Bed £140, Mattress £60. Mattress half price when you buy a bed and mattress together.
➢ **Bed Shop D:** Bed £140, Mattress £100. Get 1/3 off when you buy a bed and mattress together.
➢ **Bed Shop E:** Bed £175. All beds come with a free mattress.

Which is the cheapest bed shop for Alex to buy the bed and mattress from?

A. A   B. B   C. C   D. D   E. E

Question 222:

In Joseph's sock drawer, there are 21 socks. 4 are blue, 5 are red, 6 are green and the rest are black. How many socks does he need to take from the drawer in order to guarantee he has a matching pair?

A. 3   B. 4   C. 5   D. 6   E. 7

Question 223:

Printing a magazine uses 1 sheet of card and 25 sheets of paper. It also uses ink. Paper comes in packs of 500 and card comes in packs of 60 which are twice the price of a pack of paper. Each ink cartridge prints 130 sheets of either paper or card. A pack of paper costs £3. Ink cartridges cost £5 each.

How many complete magazines can be printed with a budget of £300?

A. 210   B. 220   C. 230   D. 240   E. 250

Question 224:
Rebecca went swimming yesterday. After a while she had covered one fifth of her intended distance. After swimming six more lengths of the pool, she had covered one quarter of her intended distance.

How many lengths of the pool did she intend to complete?
A. 40   B. 72   C. 80   D. 100   E. 120

Question 225:
As a special treat, Sammy is allowed to eat five sweets from his very large jar which contains many sweets of each of three flavours – Lemon, Orange and Strawberry. He wants to eat his five sweets in such a way that no two consecutive sweets have the same flavour.

In how many ways can he do this?
A. 32   B. 48   C. 72   D. 108   E. 162

Question 226:
Granny and her granddaughter Gill both had their birthday yesterday. Today, Granny's age in years is an even number and 15 times that of Gill. In 4 years' time Granny's age in years will be the square of Gill's age in years. How many years older than Gill is Granny today?

A. 42   B. 49   C. 56   D. 60   E. 64

Question 227:
Pierre said, "Just one of us is telling the truth". Qadr said, "What Pierre says is not true". Ratna said, "What Qadr says is not true". Sven said, "What Ratna says is not true". Tanya said, "What Sven says is not true".

How many of them were telling the truth?

A. 0   B. 1   C. 2   D. 3   E. 4

Question 228:

Two entrants in a school's sponsored run adopt different tactics. Angus walks for half the time and runs for the other half, whilst Bruce walks for half the distance and runs for the other half. Both competitors walk at 3 mph and run at 6 mph. Angus takes 40 minutes to complete the course.

How many minutes does Bruce take?

A. 30   B. 35   C. 40   D. 45   E. 50

Question 229:

Dr Song discovers two new alien life forms on Mars. Species 8472 have one head and two legs. Species 24601 have four legs and one head. Dr Song counts a total of 73 heads and 290 legs in the area.

How many members of Species 8472 are present?

A. 0   B. 1   C. 72   D. 73   E. 145

Question 230:

A restaurant menu states that:

"All chicken dishes are creamy and all vegetable dishes are spicy. No creamy dishes contain vegetables."

Which of the following **MUST** be true?

A.   Some chicken dishes are spicy.
B.   All spicy dishes contain vegetables.
C.   Some creamy dishes are spicy.
D.   Some vegetable dishes contain tomatoes.
E.   None of the above

Question 231:

Simon and his sister Lucy both cycle home from school. One day, Simon is kept back in detention so Lucy sets off for home first. Lucy cycles the 8 miles home at 10mph. Simon leaves school 20 minutes later than Lucy.

How fast must he cycle in order to arrive home at the same time as Lucy?

A. 10 mph   B. 14 mph   C. 17 mph   D. 21 mph   E. 24 mph

Question 232:

Adam buys 2000 shares in a company at a rate of 50p per share. He then sells the shares for 58p per share. Subsequently he buys 1000 shares at 55p per share then sells them for 61p per share. There is a charge of £20 for each transaction of buying or selling shares. What is Adam's total profit?

A. £ 140   B. £ 160   C. £ 180   D. £ 200   E. £ 220

Question 233:

Jina is playing darts. A dartboard is composed of equal segments, numbered from 1 to 20. She takes three throws, and each of the darts lands in a numbered segment. None land in the centre or in double or triple sections.

What is the probability that her total score with the three darts is odd?

A. $^1/_4$ B. $^1/_3$ C. $^1/_2$ D. $^3/_5$ E. $^2/_3$

Question 234:

John Morgan invests £5,000 in a savings bond paying 5% interest per annum. What is the value of the investment in 5 years' time?

A. £6,250   B. £6,315   C. £6,381   D. £6,442   E. £6,570

Question 235:

Joe is 12 years younger than Michael. In 5 years the sum of their ages will be 62. How old was Michael two years ago?

A. 20   B. 24   C. 26   D. 30   E. 32

Question 236:

A book has 500 pages. Vicky tears every page out that is a multiple of 3. She then tears out every remaining page that is a multiple of 6. Finally, she tears out half of the remaining pages. If the book measures 15 cm x 30 cm and is made from paper of weight 110 gm^{-2}, how much lighter is the book now than at the start?

A. 1,648 g   B. 1,698 g   C. 1,722 g   D. 1,790 g   E. 1,848 g

Question 237:

A farmer is fertilising his crops. The more fertiliser is used, the more the crops grow. Fertiliser costs 80p per kilo. Fertilising at a rate of 0.2 kgm^{-2} increases the crop yield by £1.30 m^{-2}. For each additional 100g of fertiliser above 200g, the extra yield is 30% lower than the linear projection of the stated rate. At what rate of fertiliser application is it no longer cost effective to increase the dose?

A. 0.5 kgm^{-2} B. 0.6 kgm^{-2} C. 0.7 kgm^{-2} D. 0.8 kgm^{-2} E. 0.9 kgm^{-2}

Question 238:

Pet-Star, Furry Friends and Creature Cuddles are three pet shops, which each sell food for various types of pets.

Type of pet food	Amount of food required per week	Price per Kg in:		
		Pet-star	Furry Friends	Creature Cuddles
Guinea Pig	3 Kg	£2	£1	£1.50
Cat	6 Kg	£4	£6	£5
Rabbit	4 Kg	£3	£1	£2.50
Dog	8 Kg	£5	£8	£6
Chinchilla	2 Kg	£1.50	£0.50	£1

Given the information above, which of the following statements can we state is definitely **NOT** true?

A. Regardless of which of these shops you use, the most expensive animal to provide food for will be a dog.
B. If I own a mixture of cats and rabbits, it will be cheaper for me to shop at Pet-star.
C. If I own 3 cats and a dog, the cheapest place for me to shop is at Pet-star
D. Furry Friends sells the cheapest food for the type of pet requiring the most food
E. If I only have one pet, Creature Cuddles will not be the cheapest place to shop regardless of which type of pet I have.

Question 239:

I record my bank balance at the start of each month for six months to help me see how much I am spending each month. My salary is paid on the 10th of each month. At the start of the year, I earn £1000 a month but from March inclusive I receive a pay rise of 10%.

Date	Bank balance	Date	Bank balance
January 1st	1,200	April 1st	1,050
February 1st	1,029	May 1st	925
March 1st	1,189	June 1st	1,025

In which month did I spend the most money?

A. January   B. February   C. March   D. April   E. May

Question 240:

Amy needs to travel from Southtown station to Northtown station, which are 100 miles apart. She can travel by 3 different methods: train, aeroplane or taxi. The tables below show the different times for these 3 methods. The taxi takes 1 minute to cover a distance of 1 mile. Aeroplane passengers must be at the airport 30 minutes before their flight. Southtown airport is 10 minutes travelling time from Southtown station and Northtown airport is 30 minutes travelling time from Northtown station.

If Amy wants to arrive by 1700 and wants to set off as late as possible, what method of travel should she choose and what time will she leave Southtown station?

Train	Departs Southtown station	1400	1500	1600
	Arrives Northtown station	1615	1650	1715
Flights	Departs Southtown airport	1610		
	Arrives Northtown airport	1645		

A. Flight, 1530   D. Train, 1500
B. Train, 1600   E. Flight, 1610
C. Taxi, 1520

Question 241:

In this multiplication grid, given below, a, b, c and d are all integers, what does d equal?

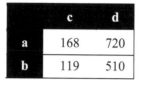

	c	d
a	168	720
b	119	510

A. 18   B. 24   C. 30   D. 40   E. 45

Question 242:

A sixth form college has 1,500 students. 48% are girls. 80 of the girls are mixed race. If an equal proportion of boys and girls are mixed race, how many mixed race boys are there in the college to the nearest 10?

A. 50   B. 60   C. 70   D. 80   E. 90

Question 243:

Christine is a control engineer at the Browdon Nuclear Power Plant. On Wednesday, she is invited to a party on the Friday, and asks her manager if she can take the Friday off. She acknowledged that this will mean she will have worked less than the required number of hours this week, and offers to make this up by working extra hours next week. Her manager suggests that instead, she works 5 hours this Sunday, and 3 extra hours next Thursday to make up the required hours. Christine accepts this proposal. Christine's amended schedule for the week is shown below:

	Mon	Tue	Wed	Thu	Fri	Sat	Sun
Hours worked	8	7	9	6	0	0	5

How many hours was Christine supposed to have worked this week, if she had completed her usual Friday shift?

A. 34   B. 35   C. 36   D. 38   E. 40   F. 42

Question 244:

Leonidas notes that the time on a normal analogue clock is 0340. What is the smaller angle between the hands on the clock?

A. 110°   **B.** 120°   **C.** 130°   **D.** 140°   **E.** 150°

Question 245:

Sheila is on a shift at the local supermarket. Unfortunately, the till has developed a fault, meaning it cannot tell her how much change to give each customer. A customer is purchasing the following items, at the following costs:

- A packet of grated cheese priced at £3.25
- A whole cucumber, priced at 75p
- A fish pie mix, priced at £4.00
- 3 DVDs, each priced at £3.00

Sheila knows there is an offer on DVDs in the store at present, in which 3 DVDs bought together will only cost £8.00. The customer pays with a £50 note. How much change will Sheila need to give the customer?

A. £33   **B.** £34   **C.** £35   **D.** £36   **E.** £3

Questions 246-248 are based on the following passage:

It has recently been questioned as to whether the recommended five fruit and vegetables a day is sufficient or if it would be more beneficial to eat 7 fruit and vegetable portions each day. A study at UCL looked at the fruit and vegetables eating habits of 65,000 people in England. Analysis of the data showed that eating more portions was beneficial and vegetables seemed to have a greater protective effect than fruit. The study however did not distinguish whether vegetables themselves have a greater protective effect, or whether these people tend to eat an overall healthier diet. A meta-analysis carried out by researchers across the world complied data from 16 studies which encompassed over 800,000 participants, of whom 56,423 had died.

They found a decline in death of around 5% from all causes for each additional portion of fruit or vegetables eaten, however they recorded no further decline for people who ate over 5 portions. Rates of cardiovascular disease, heart disease or stroke, were shown to decline 4% for each portion up to five, whereas the number of portions of fruit and vegetables eaten seemed to have little impact on cancer rates. The data from these studies points in a similar direction, that eating as much fruit and vegetables a day is preferable, but that five portions is sufficient to have a significant impact on reduction in mortality. Further studies need to look into the slight discrepancies, particularly why the English study found vegetables more protective, and if any specific cancers may be affected by fruit and vegetables even if the general cancer rates more greatly depend on other lifestyle factors.

Question 246:

Which of the following statements is correct?

A. The UCL study found no additional reduction in mortality in those who eat 7 rather than 5 portions of fruit and vegetables a day.

B. People who eat more fruit and vegetables are assumed to have an overall healthier diet which is what gives them the beneficial effect.

C. The meta analysis found fruit and vegetables are more protective against cancer than cardiovascular disease

D. The English study showed fruit had more protective effects than vegetables.

E. The Meta analysis found no additional reduction in mortality in those who eat 7 rather than 5 portions of fruit and vegetables a day.

F. The meta analysis suggests people who eat 7 portions would have a 10% lower risk of death from any cause than those who eat 5 portions.

G. Fruit and vegetables are not protective against any specific cancers.

Question 247:

If rates of death were found to be 1% lower in the UCL study than the meta-analysis, approximately how many people died in the UCL study?

A. 3,000   B. 3,200   C. 3,900   D. 4,550   E. 5,200

Question 248

Which statement does the article **MOST** agree with?

A. Eating more fruit and vegetables does not particularly lower the risk of any specific cancers.

B. The UCL research suggests that the guideline should be 7 fruit and vegetables a day for England.

C. The results found by the UCL study and the meta-analysis were contradictory.

D. Many don't eat enough vegetables due to cost and taste.

E. Fruit and vegetables are only protective against cardiovascular disease.

F. The UCL study and meta-analysis use a similar sample of participants.

G. People should aim to eat 7 portions of fruit and vegetables a day.

Questions 249-251 relate to the following table regarding average alcohol consumption in 2010.

Country	Total	2010 consumption	Unrecorded consumption	2020 Projection	Beer (%)	Wine (%)	Spirits (%)	Other (%)
Belarus		14.4	3.2	17.1	17.3	5.2	46.6	30.9
Lithuania	15.4	12.9	2.5	16.2		7.8	34.1	11.6
Andorra	13.8		1.4	9.1	34.6		20.1	0
Grenada	12.5	11.9	0.7	10.4	29.3	4.3		0.2
Czech Republic	13	11.8	1.2	14.1	53.5	20.5	26	0
France	12.2	11.8		11.6	18.8	56.4	23.1	1.7
Russia		11.5	3.6	14.5	37.6	11.4	51	0
Ireland	11.9	11.4	0.5	10.9	48.1	26.1	18.7	7.7

NB: Some data is missing.

Question 249:

Which of the following countries had the highest total beer and wine consumption for 2010?

A. Belarus   B. Lithuania C. Ireland   D. France   E. Andorra

Question 250:

Which country has the greatest difference for spirit consumption in 2010 and 2020 projection, assuming percentages stay the same?

A. Russia   B. Belarus   C. Lithuania D. Grenada   E. Ireland

Question 251:

It was later found that some of the percentages of types of alcohol consumed had been mixed up. If the actual amount of beer consumed by each person in the Czech Republic was on average 4.9L, which country were the percentage figures mixed up with?

A. Lithuania   C. Russia   E. Ireland
B. Grenada   D. France   F. Belarus

Questions 252-255 are based on the following information:

The table below shows the incidence of 6 different types of cancer in Australia.

	Prostate	Lung	Bowel	Bladder	Breast	Uterus
Men	40,000	25,000	20,000	8,000	1,000	0
Women	0	20,000	18,000	4,000	50,000	9,000

Question 252:

Supposing there are 10 million men and 10 million women in Australia, how many percentage points higher is the incidence of cancer amongst women than amongst men?

A. 0.007 %   B. 0.07 %   C. 0.093 %   D. 0.7 %   E. 0.93 %

Question 253:

Now suppose there are 11.5 million men and 10 million women in Australia. Assuming all men are equally likely to get each type of cancer and all women are equally likely to get each type of cancer, how many of the types of cancer are you more likely to develop if you are a man than if you are a woman?

A. 1   B. 2   C. 3   D. 4

Question 254:

Suppose that prostate, bladder and breast cancer patients visit hospital 1 time during the first month of 2015 and patients for all other cancers visit hospital 2 times during the first month of 2015. 10% of cancer patients in Australia are in Sydney, and patients in Sydney are not more or less likely to have certain types of cancer than other patients. How many hospital visits are made by patients in Sydney with these 6 cancers during the first month of 2015?

A. 10,300   C. 19,500   E. 195,000
B. 18,400   D. 28,700   F. 287,000

Question 255:

Which of the graphs correctly represents the combined proportion of men versus women with bladder cancer?

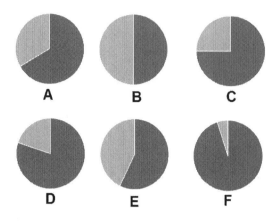

Questions 256 – 258 are based on the following information:

Units of alcohol are calculated by multiplying the alcohol percentage by the volume of liquid in litres, for example a 0.75 L bottle of wine which is 12% alcohol contains 9 units. 1 pint = 570 ml.

	Volume in bottle/barrel	Standard drinks per bottle/barrel	Percentage
Vodka	1250 ml	50	40%
Beer	10 pints	11.4	3%
Cocktail	750 ml	3	8%
Wine	750 ml	3.75	12.5%

Question 256:

Which standard drink has the most units of alcohol in?

A. Vodka   B. Beer   C. Cocktail   D. Wine

Question 257:

The recommended number of units per week for women is 14. In a week, Hannah drinks 4 standard drinks of wine, 3 standard drinks of beer, 2 standard cocktails and 5 standard vodkas. The recommended number of units per week for men is 21. In a week, Mark drinks 2 standard drinks of wine, 6 standard drinks of beer, 3 standard cocktails and 10 standard vodkas.

Who has exceeded their recommended number of units by more and by how many units more have they exceeded it by than the other person?

A. Hannah, by 1 unit   D. Mark, by 0.5 units
B. Hannah, by 0.5 units   E. Mark, by 1 unit
C. Both by the same

Question 258:

How many different combinations of drinks that total 4 units are there (the same combination in a different order doesn't count).

A. 2   B. 3   C. 4   D. 5   E. 6

Questions 259-261 relate to the table showing the population of Greentown:

	Female	Male	Total
Under 20	1,930		
20-39	1,960	3,760	5,720
40-59		4,130	
60 and over	2,350	2,250	4,600
Total	11,430	12,890	24,320

Question 259:

How many males under 20 are there in Greentown?

A. 2,650   B. 2,700   C. 2,730   D. 2,750   E. 2,850

Question 260:

How many females aged 40-59 are there in Greentown?

A. Between 3,000 and 4,000   C. Between 5,000 and 6,000
B. Between 4,000 and 5,000   D. Between 6,000 and 7,00

Question 261:

Which is the approximate ratio of females:males in the age group that has the highest ratio of males:females?

A. 1.4:1   B. 1.9:1   C. 1:1.9   D. 1:1.4

Questions 262 to 264 relate to the following graph that shows average temperatures in London (top trace) and Newcastle (bottom trace).

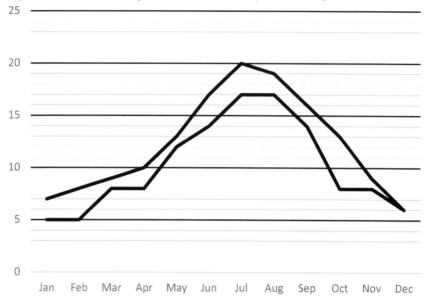

Question 262:

If the average monthly temperature is the same in every year, how many times during the period May 2007 to September 2013 inclusive is the average temperature the same in 2 consecutive months in Newcastle?

A. 20   B. 24   C. 25   D. 30

Question 263:

In how many months in the period specified in the previous question is the average temperature in London AND Newcastle lower than the previous month?

A. 19   B. 21   C. 25   D. 32

Question 264:

To the nearest 0.5 degrees Celsius, what is the average temperature difference between Newcastle and London?

A. 1.5°   B. 2 °   C. 2.5 °   D. 3 °

Questions 265 - 267 concern the following data:

The pie chart to the right shows sales of ice cream across the four quarters of a year from January to December. Sales are lowest in the month of February. From February they increase in every subsequent month until they get to the maximum sales and from that point they decrease in every subsequent month until the end of the year.

Sales of ice cream

Question 265:

In which month are the sales highest?

A. June
B. July
C. August
D. Cannot Tell

Question 266:

If total sales of ice cream were £354,720 for the year, how much of this was taken during Q1?

A. £29,480
B. £29,560
C. £29,650

D. £29,720
E. £29,800

Question 267:

Assuming total sales revenue (i.e. before costs are taken off) is £180,000, and that each tub of ice cream is sold for £2 and costs the manufacturer £1.50 in total production and transportation costs, how much profit is made during Q2?

A. £15,000
B. £30,000

C. £45,000
D. £60,000

Question 268:

Data on the amount families spend on food per month to the nearest £100 was collected for families with 1, 2 and 3 children.

The percentage of families with different spending sizes is displayed below:

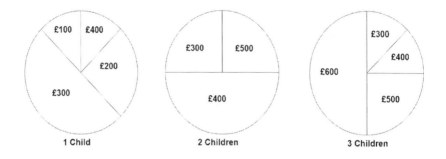

Which of the following statements is definitely true?

A. More families with 1 child than families with 2 children spent £300 a month on food.
B. The overall fraction of families spending £600 was 1/6.
C. All of the families with 2 children spent under £4000 on food per year.
D. The fraction of families with 1 child spending £400 on food per month is the same as the fraction of families with 3 children spending this amount.
E. The average amount spent on food by families with 2 children is £410 a month.

Questions 269-272 are based on the passage below:

A big secondary school recently realised that there were a large number of incidences of bullying occurring that were going unnoticed by teachers. It is possible that some believe bullying to be as much a part of student life as lessons and homework. In order to tackle the problem, the school emailed out a questionnaire to all students' parents and asked them to question their children about where they had experienced or seen bullying in school. Those children that answered yes were then asked if they had told their teachers about it, and asked why they did not if they had not. Those that had told their teacher were asked whether they had seen the teacher act upon the information and whether the bullying had stopped as a result.

Of the 2500 school students surveyed 2210 filled in the online questionnaire. The results were that, 1121 students, almost exactly half (50.7%) had seen bullying in school. Only 396 (35%) of these students told a teacher about the bullying. Of the students who told a teacher, 286 did not witness any action following sharing of the information and of those that did, 60% did not notice any direct action with the bully involved.

From those students who did not report the bullying, 146 gave the reason that they didn't think it was important. 427 cited fears of being found out. 212 students said they did not tell because they didn't think the teachers would do anything about it even if they did know. Assume that all the students who filled out the survey did so honestly.

Question 269:
To the nearest integer, what percentage of students did not respond?
A. 10 %   B. 12 %   C. 18 %   D. 8 %   E. 5 %

Question 270:
If a student saw bullying occur and did not tell a teacher about it, what is the probability that the reasoning for this is that they thought it to be unimportant?
A. 0.1   B. 0.15   C. 0.2   D. 0.35   E. 0.13

Question 271:
After reporting the bullying, how many students saw the teacher act on the information directly with the bully?

A. 66   B. 44   C. 178   D. 104   E. 118

Question 272:

Which of the following does the questionnaire indicate is the best explanation for why students at the school did not report bullying?

A.   Students do not think bullying happens at their school.
B.   Students think the teachers will do nothing with the information.
C.   Students think that bullying is a part of school life.
D.   The student's were worried about others finding out.

Question 273:

The obesity epidemic is growing rapidly with reports of a three-fold rise in the period from 2007 to 2012. The rates of hospital admission have also been found to vary massively across different areas of England with the highest rates in the North-East (56 per 100,000 people), and the lowest rates in the East of England (12 per 100,000). During almost every year from 2001-12, there were around twice as many women admitted for obesity as men. The reason for this is however unclear and does not imply there are twice as many obese women as men.

What was the approximate number of admissions per 100 000 women in the North-East in 2011-12?

A. 18	C. 37	E. 62
B. 26	D. 56	F. 74

Question 274:

Health professionals are becoming increasingly worried by the decline in exercise being taken by both children and adults. Around only 40% of adults take the recommended amount of exercise which is 150 minutes per week. As well as falling rates of exercise, a shockingly low number of individuals eat five portions of fruit and vegetables a day. Figures for children aged 5-15 fell to only 16% for boys, and 20% for girls in 2011. Data for adults was only slightly better with 29% of women and 24% of men eating the recommended number of portions.

Using a figure of 8 million children between 5-15 years (equal ratio of girls to boys) in England in 2011, how many more girls than boys ate 5 portions of fruit and vegetables a day?

A. 80,000	C. 160,000	E. 640,000
B. 120,000	D. 320,000	

Question 275:

The table below shows the leading causes of death in the UK.

| Rank | WOMEN | | MEN | |
	Cause of Death	No. of Deaths	Cause of Death	No. of Deaths
1	Dementia and Alzheimer's	31,850	Coronary Heart Disease	37,797
2	Coronary Heart Disease	26,075	Lung Cancer	16,818
3	Stroke	20,706	Dementia and Alzheimer's	15,262
4	Flu and Pneumonia	15,361	Lower Respiratory Disease	15,021
5	Lower Respiratory Disease	14,927	Stroke	14,058
6	Lung Cancer	13,619	Flu and Pneumonia	11,426
7	Breast Cancer	10,144	Prostate Cancer	9,726
8	Colon Cancer	6,569	Colon Cancer	7,669
9	Urinary Infections	5,457	Lymphatic Cancer	6,311
10	Heart Failure	5,012	Liver Disease	4,661
	Total	261,205	**Total**	245,585

Using information from the table only, which of the following statements is correct?

A. More women died from cancers than men.

B. More than 30,000 women died due to respiratory causes.

C. Dementia and Alzheimer's is more common in women than men.

D. No cause of death is of the same ranking for both men and women.

E. None of the above.

Question 276:

The government has recently released a campaign leaflet saying that last year waiting times in NHS A&E departments decreased 20% compared to the year before. The opposition has criticised this statement, saying that there are several definitions which can be described as "waiting times", and the government's campaign leaflet does not make it clear what they mean by "waiting times in A&E".

The NHS watchdog has recently released the following figures describing different aspects of A&E departments, and the change from last year:

Assessment Criterion	2014	2013
Average time spent before being seen in A&E	1 hour	90 minutes
Average time between dialling 999 and receiving treatment in A&E	2 hours	3 hours
Number of people waiting for over 4 hours in A&E	3200	4000
Number of high-priority cases waiting longer than 1 hour	900	1000
Average waiting time for those seen in under 4 hours	50 minutes	40 minutes

Assuming these figures are correct, which criterion of assessment have the government described as "waiting times in A&E" on their campaign leaflet?

A. Number of people waiting for over 4 hours in A&E.
B. Number of people waiting for under 4 hours in A&E.
C. Number of high-priority cases waiting longer than 1 hour.
D. Average time spent before being seen in A&E.
E. Average time between dialling 999 and receiving treatment in A&E.
F. Average waiting time for those seen in less than 4 hours.

Questions 277– 279 refer to the following information:

The table below shows the final standings at the end of the season, after each team has played all the other teams twice each (once at home, once away). The teams are listed in order of how many points they got during the season. Teams get 3 points for a win, 1 point for a draw and 0 points for a loss. No team got the same number of points as another team. Some of the information in the table is missing.

Team	W	D	L
United	8	1	
Athletic	7		
City	7	2	
Town	1	4	
Rovers		0	9
Rangers		2	8

Question 277:
How many points did Rovers get?

A. 0

B. 3

C. 6

D. 9

E. More information needed.

Question 278:
How many games did Athletic lose?

A. 0

D. 1

C. 2

D. 3

E. More information needed.

Question 279:
How many more points did United get than Rangers?

A. 7

B. 15

C. 23

D. 25

E. More information needed.

Questions 280-282 use information from the graph recording A&E attendances and response times for NHS England from 2004 to 2014.

Type 1 departments are major A&E units, type 2&3 are urgent care centres or minor injury units. The old target (2004 – June 2010) was 97.5%; the new target (July 2010 – 2015) is 95%.

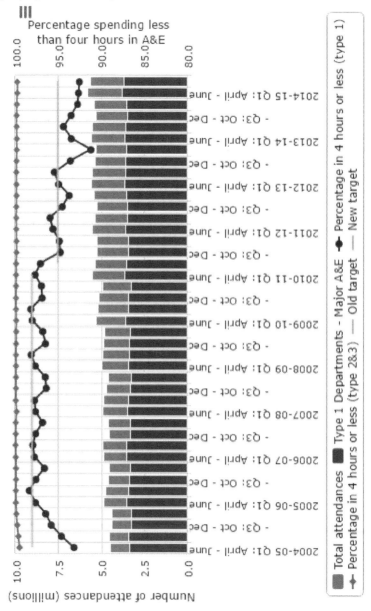

Question 280:

Which of the following statements is **FALSE**?

A. There has been an overall increase in total A&E attendances from 2004-2014.
B. The number of attendances in type 1 departments has been fairly constant from 2004-2014.
C. The new target of 4 hours waiting time has only been reached in two quarters by type 1 departments.
D. The change in attendances is largely due to an in increase people going to type 2&3 departments.

Question 281:

What percentage has the number of total attendances changed from Q1 2004-5 to Q1 2008-9?

A. +5%   C. +10%   E. +15%
B. −5%   D. −10%   F. −15%

Question 282:

If the new target was achieved by type 1 departments 4 times, in what percentage of the quarters was the target missed?

A. 25%   B. 60%   C. 75%   D. 90%

Questions 283-284 relate to the following data:

Ranjna is travelling from Manchester to Bali. He is required to make a stopover in Singapore for which he wants to allow at least 2 hours. It takes 14 hours to fly from Manchester to Singapore, and 2 hours from Singapore to Bali. The table below shows the departure times in local time [Manchester GMT, Singapore GMT + 8, Bali GMT + 8]:

Manchester to Singapore			Singapore to Bali			
Mon	Wed	Thu	Mon	Tue	Wed	Thu
08.00	09.30	02.30	13.00	00.00	15.30	13.00
10.45	14.00	08.30	15.30	07.30	18.00	16.00
13.30	18.00	12.30	21.00	08.30	20.30	19.00
15.00	20.00	19.00		12.00		

Question 283:

What is the latest flight Ranjna can take from Manchester to ensure she arrives at Bali Airport by Thursday 22:00?

A. 18:00 Tuesday
B. 14:00 Wednesday
C. 18:00 Wednesday

D. 20:00 Wednesday
E. 02:30 Thursday
F. 08:30 Thursday

Question 284:

Ranjna takes the 08:00 flight from Manchester to Singapore on Monday. Allowing 1 hour to go through customs and collect her luggage at Bali Airport and a 45 minute taxi to her hotel. At what time will she arrive at the hotel?

A. 16.45 Monday
B. 04:15 Tuesday

C. 10:30 Tuesday
D. 12:15 Tuesday

E. 12:30 Tuesday
F. 20:30 Tuesday

Question 285:

The graph below represents the percentage of adult smokers in the UK from 1974 to 2010. The top trace represents men and the bottom trace represents women.

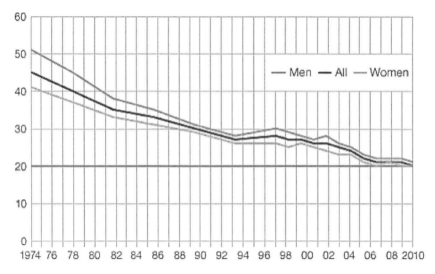

Which of the following statements **CAN** be concluded from the graph?

A. The 2007 smoking ban increased the rate in decline of smokers.
B. There has been a constant reduction in percentage of smoker since 1974.
C. The highest rate in decline in smoking for women was 2004-2006.
D. From 1974 to 2010, the smoking rate in men decreased by a half.
E. There has always been a significant difference between the smoking habits of men and women.

Question 286:

The name, age, height, weight and IQ of 11 people were recorded below in a table and a scatter plot. However, the axis labels were left out by mistake,

Name	Age	Height (cm)	Weight (kg)	IQ
Alice	18	180	68	110
Ben	12	160	79	120
Camilla	14	170	62	100
David	25	145	98	108
Eliza	29	165	75	96
Fred	15	190	92	111
George	20	172	88	104
Hannah	22	168	68	115
Ian	13	182	86	98
James	17	176	90	102
Katie	27	151	66	125

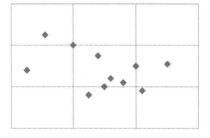

Which variants are possible for the X and Y axis?

	X axis	Y axis
A	Height	Weight
B	IQ	Height
C	Age	IQ
D	Height	IQ
E	Height	Age
F	IQ	Weight

Question 287:

A group of students looked at natural variation in height and arm span within their group and got the following results:

Name	Arm span (cm)	Height (cm)
Adam	175	168
Tom	188	175
Sam	172	184
Mary	148	142
Alice	165	156
Sarah	166	168
Emily	159	160
Matthew	165	172
Michael	185	183

They then drew a scatter plot, but forgot to include names for each point. They also forgot to plot one student.

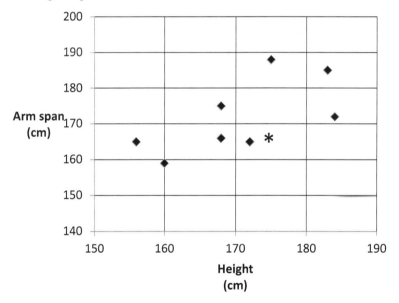

Which student is represented by the point marked with a *?

A. Alice   D. Adam
B. Sarah   E. Emily
C. Matthew   F. Michael

Questions 288 - 294 are based on the following information:
The rectangle represents women. The circle represents those that have children. The triangle represents those that work, and the square those that went to university.

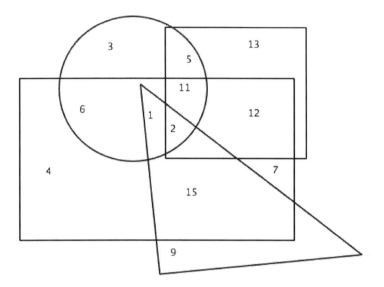

Question 288:
What is the number of non-working women who have children and who did not go to university?

A. 3   B. 5   C. 6   D. 7   E. 9

Question 289:
What is the total number of women who have children and work?

A. 1   B. 2   C. 3   D. 11   E. 14

Question 290:
How many women were surveyed in total?

A. 49   B. 51   C. 58   D. 67   E. 85

Question 291:
What is the number of people who went to university and had children?

A. 5   B. 11   C. 13   D. 16   E. 18

Question 292:

What is the total number of people who went to university, or have children but not both?

A.　18　　　　B.　28　　　　C.　35　　　　D.　41　　　　E.　53

Question 293:

The total number of men who went to university and had children was?

A.　3　　　B.　4　　　C.　5　　　D.　12　　　E.　13　　　F.　18

Question 294:

Which of the following people were not surveyed? Choose **TWO** options.

A.　A non-working woman who went to university but did not have children.
B.　A working man who went to university and has children.
C.　A working woman who had children but did not go to university.
D.　A non-working man who did not have children and did not go to university.
E.　A working woman who went to university but did not have children.

Question 295:

Savers 'R 'Us is national chain of supermarkets. The price of several items in the supermarket is displayed below:

Item	Price
Beef roasting joint	£8.00
Chicken breast fillet	£6.00
Lamb shoulder	£7.00
Pork belly meat portion	£4.00
Sausages – 10 pack	£3.50

This week the supermarket has a sale on, with 50% off the normal price of all meat products. Alfred visits the supermarket during this sale and purchases a beef roasting joint, a 10 pack of sausages and a lamb shoulder, paying with a £20 note.

How much change does Alfred get?

A.　£1.50　　　B.　£5.00　　　C.　£10.75　　　D.　£11.75　　　E.　£12.50

Question 296:

The local football league table is shown below, but the number of goals scored against Wilmslow is missing. Each team played the other teams in the league once at home and once away during the season.

Team Name	Points	Goals For	Goals Against
Sale	20	16	2
Wilmslow	16	11	?
Timperley	14	8	7
Altrincham	13	7	9
Mobberley	10	8	12
Hale	8	4	14

How many goals must Wilmslow have conceded?

A. 8   B. 9   C. 10   D. 11   E. 12   F. 14

Question 297:

The heights and weights of three women with BMI's 21, 22 and 23 were measured. If Julie and Lydia had different weights but the same height of 154 cm, and the weight of Emma, Lydia and Julie combined was 345 lbs, what was Emma's height?

Weight (lbs)

		100	105	110	115	120
	152	19	20	22	24	26
	154	18	19	21	23	25
	156	17	18	20	22	24
	158	15	17	19	21	23
Height	160	14	15	18	20	22
(cm)	162	13	14	17	19	21
	164	12	13	15	18	20
	166	11	12	14	17	19
	168	10	11	13	15	18
	170	9	10	12	14	17

A. 158 cm   C. 160 cm   E. 165 cm
B. 162 cm   D. 164 cm

Question 298:

The measurements for different types of fish appear below:

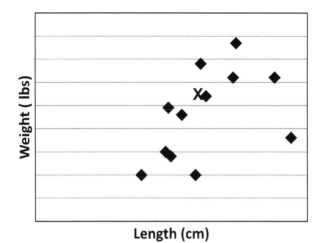

Length (cm)

	Length (cm)	Weight (lbs)
Bluecup	78	40
Silverfinn	96	60
Starbug	98	98
Jawless	100	56
Lamprene	108	92
Scarfynne	118	40
Rayfish	122	136
Lobefin	126	108
Eringill	146	124
Whaler	148	154
Magic fish	176	124
Blondeye	188	72

Which fish is shown by the point marked **X**?

A.   Silverfinn
B.   Starbug
C.   Lobefin
D.   Blondeye
E.   Eringill

The following graphs are required for questions 299-300:
The graph below shows the price of crude oil in US Dollars during 2014:

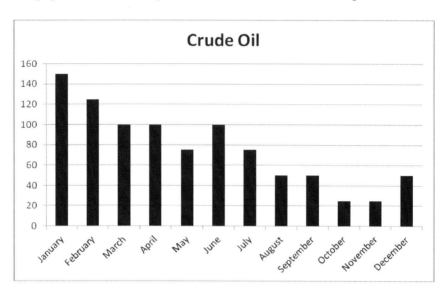

The graph below shows total oil production, in millions of barrels per day:

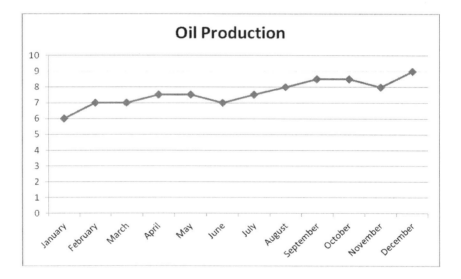

Question 299:

What was approximate total oil production in 2014?

A. 1,750 million barrels
B. 2,146 million barrels
C. 2,300 million barrels
D. 2,700 million barrels
E. 3,500 million barrels

Question 300:

How much did oil sales total in July 2014?

A. $0.56 Billion
B. $16.9 Billion
C. $17.4 Billion
D. $21.1 Billion

SECTION 2

What is the writing task?

The writing task forms the second section of the Thinking Skills Assessment and is only taken by Oxford applicants. Whilst the first part of the assessment is intended to examine the problem solving and critical thinking skills of candidates through a series of short multiple choice questions, the **writing task section examines an applicant's verbal reasoning ability**. Candidates are therefore required to produce a short essay in response to a pre-set question. Most Oxbridge subjects that require that TSA also have some level of essay writing as part of the course. Thus, the writing task is designed to test whether those sitting the assessment can form logical, structured arguments, and to better understand the ways in which they communicate ideas.

What is the format of the writing task?

The Writing Task is sat as Section 2 of the Oxford Thinking Skills Assessment, immediately following Section 1. Candidates have thirty minutes in which to complete their essay, including any time they dedicate to planning. Applicants are presented with **four potential essay questions**, and are asked to **choose one to answer**. All **questions are not subject specific**, and are designed in a way which means that they do not require applicants to have high levels of prerequisite knowledge in any one field. Answer sheet is provided for the writing task, upon which the entire essay must be completed. This means that essay answers can be **no more than two full sides of A4**. Candidates will also be provided with additional paper for planning or rough work, but this will not be submitted or marked.

How is the writing task marked?

Although the writing task is set independently by the Admissions Testing Service, they will not mark the essay submitted. The **essay will instead be passed directly to Oxford tutors** along with the data collected regarding the applicant's marks for Section 1. Individual tutors will have different ways of marking the writing task. Some may consider it in the same way they assess essay submissions from current undergraduates, whilst others may view it as a unique task and consider it under slightly different criteria. Similarly, some tutors may give the essay a numerical score, or a grade; others might provide more verbal feedback. Regardless of unique marking styles, all tutors will be looking for **the ability to organise ideas in a clear and concise manner**, and to communicate them effectively in writing. The essay is not returned to applicants by the Admissions Testing Service, and is kept by tutors for reference throughout the application.

How important is the writing task?

The writing task is just one part of a multitude of information Oxford tutors receive about candidates. Each tutor will give the essay **different weighting** in their consideration of an applicant. Some tutors see the essay as the most accurate reflection of the standard of work they can expect from potential students should they go on to study at Oxford, and thus will treat the writing task as a hugely important source for consideration. However, other tutors may hold the opinion that A-Level grades are a much better method of predicting the quality of work they should expect, and as a result will place less weight on the essay. All tutors will, at the very least, read the essay carefully and **use it to form a judgement on a candidate's ability**. It is relatively common practice for tutors to refer to the essay in interviews, and question applicants on the arguments they have formed. You should therefore **treat the essay as seriously as the rest of your application**, under the assumption that tutors will do the same.

Considering Essay Titles

How are essay titles determined?

Candidates are presented with four potential essay titles in the exam paper, which will have been decided in advance by the Admission Testing Service. Every candidate receives the same options, regardless of the subject they have applied for or any other differentiating factors. You must choose to answer **one question from the four potential titles** provided, and has as much time as they wish to come to a decision. It is worth remembering that applicants are allowed to submit just one answer sheet, with essays limited to a **maximum of two sides of A4**. Therefore, if you choose to change answers having already started writing an essay, your time and space will be severely restricted and only one of the responses will be considered by tutors.

Are there general themes amongst essay titles?

All of the questions posed in the writing task will have been specifically chosen by the Admissions Testing Service based on a number of criteria. All of the questions are designed to facilitate discussion, and often **there will be no single 'correct' answer**. Instead, the essay titles are intended to explore a number of different arguments, which may support or dispute one another. The questions generally invite good candidates to display their theoretical knowledge, yet they tend to **focus on real world issues** and therefore require you to have an understanding of how such theory can be applied in reality. All of the essay titles allow a conclusive judgement to be made, as the ability to reach conclusions is a key skill the assessors are looking for in successful applicants.

What makes an attractive essay title?

When identifying which question you want to answer, **it is crucial that you understand what the question is looking for**. If you don't, there is a real danger that your essay will not address the key issues, and the answer you provide may not meet the expectations that tutors hold about the abilities of successful applicants.

Some candidates will be drawn into the mistake of deciding upon a question before considering all of the options fully, particularly in a stressful examination situation. You should therefore **ensure that you read all of the questions in full** before deciding upon a question. Furthermore, it is highly recommended that you **avoid any questions you don't fully understand**, including if you are unsure of the definition of any key words in the question. Tutors are able to tell if a student is unsure about the meaning of a question, and thus it is important that you feel confident in your ability to answer the question at hand before proceeding with writing your essay.

Some questions will be more appropriate to candidates for specific courses, but candidates should be able to approach almost every question, and should not be deterred from answering a question that does not seem obviously related to their subject. **A good essay on a seemingly unrelated topic will be looked upon far more preferably than a poor attempt at addressing a relative issue.** However, it is worth remembering that the essay will be read by a tutor in that subject, and they will be assessing the writing task in the hope of determining applicants' suitability for the course. Therefore, if you don't feel comfortable that you will be able to display the qualities required for your course in answering a specific question, then the question should perhaps be avoided.

Is it useful to look at past questions?

Looking at previous essay titles is very useful in understanding the types of question you can expect on your writing task. It is extremely unlikely that you will be able to predict the questions in advance of the assessment, as they cover such a broad spectrum of topics; looking at past essay questions will help you prepare for the style of essay you need to write. You will find that **the essays generally lend themselves to conclusive responses**, often taking the form of a yes/no question. However, it is important to remember that although a clear conclusion is needed, **you remain perfectly entitled to argue that there is not one correct answer**. A conclusion based around the idea that "it depends…" or "we cannot tell…" can be completely valid, so long as it is well justified.

As mentioned previously, some questions are better suited to those with an interest in a specific subject. By examining previous papers for yourself, you will be able to better identify these trends. For example, **there is often a question posed which lends itself to an economic approach**, and is very accessible for students applying for Economics and Management or Philosophy, Politics and Economics. Similarly, it is common for **questions regarding morality and the human psyche**, which may be appropriate for a candidate with an interest in Philosophy and Psychology. Nevertheless, the most important factor when considering potential essay titles is not whether you feel the question is aimed at candidates for your subject, but that you feel confident that you can answer the question well, and display the qualities tutors are looking for in the process.

Planning the Essay

Why should I plan my essay?

Planning is a crucial part of essay writing, and ensures that you are prepared to write an effective essay. With a time limit of half an hour to complete section 2 of the assessment, a lot of candidates panic and neglect the planning stage of the writing task. Yet, when you consider that the essay itself is limited to a maximum of two A4 sides, **half an hour is more sufficient to write the essay**. A few minutes spent planning remains an efficient use of time even in the face of a tight time limit. Planning ensures that candidates can organise their thoughts in advance of beginning to write, and provides you with an opportunity to consider the format of your essay. Planning is a good way to ensure that you have not missed any points, and will help you to form your own arguments and reach more well-founded conclusions.

How much time should be given to planning an essay?

There is no set period of time that should be dedicated to planning in the Thinking Skills Assessment, and everyone will dedicate a different length of time to the planning process. You should spend as long planning your essay as you require, but it is essential that you leave enough time to complete the essay.

A candidate may possess a great essay plan, but it is likely to be held on rough paper which is not submitted for marking. If the same applicant then fails to complete the essay in the time allowance, the tutor marking their paper will not be able to appreciate the well-structured plan – and will instead see a candidate with poor time management skills who has failed to write an effective structure. As a rough guide, it is usually worth **spending about five minutes completing the planning process**, as this should allow a useful plan to be formed, whilst still leaving plenty of time to complete the essay. However, this is not a strict rule, and you are advised to tailor your time management to suit your individual style.

What is the planning process trying to achieve?

The planning process exists to produce a **brief skeleton argument**, from which applicants can write a clear and concise essay. Once you understand the structure your essay is likely to take, it becomes much easier to **link points and present ideas in a well organised manner**. This is important as tutors are looking for students who can communicate their ideas effectively. Oxford students are expected to write a number of essays during their time at university, and tutors use the writing task to spot those candidates with the potential to produce a number of good essays during this time. This means they are looking for candidates with the ability to organise ideas, structure arguments and reach valid conclusions. Planning can contribute significantly to ensuring you meet these criteria, and for that reason it is highly recommended that you take the planning process seriously.

How should I go about the planning process?

There is a general format for the planning process which can be used as a framework by all candidates, but everyone will have their own ideas about how best to reach a solid final plan. The first step is generally to **gather ideas relevant to the question**, which will form the basic arguments around which the essay is to be built. Individual candidates will have unique methods of gathering these arguments. Some may choose to form a list of bullet points, whilst others will prefer mind-maps or a for and against table. Again, this is a case of personal preference, and you should **use whatever method suits you best**.

Once these core arguments have been decided, you can then begin to structure the general formatting of your essay, including the way that points will become linked. At this stage, you should **evaluate the balance of your argument**, and confirm that you have reflected arguments from both sides of the debate. Once this general structure has been established, it is useful to consider any examples or real world information that might help to support your arguments. Finally, you can begin to assess the plan as a whole, and establish what conclusions the essay will reach based on the arguments proposed. The **final product is likely to resemble a mini-essay**, with a series of interconnected points.

Essay Structure

What should the general structure of my essay be?

The essay should begin with an **introduction that gives a balanced overview** of the issue in question, introducing any background information and the arguments which will be proposed for both sides. This should be followed by the main body of the essay. This section should give a balanced approach to the question, exploring **at least two distinct ideas and considering each point equally**. Supporting evidence should be provided throughout the essay, with examples referred to when possible. The essay should finish with **a conclusion, which summarises the ideas considered** throughout the main body of text. The conclusion should bring together all sides of the argument, reaching a clear and concise answer the question. There should be an obvious logical structure to the essay, which reflects careful planning and preparation.

How should I format my essay?

Paragraphs are a very important formatting tool, which display to anyone who reads the essay that you have thought clearly about your arguments and are able to structure your ideas clearly. **A new paragraph should be used every time a new idea is introduced**, and should be developed until the argument at hand is clear. Given the space restrictions, you should ensure you leave room to include all the ideas that you wish to discuss, including the conclusion. **Use indents to show new paragraphs**- not empty lines!

However, the emphasis should remain on quality and not quantity. An essay with fewer paragraphs, but with well-developed ideas, is much more effective than a number of short, unsubstantial paragraphs which fail to fully grasp the question at hand. Similarly, a short, well-structured essay is likely to be more effective than a longer essay which fails to address the key issues. Some candidates may choose to compose their essay of alternating 'for' and 'against' paragraphs, whilst others may choose to present all arguments in proposition before moving onto opposition. There is no single correct way to arrange paragraphs, but **it is important that each paragraph flows smoothly from the last**. A slick, interconnected essay displays that an applicant has the ability to communicate their ideas efficiently, and will be looked about kindly by a tutor.

Writing an Introduction

Why are introductions important?

An introduction provides tutors with their first opportunity to examine applicants' work. The introduction is where first impressions are formed, and these first impressions can be extremely important in producing a convincing argument. A well-constructed introduction shows that the writer has seriously considered the question at hand, and can **indicate the logical flow of arguments that is to come**. The format a good essay should take in the writing task mirrors that which would be expected in the highest levels of academic practice. This includes a strong, concise introduction which entices the reader and clearly outlines the structure of the piece.

What should an introduction do?

A good introduction should briefly **introduce the arguments for both sides** and give any relevant background information in a concise manner. It is not necessary for any real depth to be given here, but evidence of some knowledge of the topic should be made clear. The introduction **should not merely repeat the question** in a different manner, but should make reference to points which will be explored later in the essay in a couple of sentences.

The reader should be able to have a strong idea of what the rest of the essay will contain, including the conclusion that will be reached, after reading the introduction. The introduction is the first opportunity to suggest an answer to the question posed, with the main body of text providing an investigation as to whether this answer is justified.

Although background information about the topic can make a nice addition to an introduction, it should not be the focus of the opening paragraph. Instead, the emphasis should be placed on responding to the question.

The Main Body

How do I go about making a convincing point?

Each ideas proposed during the writing task need to be supported and justified, in order to build a convincing overall argument. In this case, the simplest method for presenting arguments is often the best. A point can be solidified through a basic **Point → Evidence → Evaluation** process. An idea should be introduced at the start of the paragraph, in order to signal the flow that the argument is taking. This should be followed by the evidence upon which the argument is based, in order to justify the point being made. Finally, an evaluation of the point can be used to assess the strengths and weaknesses of the argument. By following this process, you can **ensure each sentence builds upon the last**, and that all ideas presented are well solidified.

How do I achieve a logical flow between ideas?

One of the most effective ways of displaying a good understanding of the question is to keep a logical flow throughout your essay. This means **linking points effectively between paragraphs**, and creating a logical train of thought for the reader as the argument develops.

A good way to generate this flow of ideas is by starting each paragraph with a direct reference to how it develops from the last. You should also **provide ongoing comparisons of arguments**.

What else needs to be considered?

In order for an argument to be convincing, it needs to show **a balanced consideration of both sides** of a debate. Even if a one-sided conclusion is reached, discussing opposing viewpoints is a good way to highlight why one suggestion may be more robust than another.

An unbalanced essay can suggest that an applicant is not confident in their reasoning ability to argue their viewpoint convincingly. Another way to build a comprehensive essay is to **clearly state your logical reasoning** as you move through the essay. This can clarify to readers how opinions have been formed throughout, and tutors are more likely to be persuaded by your arguments if they can see where they stem for. Furthermore, **opinions should always be supported with existing knowledge** whenever possible.

Should I use examples?

Examples or real world data can help boost the validity of arguments, and can help display high quality writing skills. Examples can add a lot of weight to an argument and make an essay much more relevant to the reader. When using examples, you should **ensure that they are relevant to the point being made**. Examples can be added wherever they appear to fit, and **there is no set rule about how many to include.** Some questions will provide more opportunities to include examples than others, and the judgement about how many to use remains at the discretion of the applicant. However, in an essay limited to two A4 sides, it is important not to devote too much space to examples at the expense of creating a coherent, well organised essay. Therefore, if you feel as if you don't have space to conclude your essay convincingly, it may be worth sacrificing examples in order to produce a logical, comprehensive essay.

Writing a Conclusion

Why are conclusions important?

The conclusion is one of the most important parts of the writing task. It provides an opportunity to **emphasise the overall sentiment of your essay** to a reader, and also display an ability to reach your own conclusions.

A conclusion provides a final opportunity to show that they have fully engaged with the issues at hand. Similarly to an introduction, a conclusion is a key part of academic articles, and the format tutors are looking for in a good writing task reflects this practice.

What should a conclusion do?

The conclusion should be **one clear paragraph at the end** and should summarise what has been discussed during the main body of text and answering the question decisively. The conclusion provides readers with a **lasting message to take away from the essay**, and candidates should therefore be sure to include anything that they want to discuss.

You can also use the conclusion to **introduce a new idea that has not already been presented**. This can sometimes be an interesting addition to an essay, and can help differentiate a candidate; however you must be careful to do so effectively. Such ideas can easily seem like an afterthought, without adding anything to the essay. In general, a well-organised, "standard" conclusion is likely to be more effective than an adventurous, poorly executed one.

Common Mistakes

1) Ignoring the other side of the argument

Even if you are clearly in support of one side of the debate, it is important to **consider arguments from both sides of the discussion**. A good way to do this is to propose an argument that might be used against you, and then to argue why it doesn't hold true or seem relevant. You may use the format: *"some may say that...but this doesn't seem to be important because..."* in order to dispel opposition arguments, whilst still displaying that you have considered them.

For example, *"some may say that fox hunting shouldn't be banned because it is a tradition. However, witch hunting was also once a tradition – we must move on with the times"*.

2) Answering the topic/Answering only part of the question

One of the most common mistakes is to only answer a part of the question whilst ignoring the rest of it. Alternatively, some students misinterpret the question- or worse, write down pre-prepared essays.

3) Long Introductions

Some students can start rambling and make introductions too long and unfocussed. Although background information about the topic can be useful, it is normally not necessary. Instead, the **emphasis should be placed on responding to the question**. Some students also just **rephrase the question** rather than actually discussing it. The tutors know what the question is, and repeating it in the introduction is simply a waste of space.

4) Not including a Conclusion

An essay that lacks a conclusion is incomplete and can signal that the answer has not been considered carefully or that your organisation skills are lacking. The **conclusion should be a distinct paragraph** in its own right and not just a couple of rushed lines at the end of the essay.

5) Sitting on the Fence

Students sometimes don't reach a clear conclusion. You need to ensure that you **give a decisive answer to the question** in your conclusion, and clearly explain how you've reached this judgement.

6) Exceeding the two page limit

The page limit is there for a reason – don't exceed it under any circumstances including crossings out as the material outside the limit won't be marked and it will appear that you haven't read the instructions.

7) Not using all the available space

Remember that you only have two A4 sides- so ensure you **make the maximum use of the space available** to you. Don't leave lines to show paragraphs – instead, you should use indents. Similarly, you should also **use the top-most line in the response sheet** and avoid crossing entire sentences out.

Example Essays

Example Essay 1

Is globalisation a threat to nations?

Globalisation is best described as the removal of international barriers, and the integration of people on a global scale. Many factors behind globalisation, such as the development of international transport and communication networks, are lauded as a route to global prosperity. Meanwhile other factors are widely criticised. For example, the free movement of labour between nations, and the resulting increase in levels of immigration into developed economies, is often criticised by many. There are a number of socio-economic benefits that can be derived from globalisation, such as the enhanced diffusion of ideas and improved free trade. However, there are also a number of drawbacks to globalisation. It has brought about significant environmental costs, and could be argued to lead to less cultural diversity. I would argue that globalisation can provide both opportunities and threats for nations, and that the overall impact is dependent on the context under which you examine the issue.

One argument in support of globalisation is that it can bring about significant economic benefits for all nations. Globalisation makes international communication and transportation easier, and allows businesses and governments access to a wider pool of resources. For example, a business domesticated in a nation with little or no oil may see their costs reduced by globalisation, through access to international oil suppliers. Likewise, immigration may allow a business to utilise skilled labour from overseas. Having access to these international resources can obviously benefit a country through increased economic growth. Furthermore, improvements in free trade can lead to more efficient international markets, which in turn can lead to consumers facing greater choice and lower prices.

Yet where some countries profit, others usually suffer. A common criticism of globalisation is that it has led to the exploitation of developing countries, particularly in Africa and Asia. It could be said that this presents a serious economic threat to some nations. With multinational firms able to buy up resource centres like oil fields and mines for use elsewhere, domestic citizens in these developing countries often fail to benefit from globalisation. Similarly, with workers from less established economies free to move elsewhere, the progress of these poorer countries may actually be impaired by globalisation. On a purely economic basis, it is hard to argue whether globalisation is a threat or an opportunity for nations. Whilst it can definitely benefit nations, it may present a threat to those who are not suitably prepared to capitalise. Instead, developing economies may in fact be impaired by the additional power globalisation provides to the so called "big players".

Aside from the economic impacts, there are a number of other factors to consider when determining whether or not countries benefit from globalisation. We must also consider impacts on other aspects of society, such as the cultural effects. Globalisation in the last half century has brought with it a greater diffusion of cultural ideas across the globe. As nations have learnt to adopt facets of contrasting cultures, there has been a rise in multiculturalism within individual countries. There is potential for this to benefit society, in as much as they are provided with an opportunity to engage with arts, literature, music etc. from a huge variety of places. Some may even take the standpoint that multiculturalism is beneficial as it surmounts the socially constructed idea of international borders. It could be said that globalisation is the first step in overcoming the principle of competition between countries, and moving toward increased international harmony.

Nonetheless, increases in multiculturalism facilitated by the removal of labour mobility barriers, may be seen as undesirable by many. It is often suggested that this immigration stimulates a dilution of national identity. Countries with high levels of immigration may move away from traditional patriotic practices, which may not be to the liking of some individuals and could be seen as a "threat to nations". Indeed, immigration and high levels of multiculturalism have triggered a growth in neo-nationalism across many European countries, with the rise of a number of far-right political groups in UK and beyond. If the rise of these far-right groups is any indication, it would appear that globalisation has done more to trigger hostility than harmony. There is a strong case to be made that globalisation leads nations to converge culturally. Whether or not this presents a social threat to nations is difficult to determine, and hinges multiculturalism vs. patriotism debate.

The environmental impact of globalisation is often under-considered, but may present a real long term threat not only to individual nations, but to all citizens worldwide. The increased transport of goods worldwide has increased the use of non-renewable resources, and has contributed to increased pollution levels. Globalisation allows firms to outsource production to where environmental standards are less strict. The long run effects of pollution and climate change present a real threat to society. However, it could be argued that these impacts are not a result of globalisation itself, but rather of poor regulatory management of economic growth. If international trade could be remodelled into a more sustainable form, with reduced reliance on unrenewable energy, then this issue would not need to be considered by future generations.

There are a number of effects of globalisation in a number of areas, some positive and some negative, and the impact varies significantly between countries. Overall, it seems to have provided more opportunities to nations than threats, but future globalisation needs to be carefully managed to ensure it does not harm international development.

Examiners Comments:

Initial Comments:
This is generally a well-structured, organised essay that displays many of the qualities that are looked for in a candidate. The answer clearly addresses the question at hand, and analyses the debate from a number of different perspectives. The essay seems indicative of a potential **Politics, Philosophy and Economics student**, given that the applicant undertakes a socio-economic interpretation of the issue. The candidate has clearly allowed themselves enough time and space to complete their essay fully, suggesting that they have carefully planned the structure of their response in advance.

Introduction:
Although the introduction provides a good opening, it is arguably **too long** for this type of essay. The general sentiment of the introduction is good, and the **definition of one of the keywords mentioned** in the title shows a solid understanding of the issue at hand. Similarly, the way the writer outlines the arguments that will follow shows a good organised approach to the question. Nonetheless, the middle segment of the paragraph could have been omitted.

Main Body:
The notions raised are well considered, although at times some of the arguments seem slightly rushed, and without thorough justification. The candidate uses plenty of references to real life to support their points, and displays a good knowledge of relevant issues. The first couple of points are given the most robust analysis.

The candidate could have reinforced some of the later arguments in order to strengthen the essay. The fourth and fifth paragraphs in particular attempt to include **too many ideas at once**, and as a result fail to provide the rigour that the rest of the essay achieves. In this case, the moral investigation into multiculturalism as a way to "surmount the socially constructed idea of international borders" may have been omitted, although it did raise an interesting point.

The flow of the arguments is relatively sound, although the movement between paragraphs could have been better managed at times. The candidate uses the first and last sentences of each paragraph to link ideas well in some parts of the essay, and neglects to do so in others. However, there is a **congruent train of thought throughout** the majority of the essay – which is a good indication of an applicant with impressive essay writing skills.

Conclusion:

The conclusion is a fair one, and shows good understanding of the importance of context when dealing with such issues. This essay highlights the fact that there is **no obligation to give a simple yes or no answer** when presented with a question of this nature. However it could have been slightly more assertive in its final judgement. Whilst the introduction was too long, this conclusion seems **too short**.

Final Comments:

The format of the essay is generally good. There is a clear introduction, followed by a main body of text that addresses a variety of viewpoints, and finally a conclusion which reaches a relatively well-defined answer. The **paragraphs address distinct points**, and the argument is clearly well planned and organised.

The general principles and structure are solid, and the candidate displays many positive writing skills, however the essay is **not as concise as it could be**, and at times some of the points become blurred. The essay has less of an impact on the reader as a result.

Overall, given the constraints that are applied to the writing task, the essay is of a good standard and the author deserves credit.

Example Essay 2

Is globalisation a threat to nations?

Globalisation, the process by which people and countries become more closely integrated across the planet, brings with it a number of benefits to individuals, businesses, and countries. These include the development of free trade and improvements to the mobility of labour. However, it also brings with it certain dangers, including environmental harm and exploitation of developing nations. Despite these dangers, globalisation presents more of an opportunity to nations than it does a threat.

Globalisation is generally considered to be an economic issue. The removal of barriers between nations allows for increased interaction, and opens up a truly international marketplace. Over the last century, technological developments in the fields of transport and communication have allowed for a significant increase in worldwide trade. The birth of the internet and the expansion of the aerospace industry have made the world a much more connected place, and businesses have capitalised on these advancements. Imports and exports, once considered a rarity, are now a huge part of day to day life and consumers reap the rewards. Increased choice and lower prices are just some of the economic benefits to consumers brought about by globalisation, whilst businesses profit from access to new output markets. Nations have benefited from an increased quality of life, driven by the availability of import markets, and higher economic growth, driven by the availability of export markets.

A second economic benefit stemming from globalisation has been the increased free movement of labour. Globalisation has allowed workers to move between nations more freely, due to the removal of many existing barriers to geographical mobility of labour. This issue is a controversial one, with many citizens of developed western economies unhappy at the additional strain immigrants who fail to work place on their welfare system, but theoretically advantages all nations. Those economies with high levels of unemployment will see their workers move elsewhere for jobs, relieving the strain on the nation's welfare system. Simultaneously, those countries which have excess jobs that need filling gain access to a vastly expanded labour market, and can use immigrants to promote the economic growth they are pursuing. This has seen to be effective in areas such as the EU, where the removal of labour mobility barriers has caused many Eastern Europeans to migrate west.

However it is worth considering that these perceived economic benefits may come at a price for some nations. One threat of globalisation is that it makes developing economies increasingly vulnerable to exploitation from external sources. In particular, the increased access multinational corporations have to the resources of underdeveloped nations has the potential to be extremely damaging. Many struggling countries in Africa and Asia have seen increased activity from these international businesses, which are afforded the opportunity to extract resources for less than they would pay in a more established economy. This "investment" may initially seem beneficial to the nations involved, but in reality they would be better served using such resources domestically. Similarly, the global labour market may provide a "drain" which absorbs skilled workers away from the nation to take up positions abroad. These events are likely to impair the economic development of such nations, rather than provide the expected benefits of globalisation.

One further threat brought about by globalisation is that of environmental damage. As has been established, globalisation assists international capitalism through improved transport and communication links. However these links rely heavily on use of non-renewable, carbon based energy sources. Globalisation stimulates huge demand for such resources, to power everything from aeroplanes to computers, and nations suffer serious environmental damage as a result. Rising pollution levels and climate change pose real threats to the future of all countries, which if left unaddressed may result in serious international problems. It has been argued that this is not so much an issue with globalisation, but rather with the current methods of supporting globalisation. It is true that this is a threat that may be rectified in the future, but that makes it no less of a threat.

With careful consideration of all these arguments, globalisation should be seen as an opportunity for nations to benefit economically through increased trade and labour mobility. However, this does not mean that globalisation comes with no dangers. Legislators and governments must ensure that globalisation does not lead to the exploitation of developing nations, or to the exploitation of non-renewable resources, or they risk allowing globalisation to become a threat to nations.

Examiners Comments:

Initial Comments:

Upon first examination, this essay appears carefully considered, well structured, and concisely executed. The format is exactly what is expected, with a **clear introduction and conclusion** forming crucial elements of the overall structure. There appears to be a balanced consideration of more than one argument, with a logical judgement reached. One possible criticism may be that the candidate addresses the question purely from an economics perspective, and fails to investigate other interpretations of the issue. However, the response is a perfectly valid if they are applying to an **Economics related course**.

Introduction:

This is a very strong introduction. It is clear, concise, and immediately addresses the question. The applicant introduces the arguments which will follow, without wasting any time or space delving deeper than they need to. It is **easy to predict how this essay will unfold** after reading the introduction, which is a good indicator of a well-crafted opening.

Main Body:

The candidate clearly raises two arguments in support of the question, and two against it, and provides a well-balanced argument. There are a suitable number of points raised to allow each one to be explored fully without rushing. The candidate successfully **addresses one idea per paragraph**, and all the points are justified well. The points made are well supported to form a solid progression of ideas.

The logical flow of arguments is good, with **clear signposting used** throughout to indicate the direction the essay is taking. The candidate chooses to examine all arguments in favour of globalisation, and ensures that these are fully addressed, before moving on to criticisms. This provides a nice structure to the essay, and allows the reader to develop their own judgement alongside that of the applicant.

Conclusion:

The conclusion reaches a definitive judgement, and shows that the applicant has formed their own opinions on the subject. There is no correct answer to a question such as this, and the **conclusion is rationalised well**. The final point, which suggests that if governments are not careful, globalisation could move from being an opportunity to a threat, is a nice addition that displays careful consideration of all the factors at work. Overall, the conclusion accomplishes its purpose well.

Final Comments:

From start to finish, this is an impressive essay. The question seems to have been seriously considered, and the response itself is very carefully constructed. The one criticism that may be raised is that the essay is rather **conventional and prosaic**, but given the constraints of the task this is not surprising. The applicant clearly demonstrates great ability to communicate their ideas effectively, and engages with the question thoroughly to reach a personal conclusion. Overall, the work seems representative of that of a strong Oxford candidate.

Example Essay 3

Is globalisation a threat to nations?

Globalisation is the process by which countries become more connected on an international scale. It occurs through things that improve links between different countries, like the internet for example. It can also be through the movement of people across borders – increased immigration has been a big contributor to globalisation in recent years. Given the technological improvements that continue to be made in today's society, globalisation seems to be happening more and more. However, does it pose a threat to countries or is it something to be embraced?

One reason that globalisation may be a threat to nations is that it may allow people to look elsewhere for goods. If consumers can buy a product cheaper from China than the USA, then they will obviously do so. In this case globalisation is a threat to the USA, as they cannot compete effectively in a globalised market. The internet, amongst other things, makes it easier for people to buy from abroad, and this can damage countries that are not able to compete as successfully. The economies of these countries suffer, as demand for their goods falls.

Globalisation can break down barriers between nations, and allow people to move from country to country more freely. For example, legislation in the EU means that workers can move to any EU member state to undertake jobs. This might seem like a good thing, but immigration could pose a threat to nations. Those nations with high levels of immigrants may become overcrowding, putting additional strain on resources and lowering quality of life for domestic residents. They might see their welfare system become too burdened, and government spending may have to increase as a result. All of these things can damage a country if the government are not careful.

Immigration can also cause political unrest. People in countries with lots of immigrants may feel as if they are not being prioritised by the government, and there may be tensions between locals and immigrants. This can cause problems for countries, as divisions can rise amongst citizens. This unrest may even lead to conflict, which is definitely a threat to nations. Globalisation may not directly cause disagreements, but it can facilitate them and cause a possibility of violence breaking out.

There are also environmental costs to globalisation. Whilst the increased availability of exports and imports might seem like a global initially, in the long run globalisation places has serious environmental impacts. The increased use of long haul transport causes a rise in the use of fossil fuels, which not only reduces the availability of these resources but also contributes to climate change. Environmental problems may be dismissed by politicians and others because the impacts are not easy to see in the short run, but the long run effects of increased pollution are definitely a threat to nations.

Some people might say that despite all these individual fears, globalisation as a whole does not represent a threat to nations. They may argue that the benefits of globalisation are far greater than the drawbacks, and that the net impact of globalisation is positive overall. The benefits of globalisation are the improved connectivity of people worldwide. Increased communication and transport links make it easier for businesses to expand, for people to experience new culture, and for governments to negotiate with one another. These benefits can be significant, and globalisation has improved the lives of billions worldwide in one way or another.

It is hard to know whether the benefits of globalisation outweigh the costs. There are certainly many positives effects of improving connections between countries. However, as discussed, there are also a number of disadvantages which are often less publicised in the discussion about globalisation. Everyone will have a different view on the matter, and well some may enjoy the improved quality of life brought about by globalisation, others will argue that it is a sign of unsustainable capitalist growth.

Examiners Comments:

Initial Comments:

The candidate has clearly made some attempt to address the question at hand; however the essay is poorly constructed and **inadequately balanced**. There doesn't seem to be a logical flow of arguments, and there is **insufficient depth** to many of the points raised. The essay seems to have been written with **little or no planning**, and lacks a clear conclusion.

Introduction:

This introduction is more reflective of **GCSE standard** than a potential Oxford undergraduate. Although there is some consideration of what globalisation is, and how it occurs, the applicant **fails to address the question** at hand. Instead, they present a paragraph of background knowledge and a **vague rewording of the question** posed. This is a waste of time and space: the reader already knows the question and there is no suggestion of any potential answer. Addressing the question should be the primary purpose of any such opening, and this attempt falls well short of the standards set by Oxford tutors.

Main Body:

The majority of this essay is formed of a string of points that could be made as to why globalisation might be a threat. Individually, these arguments are relatively strong. The candidate raises some interesting points, and provides some level of justification to each idea. However, the essay as a whole is horribly **one sided**, and gives very little attention to the possibility that globalisation is not in fact a threat. The penultimate paragraph does address the benefits of globalisation, but provides far too little consideration for the essay to be considered balanced.

The candidate seems to have forgotten the question at hand, and instead seems to get carried away attempting to come up with suggestions as to why globalisation is a threat to nations. **Not answering the question** is a fatal flaw, and reduces the effectiveness of the essay dramatically. Furthermore, there is little or no sense of flow between ideas, and the **essay reads more like a list of points** than a structured argument. This simply furthers the impression that the essay was written off the cuff, rather than being produced as result of serious deliberation regarding the question at hand.

Conclusion:

In similar fashion to the introduction, the conclusion is noticeably indecisive, and as a result is extremely ineffective. The candidate remarks that "everyone will have a different view on the matter". Whilst this may be true, the objective of the writing task is to **clearly express your own personal judgement** on the issue. The candidate has failed to do this; producing an essay without a concise conclusion suggests that they have **failed to engage fully** with the task.

Final Comments:

Overall, this essay is of a poor standard. The candidate has shown some knowledge of the subject matter, and has attempted to explore the issues surrounding the question posed. However, the **structure of the essay is dreadful**. The response submitted is unbalanced in its consideration of the issues, lacks consistent flow, and fails to reach a clear conclusion. As a result the essay seems **rushed, poorly planned and indecisive**. This essay does not represent the work of a strong Oxford candidate.

General Advice

✓ Always answer the question clearly – this is the key thing tutors look for in an essay.

✓ Analyse each argument made, justifying or dismissing with logical reasoning.

✓ Keep an eye on the time/space available – an incomplete essay will be taken as a sign of a candidate with poor organisational skills.

✓ Use pre-existing knowledge when possible – examples and real world data can be a great way to strengthen an argument.

✓ Present ideas in a neat, logical fashion.

✓ Complete some practice papers in advance, in order to best establish your personal approach to the paper (timings, planning etc).

✗ Attempt to answer a question without fully understanding it or ignoring part of it.

✗ Rush or attempt to use too many arguments – it is much better to have fewer, more substantial points.

✗ Attempt to be too clever, or present false knowledge to support an argument – a tutor may call out incorrect facts at your interview!

✗ Panic if you don't know the answer the examiner wants – there is no right answer, **the essay is not a test of knowledge but a chance to display reasoning skill**.

✗ Leave an essay unfinished – if time/space is short, wrap up the essay early in order to provide a conclusive response to the question.

Practice Essays

1. Is murder ever a rational act?
2. Does a growing global population help or hinder the progress of humanity?
3. Is it science or the arts which shapes the world we live in?
4. Has the "digital age" destroyed the human right to anonymity?

ANSWERS

Answers Key

Q	A	Q	A	Q	A	Q	A	Q	A
1	A	31	A	61	D	91	A	121	B
2	C	32	C&E	62	B	92	A	122	C
3	A	33	B	63	C	93	D	123	C
4	A	34	B	64	B	94	B	124	D
5	C	35	D	65	B	95	E	125	B
6	D	36	A	66	D	96	E	126	C
7	D	37	A	67	E	97	D	127	B
8	A	38	B	68	E	98	E	128	E
9	A	39	D	69	D	99	E	129	B
10	B	40	A	70	D	100	A	130	D
11	D	41	B	71	F	101	C	131	D
12	C	42	B	72	B	102	D	132	C
13	D	43	E	73	A	103	C	133	C
14	A	44	B	74	C	104	E&F	134	B
15	D	45	D	75	D	105	D	135	C
16	A	46	E	76	A	106	C	136	C
17	B	47	B	77	B	107	B	137	C
18	B	48	D	78	D	108	A	138	D
19	A	49	B	79	A	109	C	139	C
20	B	50	D	80	B	110	B	140	E
21	A	51	A	81	E	111	C	141	D
22	C	52	B	82	B	112	D	142	C
23	C	53	D	83	C	113	B&C	143	A
24	C	54	A	84	C	114	B	144	A
25	B	55	C	85	D	115	B&D	145	C&E
26	A	56	D	86	C	116	D	146	D
27	D	57	C	87	C	117	F	147	D
28	A	58	A	88	A	118	D	148	B
29	A	59	D	89	C	119	D	149	D
30	B	60	D	90	C	120	B&D	150	A

Q	A	Q	A	Q	A	Q	A	Q	A
151	B	181	A	211	B	241	C	271	B
152	C	182	B	212	E	242	E	272	D
153	B	183	F	213	D	243	D	273	F
154	C	184	C	214	C	244	C	274	C
155	D	185	E	215	B	245	B	275	B
156	D	186	B	216	E	246	E	276	A
157	C	187	B	217	C	247	C	277	B
158	C	188	C	218	C	248	B	278	A
159	C	189	C	219	E	249	E	279	C
160	A	190	C	220	B	250	D	280	C
161	C	191	F	221	D	251	C	281	C
162	A	192	C	222	C	252	B	282	C
163	E	193	A	223	D	253	C	283	C
164	C	194	C	224	E	254	D	284	D
165	B	195	A	225	B	255	A	285	C
166	B	196	B	226	C	256	D	286	D
167	C	197	B	227	C	257	B	287	C
168	B	198	E	228	D	258	D	288	C
169	C	199	E	229	B	259	D	289	C
170	E	200	C	230	E	260	C	290	C
171	D	201	B	231	C	261	C	291	E
172	C	202	C	232	A	262	C	292	C
173	B	203	D	233	C	263	A	293	C
174	E	204	C	234	C	264	B	294	D& E
175	D	205	B	235	D	265	D	295	C
176	A	206	D	236	A	266	B	296	C
177	C	207	C	237	D	267	A	297	C
178	A	208	C	238	D	268	D	298	C
179	B	209	A	239	C	269	B	299	D
180	C	210	C	240	C	270	C	300	C

Worked Answers

Question 1: A
Whilst **B**, **C** and **D** may be true, they are not completely stated, **A** is clearly stated and so is the correct answer.

Question 2: C
The main argument of the first paragraph is to propose the point that it is more society that controls gender behaviour not genetics. **A** and **D** do not indicate either as they only allude to the end result of gender behaviour and so are incorrect. Hormonal effects are not mentioned in the first paragraph and so **B** is incorrect. **C** would undermine the argument that society *predominately* controls gender, and so is correct.

Question 3: A
B, **C** and **D** are not stated and so are incorrect. **A** is directly stated and so is correct.

Question 4: A
B and **D** are contraindicated by the statement and so are incorrect. **C** could be true but implies children always like the same thing as their same-gendered parent irrelevant of how they are treated as a child, which is contrary to the statement and so is not correct. **A** is correct as is the overall message.

Question 5: C
D may help prevent problems with sexual identity but does not prevent stereotyping and so is incorrect. **A** is not stated, and **B** is implied but not stated and so are incorrect. **C** is the end message of how to prevent gender stereotyping and so is correct.

Question 6: D
The argument follows the reasoning of "A **must** happen for B to happen. B happens, therefore A **must** have happened". Only D) follows this reasoning. Answers A), C) and E) are incorrect, as the conclusions they draw do not necessarily follow from the events described in the sentence. Meanwhile, B) reasons as "If A happens, B **will** happen". This is not the same as saying that A **must** happen for B to happen. In B), Darlington may have won the league anyway, so the reasoning is not the same as in the question.

Question 7: D

The text states that 'Those who regularly took 30-minute naps were more than twice as likely to remember simple words such as those of new toys.' Which means those who napped were twice as likely to remember teddy's name than the 5% who did not, 5% x 2 = 10%, which would be twice as likely, ruling out **A** and **B**. But being 'more than twice' the only possible answer is **D.**

Question 8: A

The answer is to work out 10% (the percentage of napping toddlers more likely to suffer night disturbances) of 75% (the percentage of toddlers who regularly nap). Hence 10 % of 75% is 7.5%

Question 9: A

B, C and **D** may be true but there is nothing in the text to support them. **A** is suggested, as the passage states 'non-napping counterparts, who also had higher incidences of memory impairment, behavioural problems and learning difficulties'. If the impaired memory were the cause, as opposed to the result, of irregular sleeping then it would offer an alternative reason why those who nap less remember less.

Question 10: B

A and **C** are possible implications but not stated and so are incorrect. It is said that parents cite napping having 'the benefits of their child having a regular routine' so hence **B** is more correct than **D** as it refers to the benefit to the toddlers' rather than the parents.

Question 11: D

B, if true would counteract the conclusion, as it would imply that, the study is skewed. The same is true of **C,** which if true would imply unreliable results as the toddler sample are all the same age within a year, but not within a few weeks. **A,** if true, would not provide any additional support to the conclusion and so is incorrect. **D** if true would provide the most support for the conclusion as it proposes using groups with a higher incidence of napping in comparison to those with a lower incidence.

Question 12: C

Although it can be argued that **A, B, D** and **E** are true they are not the best answer to demonstrate a flaw in Tom's father's argument. **C** is the best because it accounts for other factors determining success for the Geography A-level exam such as aptitude for the subject.

Question 13: D

A is never stated and is incorrect. **B** and **C** are referred to being 'many people's' beliefs, and are cited as others' opinions not an argument supported by evidence in the passage, and so are not valid conclusions. It is implied that the NHS may have to reduce its services in the future, some of which could be fertility treatments hence **D** is the most correct answer.

Question 14: A

C does not severely affect the strength of the argument, as it is only relevant to the length of the time taken for the effects of the argument to come into place. **D** is incorrect, as people breaking speed limits already would not negate the argument that speed limits should be removed, but could even be seen as supporting it. These people may count as the 'dangerous drivers' who would be ultimately weeded out of the population.

B may affect part of the argument's logic (as it undermines the idea that dangerous drivers are born to dangerous drivers), but the final conclusion that dangerous drivers will end up killing only themselves still stands, and so the ultimate population of only safe drivers may be obtained. The fact that one dead dangerous driver could have produced a safe one does not necessarily challenge the main point of this argument.

A if true would most weaken the argument as it states that fast driver is more likely to harm others and not the driver itself, which would negate the whole argument.

Question 15: D

Whilst is it stated that the Government assesses risk it is not described as an obligation, hence **A** is incorrect. The overall conclusion of the statement is that on balance the Government was justified in not spending money on flooding preparation, as it was unlikely to occur, so **C, B** and **E** are incorrect and **D** is correct.

Question 16: A

C is incorrect and D is a possible course of action rather than a conclusion. B and E are possible inferences but not the conclusion of the statement. The overall conclusion of the statement is that the way that children interact has changed to the solitary act of playing computer games.

Question 17: B

The passage does state that in this case the £473 million could have been put to better use, however, there is no mention that no drug should ever be stockpiled for a similar possible pandemic. The passage discusses the lack of evidence behind Tamiflu and therefore is stating that in a situation where there is a lack of evidence, there may not be justification for stockpiling millions of pounds worth of the drug. Stockpiling in the case of drugs with high effectiveness is not discussed so we should not assume this is a generic argument against preparation for any pandemic and stockpiling of any drug.

Question 18: B

The passage discusses the fact that unhealthy eating is associated with other aspects of an unhealthy lifestyle so the argument that tackling only the unhealthy eating aspect does not logically follow. The other statements are all possible reasons why the solution given may not be optimal, but are not directly referred to in the passage.

Question 19: A

This is a tricky question in which A, B, C and D are all true. However, the question asks for the conclusion of the passage, which is best represented by A. B is a premise that gives justification for why the elderly should take care of themselves and C provides a justification for why they may not.
D is implied in the text but statement A is explicitly stated. E is incorrect as the passage implies that people should spend the money that they have in old age, not stop saving altogether.

Question 20: B

The passage states stem cell research is an area where there are possible high financial and personal gains, however there is no mention of these being the main driving factors in either this area of research or others. Although rivalry between groups may be a reason driving publishing, this is not mentioned in the passage. The image discrepancies were in only one paper but the passage implies the protocol and replication problems were in both papers.

Question 21: A

D actually weakens the argument, and is therefore not a conclusion. **C** is simply a fact stated to introduce the argument, and is not a conclusion. **B** is a reason given in the passage to support the main conclusion. If we accept **B** as being true, it helps support the statement in **A**. **E** is not discussed in the passage. **A** is the main conclusion of this passage

Question 22: C

The passage describes improved safety features and better brakes in cars, and concludes that this means the road limit could be increased to 80mph without causing more road fatalities. However, if **C** is not true, this conclusion no longer follows on from this reasoning. At no point is it stated that **C** is true, so **C** is therefore the assumption in the passage. The statements in **B** and **D** are not *required* to be true for the argument's conclusion to lead on from its reasoning. **A** is a statement which is strengthened by this passage, and is not an assumption from the passage. **E** is not relevant to the conclusion or mentioned in the passage.

Question 23: C

Answers **A** and **D** are both reasons given to explain fingerprints under the theory of evolution, and contribute towards the notion given in **C**, that they do not offer support to intelligent design. Thus, **A** and **D** are reasons given in the passage, and **C** is the main conclusion. **B** is simply a fact stated to introduce the passage, whilst **E** actually contradicts something mentioned in the argument (namely that Intelligent Design is religious-based, and scientifically discredited). Neither of these options are conclusions.

Question 24: C

The question follows the reasoning of "**If** A happens, B **will** happen. **If** B happens, **C will** happen. Therefore, **If** A happens, C **will** happen". Only C) follows this reasoning correctly.

A) and B) are both incorrect because they assume things will happen which have not been stated in the reasoning. In A), it is not stated that David will lose his job if he cannot travel to work, therefore this is incorrect. In B), John's car may not necessarily pass a speed camera, so B) is incorrect. E) also contains incorrect reasoning. It is not stated that either of the things mentioned are *necessary* for crops to be ripe earlier, so we cannot know from what is stated that Country X is further south than Country A.

D) is correct, but follows different reasoning. D) reasons as "A **must** happen for B to happen. B **must** happen for C to happen. Therefore if C happens, A **must** have happened". This is not the same as saying If A happens, B **will** happen. Grace could visit a petrol station yet still not arrive home.

Question 25: B

The passage states that the average speed *including* time spent stood still at stations was 115mph. Thus, **A** is incorrect, as the stopping points have already been included in the calculations of journey time. Similarly, the passage states that the train completes its journey at Kings cross, so **D** is incorrect. **C** is not correct because we have been given the total length of the journey. Whether it took the most direct route is irrelevant. **E** is completely irrelevant and does not affect the answer. **B** is an assumption, because we have only been given the *scheduled* time of departure. If the train was delayed in leaving, it would not have left at 3:30, and so would have arrived *after* 5:30.

Question 26: A

The argument discusses healthcare spending in England and Scotland, and whether this means the population in Scotland will be healthier. It says nothing about whether this system is fair, and does not mention the expenditure in Wales. Thus, **C** and **D** are incorrect. Similarly, the argument makes no reference to whether healthcare spending should be increased, so **B** is incorrect. **E** is true but not the main message of the passage. The passage does suggest that the higher healthcare expenditure per person in Scotland does not necessarily mean that the Scottish population will be healthier, so **A** is a conclusion from this passage.

Question 27: D

C is an incorrect statement, as the passage says that Polio *hasn't* been eradicated yet. **A** and **B** are reasons given to support the conclusion, which is that given in **D**. **E**, meanwhile, is an opinion given in the passage, and is not relevant to the passage's conclusion.

Question 28: A

This passage provides various positive points of the Y chromosome, before describing how all of this means it is a fantastic tool for genetic analysis. Thus, the conclusion is clearly that given in **A**. The statement in **B** is a further point given to provide evidence of its utility, as stated in the passage. Thus **B** is not a conclusion in itself, but further evidence to support the main conclusion, given in **A**. **C** is also a reason given to support the conclusion in **A**, whilst **D** is simply a fact stated to introduce the passage. As for **E**, there is no mention of Genghis Khan's children (only his descendants).

Question 29: A

Answers **C** and **E** are not valid assumptions because the argument has *stated* that a patient *must* be treated with antibiotics for a bacterial infection to clear. B is not a flaw, because this does not affect whether the antibiotics would clear the infection if it were bacterial. D is an irrelevant statement, and also disagrees with a stated phrase in the passage (that antibiotics are required to clear a bacterial infection). A is a valid flaw, because the passage does not say that antibiotics are *sufficient* or *guaranteed* to clear a bacterial infection, simply that they are *necessary*. Thus, it is possible that the infection *is* bacterial but the antibiotics failed to clear it.

Question 30: B

A, C and D, if accepted as true, all contribute towards supporting the statement given in **B**, which is a valid conclusion given in this passage. Thus, **A**, **C** and **D** are all reasons given to support the main conclusion, which is the statement given in **B**. **E** is not a valid conclusion, as the passage makes no reference to action that should be taken relating to smoking, it simply discusses its position as the main risk factor for lung cancer.

Question 31: A

D is only given as a method, with no mention of its effectiveness. We do not know if C is true because it is not stated. B is not discussed in the passage. Whilst statement E is true, it is supporting evidence for the conclusion, not the conclusion itself.

Question 32: C & E

Whilst **A** and **B** may be true, cost is not mentioned as a deterring factor and we are only concerned with use in the UK, so they are irrelevant. Whether cannabis was the only class C drug is not important to the argument so **D** is not correct. **C** and **E** are the correct answers because the statement concerns the use of cannabis in the UK, directly stating use will decrease from people knowing it has been upgraded to a more dangerous category and from fearing longer prison sentences from higher-class drugs.

Question 33: B

Whilst **A** and **C** may be true, they are not part of the argument. **D** is a possible, but cannot be logically proposed from the information above. **E** would be a flaw if the argument were 'all levels of sports teams reduce bullying' but the passage explicitly states 'well-performing' teams. Hence **B** is correct as it undermines the whole argument, reversing the cause and effect.

Question 34: B

Options **A, C** and **D** do not directly weaken the argument as if any 16 year olds were buying/drinking alcohol (whether the minority or majority) – police would still be spending time catching them. The suggested benefit to reduce police time spent catching underage drinkers would be negated if **B** were true, hence it is the correct answer.

Question 35: D

A is an interpretation of the last sentence and doesn't accurately summarise the argument in the passage. **B** is untrue as there is no mention of if the government can afford to give grants or not. **C** and **E** are incorrect as the passage only talks about small businesses. **D** is correct as it best summarises the change in government policy regarding small businesses.

Question 36: A

The statement discusses a case that was reported, but aims to argue that there may be important errors occurring everyday in medicine that go unreported. Option **A** if true, would significantly weaken this argument as would negate it being a possibility. **B, C, D** and **E** may be true, but they do not negate the argument – if doctors are trained, accidents like the above may still occur. Operations that are successful do not affect those that are not, nor do unavoidable errors have any relation to avoidable ones. That the patient may have died without these errors similarly does not mean that errors, when they do occur, should not be considered errors.

Question 37: A

The main point of the statement is to highlight that although there are numerous safety precautions in place to protect patients, when the weaknesses in these precautions align big errors can occur. So **A** is correct. While **E, C, B** and **D** may well be true, they are not the overall conclusion of the statement.

Question 38: B

Though not the first to be cited, the original error is cited as being the incorrect copying of the sidedness of the kidney to be removed, hence **B** is the correct option. The other options represent errors that in the 'Swiss cheese model' would have not been allowed to occur if the original had not taken place.

Question 39: D

In this instance the 'tip of the iceberg' refers to the number of medical errors reported, implying there may be a significantly larger proportion that go unreported, hence the correct option is **D**, and not **B.**

Question 40: A

The description given about the consultant's performance versus emotional arousal, is described as initially increasing then eventually decreasing over time, which is best represented by graph **A.**

Question 41: B

The consultant says that the 'public perception is that medical knowledge increases steadily over time' which is best represented by graph **B.** The consultant says the regarding the acquisition of medical knowledge, 'many doctors [reach] their peak in the middle of their careers', which is best described by the graph **D.**

Question 42: B

Obesity is not mentioned in the passage, so **E** is incorrect. There is no mention exercise specifically as it relates to old age, so **A** and **D** are also wrong. The diseases associated with lack of exercise are not specifically stated to cause early death, only that they are associated with older people, so **C** is also incorrect. The passage does, however, argue that lack of exercise is associated with illness, and so exercise would be linked to a lack of illness, or good health.

Question 43: E

The preference of women to have their babies at hospital versus home is not commented upon so **B** is incorrect. **F** is never inferred, only that midwives are capable of assisting in normal births and assessing when women need to be transferred to be to hospital, so it is wrong. **A** and **D** are possible inferences at certain points but not conclusions of the statement. **C** is never implied, only that normal home births are no more risky than those in hospital. The overall conclusion of the statement is that the home births should be encouraged where possible as they are not more risky in the cases of normal births, and hospital births are an unsustainable cost in cash-strapped NHS.

Question 44: B

While **A, C** and **D** would, if true, make the practicalities of increasing home births more difficult they would not weaken the argument as **B** would. Where the statement's whole argument rests on home births being as safe as hospital **B**, if true, would negate this.

Question 45: D

The statement says 'With the increase in availability of health resources we now, too often, use services such as a full medical team for a process that women have been completing single-handedly for thousands of years.' Thus implying **D**, 'excessive availability of health resources' is the cause of 'medicalisation of childbirth'.

Question 46: E

1 and **3** identify weaknesses in the argument. If campaigns are what help keep deaths by fire low, they can be seen as 'necessary', and their necessity may be proven by the promisingly low fire-related mortalities. If there are more people with hernias than in fires, more people can possibly die from hernias, but this does not mean the fires are less dangerous to the (fewer) individuals involved in them. **2** is irrelevant, as the argument is about how dangerous fires are in their entirety, not in relation to their constituent parts. Therefore **E**, '1 and 3 only', is correct.

Question 47: B

Since 'some footballers' that like Maths are not necessarily the same 'some' who like History we can exclude **A** and **D**. Equally, while **C** may or may not be true, we are not given any information about rugby players' preference for History, so it is incorrect. We know that all basketball players like English and Chemistry, and that none of them like History, but as we do not know about a third subject they may like **E** is incorrect.

We know all of the rugby players like English and Geography and some of them Chemistry, hence there must be a section of rugby players that like all three subjects so **B** is correct.

Question 48: D

The passage discusses the problems surrounding controlling drugs, and focuses on the rapid manufacture of new 'legal highs': it is therefore implied that this is the current major problem. The passage also suggests that as the authorities cannot keep up with drugs manufacture, the legality of drugs doesn't reflect their risks.

1 is incorrect as the passage says health professionals feel legality is less relevant now, but not that it is not still important. **3** is incorrect as the last sentence says a potential problem of legal highs is that the risks are not as clear, which contradicts the statement that the public are not concerned about any risks.

Question 49: B

The passage is discussing how banning those with the mentioned medical conditions from mountain climbing are *essential* to ensuring safety. It does not claim that this is *sufficient* to ensure safety, simply that it is *necessary*. Thus **C** is irrelevant, as risks from other activities do not affect the risk from mountain climbing. **D** is also irrelevant, because the argument discusses how it is essential to ensure safety of people on WilderTravel holidays, so those using other companies are irrelevant. **A** is an irrelevant statement because the passage is discussing what should be done *to ensure safety*, not whether this is the morally correct course of action. Thus, a discussion of whether people should choose to accept the risks is not relevant. However, **B** *is* a flaw, because the guidelines only mention those with *severe* allergies, so thinking those with less severe allergies are in danger is a false assumption that has been made by the directors.

Question 50: D

The hospital director's comments make it abundantly clear that the most important aspect of the new candidate is good surgery skills, because the hospital's surgery success record requires improvement. If we accept his reasoning as being true, then it is clear that the candidate who is most proficient at surgery should be hired, and patient interaction should not be the deciding factor. Thus, Candidate 3 should be hired, as suggested by **D**.

Question 51: A

Answers **B** and **D** are irrelevant to the argument's conclusion, since the argument only talks about how medical complications could be avoided *if* winter tyres were fitted. Whether this is possible (as in **B**) or whether there are other options (as in **D**) are irrelevant to this conclusion. C is not an assumption because the passage states that delays cause many complications, which could be avoided with quicker treatment. However, the argument does not state that winter tyres would allow ambulances to reach patients more quickly, so **A** is an assumption.

Question 52: B

The passage discusses how anti-vaccine campaigns cause deaths by spreading misinformation and reducing vaccination rates. It claims that therefore *in order to protect* people, we should block the campaigners from spreading such misinformation freely. Thus it is made clear that this action should be taken *because the campaigners cause deaths*, not simply because they are spreading misinformation. Thus, **B** is the principle embodied in the passage, and **C** is incorrect. **A** actually demonstrates an opposite principle, whilst **D** is a somewhat irrelevant statement, as the passage makes no reference to whether we should promote successful public health programmes.

Question 53: D

The passage states that the tumour has established its own blood supply (it says this was shown during the testing), and that a blood supply is *necessary* for the tumour to grow beyond a few centimetres. Thus **A** and **B** are not assumptions. **C** is not an assumption, as it actually disagrees with something the passage has implied. The passage has actually said that action *must* be taken, implying that something *can* be done to stop the tumour. However, at no point has it been said that a blood supply is *sufficient* for a tumour to grow larger than a few centimetres. If this is not true, then the argument's conclusion that we should expect the tumour to grow larger than a few centimetres, and that action must be taken, no longer readily follows on from its reasoning. It is possible the tumour will still fail to grow larger than a few centimetres. Thus, **D** is an assumption in the passage, and a flaw in its reasoning.

Question 54: A

D is incorrect, as the passage has stated the runners are people running to raise money for the GNAA. **B** and **C**, meanwhile, are incorrect as the passage is only talking about whether the GNAA *will be able to* get a new helicopter. Thus, references to whether it wishes to, or whether this is the best use of money, are irrelevant. **A**, however, is an assumption on the part of the passage's writer. The passage says that the GNAA will be able to get a helicopter if £500,000 is raised, but this does *not* mean that it won't be able to if the £500,000 is not raised by the runners. It could well be that they secure funding from elsewhere, or that prices drop. The money being *sufficient* to get a new helicopter does not mean it is *necessary* to get one.

Question 55: C

B and **D** somewhat strengthen this argument, suggesting that more people going on courses leads to better growth, and that people who have gone on these courses are more attractive to employers. **A** does not really affect the strength of the argument, as the current rate of growth does not affect whether government subsidies would lead to increased growth.

C, however, weakens the argument significantly by suggesting that people would not be more likely to attend the courses if the government were to subsidise them, as the cost has little effect on the numbers of people attending.

Question 56: D

B is simply a fact stated in the passage. It does not draw upon any other reasons given in the passage, so it is not a conclusion. **C** is not a conclusion because it does not follow on from the passage's reasoning. The passage discusses what should be done *if* Pluto is to be classified as a planet, it does not make any mention of whether this *should* happen. **A** and **D** are both valid conclusions from the passage. However, on closer examination we can see that if we accept **A** as being true, it gives us good reason to believe the statement in **D**. Thus, **D** is the *main* conclusion in the passage, whilst **A** is an *intermediate* conclusion, which goes on to support this main conclusion.

Question 57: C

A, **B** and **D** would all affect whether the calculation of the Glasgow train's arrival time is correct, but none are assumptions because all of these things have been stated in the passage. However, the passage has *not* stated that the trains will travel at the same speed, and if this is not true, then the conclusion that the Glasgow train will arrive at 8:30pm is no longer valid.

Question 58: A

C can actually be seen to be probably untrue, as the passage mentions a need to escape immune responses, suggesting that the immune system *can* tackle these cells. **E** is true but not representative of the main argument made in the passage. **B** and **D** are not *definitely* true. The passage mentions several *essential* steps that *must* occur, but this does not mean that they are *sufficient* for carcinogenesis to occur, or guaranteed to allow it. Equally, the passage makes no reference to multiple mechanisms by which carcinogenesis can occur. It could be there is only one pattern in which these steps can occur. **A**, however, can be reliably concluded, because the passage does mention several steps that are *essential* for carcinogenesis to occur.

Question 59: D

Answers **A** and **C** are stated in the passage (the passage states 'deservedly known'), so these can be reliably concluded. **B** can also be concluded, as it is stated that in over 50% of cancers, a loss of functional P53 is identified. **D** however, cannot be concluded, as the passage simply states that any cell that has a mutation in P53 *is at risk* of developing dangerous mutations. Thus, it cannot be concluded that a given cell *will* develop such a mutation.

Question 60: D

D is not an assumption because Sam's calculations are based on the *cost per 1000 miles*, not on a given amount of fuel being used up. Thus, he has *not* assumed anything about whether the fuel usage is the same for each car. All of the others are assumptions, which have not been considered. Each of these will affect the total saving he will make if they are not true. For example, if the Diesel car costs £100 more than the Petrol car, the total saving will be £1700, *not* £1800 as calculated.

Question 61: D

The passage discusses how alcohol is more dangerous than cannabis, and states that this highlights the gross inconsistencies in UK drugs policy. Thus, **D** is the main conclusion of the passage, whilst **A** is a reason given to support this conclusion. The passage simply highlights that the policy is grossly inconsistent, and does not mention whether it should be changed, or how (whether alcohol should be banned or cannabis allowed).

Thus, **B** and **C** are not valid conclusions from this passage. The fact alcohol is freely advertised only mentioned briefly in the passage to add strength to the argument that alcohol is more accessible than cannabis, but no judgment is made on whether this should not be so, so **E** is also not a valid conclusion from this passage.

Question 62: B

The passage discusses how if first aid supplies were available, many accidents could be avoided. B correctly points out that this is a flaw – first aid supplies may help treat accidents and reduce the prevalence of *injuries and deaths*, but there is no reason why first aid supplies should reduce the incidence of *accidents*. Answers C and D are irrelevant, since the argument is talking about how first aid supplies could reduce *accidents*, not *injuries* or deaths. Thus, discussing cases in which they could not treat the injuries, or whether they need other components to do so is irrelevant. Equally A is irrelevant, as the argument is simply talking about what could happen *if* first aid supplies were stocked in homes, and makes no reference to whether this is financially viable.

Question 63: C

Answers A and D are not flaws because the passage does not conclude the things mentioned in these. No mention is made to the safety of the drug, and the argument only states that it is thought the compound *may* be of use in combating cancer. No premature conclusions are drawn, only suggestions are made. B is not a flaw because we can see that the experiments *may* produce misleading results if the wrong solutions are used, suggesting that DNA replication is inhibited even if it is not. C, however, is a valid flaw because the argument erroneously concludes that the wrong solutions must have been used when it says the experiments *do not reflect what is actually happening*. This clearly indicates a conviction that the wrong solutions were used, which does not follow on from the experiments being old.

Question 64: B

The passage has not said anything about who scored the winning goal, so A is not an assumption. C is also incorrect, because the passage states that South Shields won the game. B correctly identifies that whilst beating South Shields was *sufficient* to win the league, it was *not* necessary. If Rotherham wins their other 2 games, they will still win the league, so B demonstrates an assumption in the passage. D is not relevant, as it does not affect the erroneous nature of the claim that Rotherham *will not* win the league having lost the match to South Shields.

Question 65: B

C and D actually strengthen or reinforce the CEO's reasoning, with C suggesting as time progresses Middlesbrough will have more and more people compared to Warrington, whilst D suggests that the market share in Warrington may not be as high as suggested, adding further reasons to build in Middlesbrough. A somewhat weakens the CEO's argument, but it is not a flaw in the reasoning, because the CEO is simply talking about how Middlesbrough will bring them within the range of more people, so the market share comment is a counterargument, not a flaw in his reasoning. B, however, is a valid flaw in this argument. Just because Warrington's population is falling, and Middlesbrough's is rising, does not necessarily mean that Middlesbrough's will be higher. Thus, the answer is B.

Question 66: D

1 and 2 are assumptions. The information given does *not* necessarily lead on to the conclusion that these extinction events will continue without further conservation efforts. Equally, there is nothing in the passage that says conservation efforts cannot be stepped up without increased funding. However, 3 is not an assumption, because the passage *states* that global warming has caused changed weather patterns, which have caused destruction of many habitats, which have led to many extinction events. Thus, it is given that global warming has indirectly caused these extinctions, and so the answer is D.

Question 67: E

The argument is suggesting that in Austria, the rail service's high passenger numbers and approval ratings are accounted for by the fact that road travel is difficult in much of Austria. It then concludes that the public subsidies have no effect. We can see that 1 instantly weakens this argument by providing evidence to the contrary, (in France, difficult road travel is not prevalent and so cannot account for the high passenger numbers/approval ratings the country possesses). 3 also weakens this conclusion by suggesting multiple factors affect the situation. This makes the conclusion based on the evidence from Austria less strong.

Thus, the answer is E. 2 actually strengthens the argument that the public subsidies do not cause high passenger numbers/approval ratings, as Italy has high subsidies but low passenger numbers/approval ratings.

Question 68: E

The question refers to companies selling a product despite being in full awareness of the problems that product is causing, and says that we should therefore tax this company to pay to tackle that problem. E) follows this reasoning. B) is the closest to this reasoning, but refers to individual patients paying for their own treatment, rather than referring to a company whose product is causing problems for others, and therefore paying for this damage. Meanwhile, A), C) and D) are not talking about those at fault for certain problems having to pay to fix that specific problem, and are therefore irrelevant.

Question 69: E

All of these statements cannot be concluded from the reference passage.

Question 70: D

Be careful of using your own knowledge here! Whilst **A** and **B** may be true, they are not the main message of the passage. **C** may be true but is not discussed in the passage. **E** is speculative, as the passage does not say if the transplant would be a 'good alternative'. **D** is correct as it echoes the main message of the passage.

Question 71: F

Smoking and Diabetes are risk factors for vascular disease (not a cause). Vascular disease does not always lead to infarction. The passage does not give sufficient detail about necrotic tissue to conclude **C** or **D**.

Question 72: B

A is irrelevant to the argument's conclusion. Meanwhile **E** does nothing to alter the conclusion, as the fact that schools receive similar funds does not affect the fact that more funding could provide better resources, and thus improve educational attainment. **C** actually weakens the argument; by implying that banning the richer from using the state school system would not raise many funds, as most do not use it anyway. **D** does not strengthen the conclusion as stating that a gap exists does not do anything to suggest that more funding will help close it. **B** clearly supports the conclusion that more funding, and better resources, would help close the gap in educational attainment.

Question 73: A

D and **E** are irrelevant to the argument's conclusion. **C** is actually contradicting the argument. **B** is stated in the passage, so is not an assumption of the passage. **A** describes an assumption: the increase of DVDs does not, necessarily, cause the loss of cinema customers.

Question 74: C

The question refers to aeroplanes being the fastest form of transport, and states that this means that travelling by air will allow John to arrive as soon as possible. **C** correctly points out that the argument has neglected to take into account other delays induced by travelling by aeroplane. Cost and legality are irrelevant to the question, so **B** and **E** are incorrect. Meanwhile, **D** actually reinforces the argument, and **A** refers to future possible developments that will not affect John's current journey.

Question 75: D

The argument states that people should not seek to prevent spiders from entering their homes. It does not say anything about whether people should like spiders being in their home, so **A** is incorrect. The argument also makes no allusion to the notion of people preventing flies from entering their homes, so **B** is incorrect. The argument also does not mention or implies that any efforts should be made to encourage spiders to enter homes, or that they should be cultivated, so **C** and **E** are also incorrect.

Question 76: A

A correctly identifies an assumption in the argument. At no point is it stated that bacterial infections in hospitals are resulting in deaths. **B**, **C**, **D** and **E** are all valid points but they do not affect the notion that pressure for more antibiotic research would save lives. Therefore, none of these statements affect the conclusion of the argument and as such they are not assumptions in this context.

Question 77: B

The passage does not state that John disregards arguments because of the gender of the speaker, so **D** is incorrect. **A** and **C** are also wrong, as John states he finds women with armpit hair necessarily unattractive, so a different face or the knowledge of concealed hair would not make him find the female in question more appealing to his aesthetic. John does not state Katherine wants other women to stop shaving, so **E** is incorrect.

B is the correct answer, as Katherine was simply speaking about societal norms, and at no point is it said she was trying to convince John to find her, with armpit hair, attractive.

Question 78: D

A is irrelevant to the argument, which says nothing about what will happen to Medicine in the future. The argument is describing how Sunita is incorrect, and how better medicine is not responsible for a high death rate from infectious disease in third world countries, and how better medicine will actually decrease this rate. **C** is a direct contradiction to this conclusion, so is incorrect. **E** is a fact stated in the argument to explain some of its reasoning, and is not a conclusion, therefore **E** is incorrect.

Both **B** and **D** are valid conclusions from the argument. However, **B** is not the main conclusion, because the fact that 'Better medicine is not responsible for a high death rate from infectious disease in third world countries' actually supports the statement in **D**, 'Better medicine will lead to a decrease in the death rate from infectious disease in third world countries'. Therefore, **B** is an example of an intermediate conclusion in this argument, which contributes to supporting the main conclusion, which is that given in D.

Question 79: A

The statement in A, that housing prices will be higher if demand for housing is higher, is not stated in this argument. However, it is implied to be true, and if it is not true, then the argument's conclusion is not valid from the reasoning given. Therefore **A** correctly identifies an assumption in the argument. The other statements do not affect how the reasons given in the argument lead to the conclusion of the argument, and are therefore not assumptions in the argument.

Question 80: B

A and **E** are both contradictory to the argument, which concludes that because of the new research, Jellicoe motors should hire a candidate with good team-working skills. **C** refers to an irrelevant scenario, as the argument is referring to only one candidate being hired, and at no point does it state or imply that several should be hired.

B correctly identifies the conclusion of the argument that Jellicoe motors should hire a new candidate with good team-working skills in order to boost their productivity and profits. **D** meanwhile exaggerates the consequences of not following this course of action. The argument does not make any reference to the notion that Jellicoe motors will struggle to be profitable if they do not hire a candidate with good team-working skills.

Question 81: E

D is in direct contradiction to the argument, so is not the main conclusion. Meanwhile, **B** is a reason stated in the argument to explain some of the situations described. It is not a conclusion, as it does not follow on from the reasons given in the argument. **A** and **E** are both valid conclusions from the argument. However, only **E** is the *main* conclusion. This is because both **A** goes on to support the statement in **E**. If bacterial resistance to current antibiotics could result in thousands of deaths, this supports the notion that the UK government must provide incentives for pharmaceutical firms to research new antibiotics if it does not wish to risk thousands of deaths.

Meanwhile, **C** appears to be another intermediate conclusion in the argument that also supports the main conclusion. However, on close inspection this is not the case. **C** refers to the UK government directly investing in new antibiotic research, whilst the argument refers to the government providing incentives for pharmaceutical firms to do so. Therefore, **C** is not a valid conclusion from the argument.

Question 82: B

E is completely irrelevant because the question is referring to an unsustainable solution *if* the UN's development targets are met, so the likelihood of them being met is irrelevant. **C** is irrelevant because they do not affect the fact that the situation would be unsustainable if everybody used the amount of water used by those in developed countries, as stated in the question. **A** is also irrelevant, as the passage does not mention price as a factor to be considered within the argument. Meanwhile, **D** would actually strengthen the argument's conclusion.

Therefore, the answer is **B**. **B** correctly identifies that if those in developed countries use less water, it may be possible for everyone to use the same amount as these people and still be in a sustainable situation.

Question 83: C

There is no mention of treatment, so **A** is incorrect. A need to travel abroad for the post is not stated either, so **B** is incorrect. The need for a cool head is stated explicitly, but not necessarily that this be a leader, so **D** is also wrong. Other qualities are irrelevant to the argument, so **E** is also incorrect. **C** would only be relevant if there was indeed a link between 'a specific phobia' and 'a general tendency to panic'. Thus, **C** highlights the flaw: if a fear of flying does not necessitate a general disposition of panic, the argument for not hiring this employee crumbles.

Question 84: C

The passage does not suggest there are no more university places, nor does it make a distinction between the qualities of different universities, so **A** is incorrect and **D** is irrelevant. The argument does not deny the fact that people can be successful without a university education, so **B** is also wrong. **C** is correct, as the passage specifically states 'many more graduates', but not all, are equipped with better skills and better earning potential. This suggests not all degrees produce these skill-sets in their graduates, and so not all university places will create high-earning employees.

Question 85: D

B is unrelated to the argument, as other contributing factors would not negate the damaging potential of TV. Watching sport on television would not be akin to actually playing sport, so **A** is also incorrect. The possibility of eye damage is stated as caused by TV, so **C** is incorrect. However, if people watch television *and* partake in sport, which the passage seems to imply cannot happen, they may not suffer the negative effects of obesity and social exclusion. For example, they may play sport during the day and watch television in the evening, thus experiencing the benefits of exercise and also enjoying the sedentary activity.

Therefore, various potential threats supposedly posed by watching excessive television are undermined, and **D** is correct.

Question 86: C

D directly counters the above argument, and so is incorrect. Though **A**, **B** and **D** are all suggested or stated by the passage, they each act as evidence for the main conclusion, **C**, describing the 'multiple reasons to legalise cannabis'.

Question 87: C

C is not an assumption as it has been explicitly stated in the question that the salary is fixed, and therefore it will not change. The rest of the statements are all assumptions that Mohan has made. At no point has it been stated that any of the other statements are true, but they are all required to be true for Mohan's reasoning to be correct. Therefore, they are all assumptions Mohan has made.

Question 88: A

The answer is not **B** because, although the Holocaust was a tragedy, this is not explicitly stated in the passage. It cannot be **C** or **E**, as these are also not directly stated above. **D** provides an intermediary conclusion that leads to the main conclusion of **A**: we should not let terrible things happen again, and through teaching we can achieve this, so therefore 'we should teach about the Holocaust in schools'.

Question 89: C

DVDs are irrelevant – though one could access disturbing material through a DVD, this does not mean the material to be seen on TV is less disturbing. The argument also is not concerned with adults, and the suggestion is that violence in any quantity may have a detrimental effect, even if a show is not entirely made up of it. **A, B** and **D** are thus not the correct answers. **C** contradicts the argument, as it suggests there is no link between witnessing and re-enacting what one has witnessed. Children may watch the scenes of rape and recognise the horror of the action, and so be sworn off ever committing that crime.

Question 90: C

A is irrelevant, as the passage states it *could* teach children, not that it necessarily would. **B** and **C** are also irrelevant, as the entertainment quality of the show or the likeability of its protagonist would not undermine the logic of the argument. **C** is the correct answer, as it shows how the question uses one model of success and projects it onto all other models, which is illogical: just because Frank succeeds without morality, does not mean all others must reject morality to succeed.

Question 91: A

B, **C**, **D** and **E** are all irrelevant to Freddy's argument that he cannot say a sexist thing because he is a feminist. The woman's discomfort, Neil's feminist stance, the appropriateness of making comments about men, or lewd comments in general do not affect his claim. The presumed link between the two (inability to say something sexist, and feminist self-description) is the flaw in Freddy's argument: someone may believe in equal rights for the genders, and still say a sexist thing.

Question 92: A

At no point is it stated or implied that car companies should prioritise profits over the environment, so C) is incorrect. Neither is it stated that the public do not care about helping the environment, so E) is incorrect.

B) is a reason given in the argument, whilst D) is impossible if we accept the argument's reasons as true, so neither of these are conclusions.

Question 93: D

The easiest thing to do is draw the relative positions. We know Harrington is north of Westside and Pilbury. We know that Twotown is between Pilbury and Westside. Crewville is south of Twotown, Westside and Harrington but we do not know but its location relative to Pilbury.

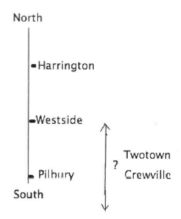

Question 94: B

By making a grid and filling in the relevant information the days Dr James works can be deduced:

	Sun	Mon	Tue	Wed	Thu	Fri	Sat
Dr Evans	X	√	X	X	√	√	√
Dr James	X	√	√	√	√	X	√
Dr Luca	X	X	√	√	X	√	√

- No one works Sunday.
- All work Saturday.
- Dr Evans works Mondays and Fridays.
- Dr Luca cannot work Monday or Thursday.
- So, Dr James works Monday.
- And, Dr Evans and Dr James must work Thursday.
- Dr Evans cannot work 4 days consecutively so he cannot work Wednesday.
- Which means Dr James and Luca must work Wednesday.
- (mentioned earlier in the question) Dr Evans only works 4 days, so cannot work Tuesday.
- Which means Dr James and Luca work Tuesday.
- Dr James cannot work 5 days consecutively so cannot work Friday.
- Which means Dr Luca must work Friday.

Question 95: E

Working algebraically, using the call out rate as C, and rate per mile as M.

So, $C + 4m = 11$

$C + 5m = 13$

Hence; $(C + 5m) - (C + 4m) = £13 - £11$

$M = £2$

Substituting this back into $C + 4m = 11$

$C + (4 \times 2) = 11$

Hence, $C = £3$

Thus a ride of 9 mile will cost $£3 + (9 \times £2) = £21$.

Question 96: E
Use the information to create a Venn diagram.
We don't know the exact position of both Trolls and Elves, so **A** and **D** are true. Goblins are mythical but not magical, so **C** is true. Gnomes are neither so **B** is true. But **E** is not true.

Question 97: D
The best method may be work backwards from 7pm. The packing (15 minutes) of all 100 tiles must have started by 6:45pm, hence the cooling (20 minutes) of the last 50 tiles started by 6:25pm, and the heating (45 minutes) by 5:40pm. The first 50 heating (45 minutes) must have started by 4:35pm, and cooling (20 minutes) by 5:20pm. The decoration (50 minutes) of the second 50 can occur anytime during 4:35pm- 5:40pm as this is when the first 50 are heating and cooling in the kiln, and so does not add time. The first 50 take 50 minutes to decorate and so must be started by 3:45pm.

Question 98: E
Speed = distance/time. Hence for the faster, pain impulse the speed is 1m/ 0.001 seconds. Hence the speed of the pain impulse is 1000 metres per second. The normal touch impulse is half this speed and so is 500 metres per second.

Question 99: E
Using the months of the year, Melissa could be born in March or May, Jack in June or July and Alina in April or August. With the information that Melissa and Jack's birthdays are 3 months apart the only possible combination is March and June. Hence Alina must be born in August, which means it is another 7 months until Melissa's birthday in March.

Question 100: A
PC Bryan cannot work with PC Adams because they have already worked together for 7 days in a row, so **C** is incorrect. **B** is incorrect because if PC Dirk worked with PC Bryan that would leave PC Adams with PC Carter who does not want to work with him. PC Carter can work with PC Bryan.

Question 101: C
Paying for my next 5 appointments will cost £50 per appointment before accounting for the 10% reduction, hence the cost counting the deduction is £45 per appointment. So the total for 4 appointments = 5 x £45 = £225 for the hair. Then add £15 for the first manicure and £10 x 2 for the subsequent manicures using the same bottle of polish bringing an overall total of £260.

Question 102: D

Elena is married to Alex or David, but we are told that Bertha is married to David and so Alex must be married to Elena. Hence David, Bertha, Elena and Alex are the four adults. Bertha and David's child is Gemma. So Charlie and Frankie must be Alex and Elena's two children. Leaving only options **A** or **D** as possibilities. Only Frankie and Gemma are girls so Charlie must be a boy.

Question 103: C

Using, x (minutes) as the, unknown amount of time, the second student took to examine, we can plot the time taken with the information provided thus:

	1st student		2nd student		3rd student
1st exam:	4x	1	2x	1	2x
Break:	8 minutes				
2nd exam:	x	1	x	1	x

Hence the total time taken, 45minutes (14:30-15:15)

Is represented by, $4x + 2x + 2x + x + x + x + 1 + 1 + 8 + 1 + 1$

$$45 \text{ minutes} = 11x \text{ (minutes)} + 12 \text{ minutes}$$
$$33 \text{ minutes} = 11x \text{ (minutes)}$$

Hence, $x = 3$ minutes, so the amount of time the second student took the first time, 2x, is 6 minutes.

Question 104: E & F

To work out the amount of change is the sum £5 - (2 x £1.65), which = £3.30. Logically we can then work out that the 3 coins in the change that are the same must be 1p as no other 3 coin combination can yield £1.70 when made up with 5 more coins. Thus we know that 3 of the coins are 1p, 1p & 1p. We can then deduce that there must also have been 2p and 5p coins in the change as £1.70 is divisible by ten. The only way then to make up the remaining £1.60 in 3 different coins is to have £1, 50p and 10p, Hence the change in coins is 1p, 1p, 1p, 2p, 5p, 10p, 50p and £1. So the two coins not given in change are £2 and 20p.

Question 105: D

If we express the speed of each train as W ms^{-1}. Then the relative speed of the two trains is 2W ms^{-1}.

Using Speed=distance/time: $2W = (140 + 140)/ 14$.

Thus, $2W = 20$, and $W = 10$. Thus, the speed of each train is 10 ms^{-1}.

To convert from metres to kilometres, divide by 1,000. To convert from seconds to hours, divide by 3,600.

Therefore, the conversion factor is to divide by $1,000/3,600 = 10/36 = 5/18$

Thus, to convert from ms^{-1} to kmph, multiply by 18/5. Therefore, the final speed of the train is $18/5 \times 10 = 36$km/hr.

Question 106: C

Taking the day to be 24 hours long, this means the first tap fills 1/6 of the pool in an hour, the second 1/48, the third $\frac{1}{72}$ and the fourth $\frac{1}{96}$.

Taking 288 as the lowest common denominator, this gives: $\frac{48}{288} + \frac{6}{288} + \frac{4}{288} + \frac{3}{288}$ which $= \frac{61}{288}$ full in one hour. Hence the pool will be $\frac{244}{288}$ full in 4 hours.

The pool fills by approximately $\frac{15}{288}$ every 15 minutes.

Thus, in 4 Hours 15: $\frac{244 + 15}{288} = \frac{249}{288}$

Thus, in 4 Hours 30: $\frac{244 + 30}{288} = \frac{274}{288}$

Thus, in 4 Hours 45: $\frac{244 + 45}{288} = \frac{289}{288}$

Question 107: B

Every day up until day 28 the ant gains a net distance of 1cm, so at the end of day 27 the ant is at 27cm height and therefore only 1cm below the top. On day 28 the 3cm the ant climbs in the day is enough to take it to the top of the ditch and so it is able to climb out.

Question 108: A

To solve this question three different sums are needed to use the information given to deduce the costs of the various items. With the information that 30 oranges cost £12, £12/30 = 40p per orange with the 20% discount, hence oranges must cost 50p at full price. With the information that 5 sausages and 10 oranges cost £8.50, we know that the oranges at a 10% discount account for 10 x 45p = £4.50 so 5 undiscounted sausages cost £4 so each full price sausage is £4/5 = 80p.

Finally we know that 10 sausages and 10 apples cost £9, at 10% discount the sausages cost 72p each thus accounting for 10 x 72p = £7.20 of the £9, hence the 10 apples at a 10% discount must cost £1.80, so each apple costs 18p at 10% discount. So an apple is 20p full price. Now to add up the final total: 2 oranges + 13 sausages + 2 apples = (2 x 50p) + (13 x 72p) + (12 x 18p) = £12.52.

Question 109: C

If we take the number of haircuts per year to be x, the information we have can be shown:

Membership	Annual Fee	Cost per cut	Total Yearly cost
None	None	£60	60x
VIP	£125	£50	£125 + 50x
Executive VIP	£200	£45	£200 + 45x

As we know that changing to either membership option would cost the same for the year, we can express the cost for the year, y as;

VIP: $y = £125 + 50x$

Executive VIP: $y = £200 + 45x$

Therefore: $£125 + 50x = £200 + 45x$

Simplified $5x = £75$, therefore the number of haircuts a year, x is 15.

Substituting in x, we can therefore work out:

Membership	Annual Fee	Cost per cut	Total Yearly cost
None	None	£60	£900
VIP	£125	£50	£875
Executive VIP	£200	£45	£875

Hence the amount saved by buying membership is £25.

Question 110: B

All thieves are criminals. So the circle must be fully inside the square, we are told judges cannot be criminals so the star must be completely separate from the other two.

Question 111: C

We are told that March and May have the same last number, which must be either 3 or 13. Taking the information from the question that one of the factors is related to the letters of the month names, we can interpret that 13 represents the M which starts both March and May. Therefore we know the rule is that the last number is the position of the starting letter.

Knowing that there is another factor about the letters of the month that controls the code we can work out that one of the number may code for the number of letters. Which in March would be 5, which is the second letter, so we have the rule of the 2nd number. Finally through observation we may note that the first number codes for the months' relative position in the year. Hence the code of April will be 4, (for its position), 5 (for the number of letters in the name) and 1 for the position of the starting letter 'A') and so 451 is the code.

Question 112: D

If b is the number of years older than 5, and a the number of A*s, the money given to the children can be expressed:

£5 + £3b + £10a

Hence for Josie £5 + (£3 x 11) + (£10 x 9) = £128

We know that Carson receives £44 less yearly, and his b value is 13, so his amount can be expressed:

£5 + (£3 x 13) + (£10a) = £84

Simplified: £44 + £10a = £84; I.e. £10a = £40,

So Carson's 'a' value, i.e. his number of A*s is 4, so the difference between Josie and Carson is 5.

Question 113: B & C

Using the information to make a diagram:

peaches? ————————————————⟶

oranges   <   pears   <   apples   <   grapes

least expensive   most expensive

Hence **A** is incorrect. **D** and **E** may be true but we do not have enough information to say for sure. **B** is correct as we know peaches are more expensive than oranges but not about their price relative to pears. Equally we know **C** to be true as grapes are more expensive than apples so they must be more expensive than pears.

Question 114: B

It's easy to assume all the cuts should be in the vertical plane as a cake is usually sliced, however there is a way to achieve this with fewer cuts. Only three cutting motions are needed. **Start by cutting in the horizontal plane** through the centre of the cake to divide the top half from the bottom half. Then slice in the vertical plane into quarters to give 8 equally sized pieces with just three cuts.

Question 115: B & D

After the changes have been made, at 12 PM (GMT +1):
- Russell thinks it is 11 AM
- Tom thinks it is 12 PM
- Mark thinks it is 1 PM

Thus, in current GMT+1 time zone, Mark will arrive an hour early at 11 AM, Russell an hour late at 1 PM and Tom on time at 12 PM. There is therefore a two hour difference between the first and last arrival. For options E and F, be careful: the time zone listed is **NOT** GMT +1 that everyone else is working in. 1PM in GMT +3 = 11am GMT +1 (the summer time zone just entered) so that is Mark's actual arrival time; 12pm GMT +0 is the old time zone that Russell didn't change out of so that is Russell's correct arrival time.

Question 116: D

Using Bella's statements, as she must contradicted herself with her two statements, as one of them must be true, we know that it was definitely either Charlotte or Edward. Looking to the other statements, e.g. Darcy's we know that it was either Charlotte or Bella, as only one of the two statements saying it was both of them can have been a lie. Hence it must have been Charlotte.

Question 117: F

The only way to measure 0.1 litres or 100ml, is to fill the 300ml beaker, pour into the half litre/ 500 ml beaker, fill the 300ml again and pour (200ml) into the 500ml, which will make it full, leaving 100ml left in the 300ml beaker. The process requires 600ml of solution to fill the 300ml beaker twice.

Question 118: D

If you know how many houses there are on the street it is possible to work out the average, which then you can round up and down and to find the sequence of number, e.g. if you know there are 6 houses in the street 870/ 6 = 145.

Which is not a house number because they are even so going up and down one even number consequentially one discovers that the numbers are 146, 144, 148, 150, 142 and 140. But it is not possible to determine Francis' house number without knowing its relative position i.e. highest, 3rd highest, lowest etc.

Question 119: D

Expressed through time:

Event	People Present
There were 20 people exercising in the cardio room	20
Four people were about to leave	20
A doctor was on the machine beside him (one of the original 20)	20
Emerging from his office one of the personal trainers called an ambulance.	21
Half of the people who were leaving, left (-2)	19
Eight people came into the room to hear the man being pronounced dead. (+8)	27
the two paramedics arrived, (+2)	29
the man was pronounced dead (-1)	28

Question 120: B & D

Blood loss can be described as 0.2 L/min.

For the man: 8 litres – 40% (3.2 L) = 4.8 L When he collapses, taking 16 minutes (3.2 / 0.2 = 16)

For the woman: 7 litres – 40% (2.8L) = 4.2: when she collapses, taking 14 minutes (2.8 / 0.2 = 14)

Hence the woman collapses 2 minutes before the man so **B** is correct, and **A** is incorrect. The total blood loss is 3.2L + 2.8L which = 6L so **C** is incorrect. The man's blood loss is 3.2L when he collapses so **E** is incorrect. The woman has a remaining blood volume of 4.2L when she collapses so **D** is correct. Blood loss is 0.2 L/min, which equates to 5 minutes per litre, which is 10 minutes per 2 litres not 12 L, so **F** is incorrect.

Question 121: B

Work out the times taken by each girl – (distance/pace) x 60 (converts to minutes) + lag time to start

Jenny: (13/8) x 60 = 97.5 minutes

Helen: (13/10) x 60 + 15 = 93 minutes

Rachel (13/11) x 60 + 25 = 95.9 minutes

Question 122: C

Work through each statement and the true figures.

A. Overlap of pain and flu-like symptoms must be at least 4% (56+48-100). 4% of 150: 0.04 x 150=6
B. 30% high blood pressure and 20% diabetes, so max percentage with both must be 20%. 20% of 150: 0.2 x 150 = 30
C. Total number of patients – patients with flu-like symptoms – patients with high blood pressure. Assume different populations to get min number without either. 150 – (0.56 x 150) – (0.3 x 150) = 21
D. This is an obvious trap that you might fall into if you added up the percentages and noted that the total was > 100%. However, this isn't a problem as patients can discussed two problems.

Question 123: C

This is easiest to work out if you give all products an original price, I have used £100. You can then work out the higher price, and the subsequent sale price, and thus the discount from the original £100 price. As the price increases and decreases are in percentages, they will be the same for all items regardless of the price so it does not matter what the initial figure you start with is.

Marked up price: 100 x 1.15 = £115

Sale price: 115 x 0.75 = £86.25

Percentage reduction from initial price is 100 – 86.25 = 13.75%

Question 124: D

The recipe states 2 eggs makes 12 pancakes, therefore each egg makes 6 pancakes, so the number Steve must make should be a multiple of 6 to ensure he uses a whole egg.

Steve requires a minimum of 15 x 3 = 45 pancakes. To ensure use of whole eggs, this should be increased to 48 pancakes.

The original recipe is for 12 pancakes, therefore to make 48 pancakes, require 4x recipe (48/12).

Therefore quantities: 8 eggs, 400g plain flour and 120 0ml milk.

Question 125: B
Work through the question backwards.
In 6 litres of diluted bleach, there are 4.8 litres of water and 1.2 litres of partially diluted bleach.

In the 1.2 litres of partially diluted bleach, there is 9 parts water to one part original warehouse bleach. Remember that a ratio of 1:9 means 1/10 bleach and 9/10 water. Therefore working through, there is 120ml of warehouse bleach needed.

Question 126: C
We know that Charles is born in 2002, therefore in 2010 he must be 8. There are 3 years between Charles and Adam, and Charles is the middle grandchild. As Bertie is older than Adam, Adam must be younger than Charles so Adam must be 5 in 2010. In 2010, if Adam is 5, Bertie must be 10 (states he is double the age of Adam).

The question asks for ages in 2015: Adam = 10, Bertie = 15, Charles = 13

Question 127: B
Make the statements into algebraic equations and then solve them as you would simultaneous equations. Let a denote the flat fixed rate for hire, and b the price per half hour.

Cost = a + b(time in mins/30)
Peter: a + 6b (6 half hours) = 14.50 (equation 1)
Kevin: 2a + 18b = 41, or this can be simplified to give cost per kayak, a + 9b = 20.5 (equation 2)

If you subtract equation 1 from equation 2: 3b = 6, therefore b = 2
Substitute b into either equation to calculate a, using equation 1, a + 12 = 14.50, therefore a = 2.50

Finally use these values to work out the cost for 2 hours:
2.50 (flat fee) + 4 x 2 (4half hours x cost/half hour) = £10.50

Question 128: E

It is most helpful to write out all the numbers from 0 – 9 in digital format to most easily see which light elements are used for each number. You can then cross out any numbers which don't use all the lights from the digit 7.

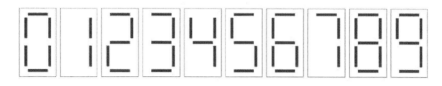

Go through the digits methodically and you can cross out: 1, 2, 4, 5, and 6. These numbers don't contain all three bars from the digit 7.

Question 129: B

In this question it is worth remembering it will take more people a shorter amount of time. Work out how many man hours it takes to build the house.

Days x hours x builders: 12 x 7 x 4 = 336 hours

Work out how many hours it will take the 7man workforce: 336/7 = 48 hours.

Convert to 8 hour days: 48/8 = 6 days

Question 130: D

By far the easiest way to do these type of questions is to draw a Venn diagram (use question marks if you are unsure about the exact position):

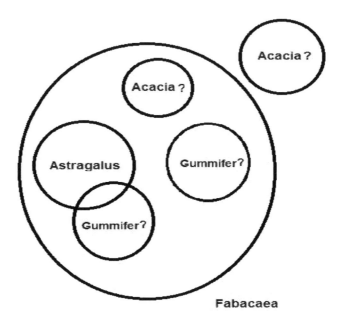

Now, it is a case of going through each statement:

A. Incorrect - Acacia may be fabacaea. Acacia are not astragalus, but does not logically follow that they therefore can't be fabacaea.

B. Incorrect – astragalus and gummifer are not necessarily separate within fabacaea.

C. Incorrect – the statement is not reversible so the fact that all astragalus and gummifer are fabacaea does not mean all facacaea are gummifer and/or astragalus. E.g. Fabacaea could be acacia

D. Correct

E. Incorrect – Whilst some acacia could be gummifer, there is no certainty that they are.

Question 131: D

Area of a trapezium = (a+b)/2 x h

Area of cushion = (50+30)/2 x 50 = 2000cm^2

Since each width of fabric is 1m wide, both sides of one cushion can fit into one width. The required length is therefore 75cm x 4 = 3m with a cost of 3 x £10 = £30.

Cost of seamstress = £25 x 4 = £100

Total cost is £130

Question 132: C

There are 30 days in September, so Lisa will buy 30 coffees.

In Milk, every 10th coffee is free, so Lisa will pay for 27 coffees at 2.40 = £64.80

In Beans, Lisa gets 20 points each day and needs 220 points to get a free coffee, which is 11 days, with 5 points left over. Therefore, in 30 days she will get 2 free coffees. The cost for 28 coffees at 2.15 is £60.20

Beans is cheaper, and the difference is £64.80 - £60.20 = £4.60.

Question 133: C

Work backwards and take note of how often each bus comes.

Must get off 220 bus at 10.57 latest. Can get 10.40 bus therefore (arrive at 10.54).

Latest can get on 283 bus is 10.15 as to make the 220 bus connection. 283 comes every 10mins (question doesn't state at what points past the hour), so Paula should be at the bus stop at 10.06 to ensure a bus comes by 10.15 at the latest. If the bus comes every 10mins, even if a bus comes at 10.05 which Paula will miss, the next bus will come at 10.15 and therefore she will still be on time.

Therefore Paula must leave at 10.01

Question 134: B

You are working out the time taken to reach the same distance (D). Make sure to take into account changing speeds of train A, and that train B leaves 20 minutes earlier.

$$Speed = \frac{distance}{time}$$

Make sure you keep the answers consistent in the time units you are using, the worked answer is all in minutes (hence the need to multiply by 60).

Train A: time for first $20km = \frac{20}{100} \ x \ 60 = 12 \ minutes$

So the distance where it equals B is $12 + (\frac{D-20}{150}) \ x \ 60$

You need to use D-20 to account for the fact you have already calculated the time at the slower speed for the first 20km

Train B: $(\frac{D}{90}) \ x \ 60 - 20$

Make the equations equal each other as they describe the same time and distance, and solve.

Simplifies to $32 + \frac{2D}{5} - 8 = \frac{2D}{3}$ so $D = 90km$

Train B will take 60 minutes to travel 90 km and train A will take 40 minutes (but as it leaves 20 minutes later, this will be point at which it passes).

Question 135: C

Work out the annual cost of local gym: 12 x 15 = £180

Upfront cost + class costs of university gym must therefore be >£180. Subtract upfront cost to find number of classes:

180 – 35 = £145

Divide by cost per class (£3) to find number of classes: 145/3 = 48 1/3

48 1/3 classes would make the two gyms the same price, so for the local gym to be cheaper, you would need to attend 49 classes.

Question 136: C

A is definitely true, since the question states that all herbal drugs are not medicines. **B** is also definitely true as all antibiotics are medicines which are all drugs. **C** is definitely false, because all antibiotics are medicine, yet no herbal drugs are medicines. **D** is true as all antibiotics are medicines.

Question 137: C

Answer **A** cannot be reliably concluded, because from the information given a non-"Fast" train could stop at Newark, but not at Northallerton or Durham. We have no information on whether *all* trains stopping at Newark also stop at Northallerton. Answer **B** is not correct because 8 is the *average* number of trains that stop at Northallerton. It is possible that on some days more than 16 trains run, and more than 8 will thus stop at Northallerton.

Answer **D** is incorrect because it is mentioned that *all* trains stopping at Northallerton also stop at Durham, giving a total 6 stops as a minimum for a train stopping at Northallerton (the others being the 4 stops which *all* trains stop at). Answer **E** is incorrect for a similar reason to **A**. We have no information on whether all trains stopping at Newark also stop at Northallerton, so cannot determine that they must also stop at Durham.

Answer **C** is correct because "Fast" trains make less than 5 stops. Since all trains already stop at 4 stops (Peterborough, York, Darlington and Newcastle), they cannot then stop at Durham, as this would give 5 stops.

Question 138: D

From the information we are given, we can compose the following image of how these towns are located (not to scale):

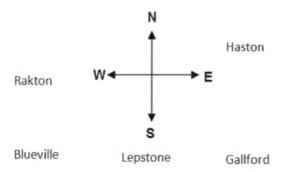

From this "map", we can see that all statements apart from **D** are true. Statement **D** is definitely *not true*, since Blueville is south west of Haston it cannot be East of Haston.

Question 139: C

We are told that in order to form a government, a party (or coalition) must have *over* 50% of seats. Thus, they must have at least 50% of the total seats plus 1, which is 301 seats. We are told that we are looking for the *minimum* number of seats the greens can have in order to form a coalition with red and orange. Thus, we are seeking for Red and Orange to have the *maximum* number of seats possible, under the criteria given. Thus we can calculate as follows:

- No party has over 45% of seats, so the maximum that the Red party can have is 45%, which is 270 seats.
- No party except for red and blue has won more than 4% of seats. We are told that the green party won the 4th highest number of seats, so it is possible that the Orange party won the 3rd highest.
- Thus, the maximum number of seats the orange party can have won is 4% of the total, which is 24 seats.
- Thus, the maximum possible combined total of the Red and Orange party's seats won is 294.

Thus, in order to achieve a total of 301 seats in a Red-Orange-Green coalition, the Green party have to have won at least 7 seats. However, in addition to satisfy the criteria of the green party coming 4th place they must have won the majority of the remaining 36 seats giving a final breakdown of votes as: Red 270, Blue 270, Orange 24, Green 13, Yellow 12, Purple 11.

Question 140: E

Expressing the amount each child receives:

Youngest	M
2nd youngest	$M + D$
3rd youngest/ 3rd oldest	$M + 2D$
4th youngest/ 2nd oldest	$M + 3D$
Oldest	$M + 4D$

Question 141: D

The total amount of money received;

£100, $= M + M + D + M + 2D + M + 3D + M + 4D$

Simplified, thus is:

£100 $= 5M + 10D$

Question 142: C

The two youngest are expressed as M and $M + D$. Simplified as $2M + D$.

The three oldest are expressed as $M + 2D$, $M + 3D$ and $M + 4D$, Simplified as $3M + 9D$

Hence 7 times the two youngest together is expressed $7(2M + D)$, so altogether the Answer is $7(2M + D) = 3M + 9D$.

Question 143: A

To work this out, simplify the two equations:

$7(2M + D) = 3M + 9D$

$14M + 7D = 3M + 9D$

$11M = 2D$

$M = \frac{2D}{11}$

Question 144: A

Substitute M into the equation £ $100 = 5M + 10D$

$5\left(\frac{2D}{11}\right) + 10D = £100$

$\frac{10D}{11} + 10D = \frac{10D}{11} + \frac{110D}{11} = \frac{120D}{11}$

Question 145: C & E

The easiest way to work this out is using a table. With the information we know:

1st		Madeira
2nd		
3rd	Jaya	
4th		

Ellen made carrot cake and it was not last. It now cannot be 1st or 3rd as these places are taken so it must be second:

1st		Madeira
2nd	Ellen	Carrot cake
3rd	Jaya	
4th		

Aleena's was better than the tiramisu, so she can't have come last, therefore Aleena must have placed first:

1st	Aleena	Madeira
2nd	Ellen	Carrot cake
3rd	Jaya	
4th		

And the girl who made the Victoria sponge was better than Veronica:

1st	Aleena	Madeira
2nd	Ellen	Carrot cake
3rd	Jaya	Victoria Sponge
4th	Veronica	Tiramisu

Question 146: D

The information given can be expressed to show the results that the teams must have had to make their points total.

Team	Points	Game Results			
Celtic Changers	2	L	L	D	D
Eire Lions	?	?	?	?	?
Nordic Nesters	8	W	W	D	D
Sorten Swipers	5	W	D	D	L
Whistling Winners	1	D	L	L	L

The results so far total 3 wins, 6 losses and 7 draws. Since, the number of draws must be even, there must have been another draw. So we know one of the Eire Lions results is a draw.

The difference between wins (3) and losses (6) is 3. Thus, there must be another 3 wins to account for this difference. So the Eire Lions results must be 3 wins and 1 draw. Thus, they scored 3 x 3 + 1 = 10.

Question 147: D

Draw a quick diagram to show the given information and it becomes obvious that only D is correct.

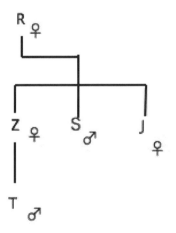

Question 148: B

After the first round; he knocks off 8 bottles to leave 8 left on the shelf. He then puts back 4 bottles. There are therefore 12 left on the shelf. After the second round, he has hit 3 bottles and damages 6 bottles in total, and an additional 2 at the end. He then puts up 2 new bottles to leave $12 - 8 + 2 = 6$ bottles left on the shelf. After the final round, John knocks off 3 bottles from the shelf to leave 3 bottles standing.

Question 149: D

Based on the information we have we can plot the travel times below. Change over times are in a smaller font.

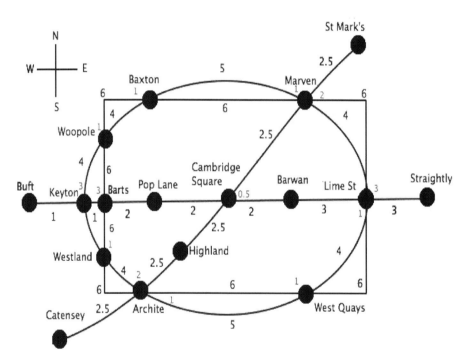

Hence, on the St Mark's line, St Mark's to Archite takes 4 x 2.5 minutes = 10 minutes.

Question 150: A

Going from stop to stop on the Straightly line end Buft to Straightly would take 14 minutes, but we are told earlier on there is an express train that goes end to end and only takes 6.

Question 151: B

The quickest route from Baxton to Pop Lane is via Marven and Cambridge Square, which takes $5 + 2 + 2.5 + 0.5 + 2 = 12$ minutes. Baxton to Pop Lane via Barts would take $4 + 1 + 6 + 3 + 2 = 16$ minutes, which is longer so **E** is incorrect. Other options include times failing to take account of, or incorrectly adding changeover times, and so are incorrect.

Question 152: C

From Cambridge Square:

- Catensey is $(2.5 \times 3 =)$ 7.5 minutes away.
- Woopole, is $(4 + 3 + 1 + 2 + 2 =)$ 12 minutes.
- Buft is $(1 + 1 + 2 + 2 =)$ 6 minutes
- Westland is $(4 + 2 + 2.5 + 2.5 =)$ 11 minutes

Question 153: B

With the new delay information we can plot the travel times as before, adjusted for the delays. Plus a 5 minute delay on the platforms when waiting on any platform for a train.

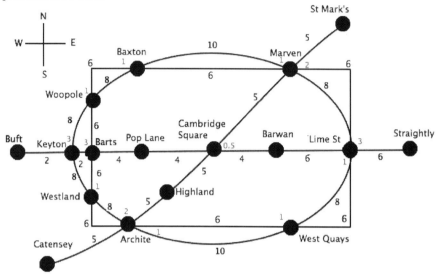

The quickest way from Westland to Marven now uses the non-delayed reliable rectangle line. Four stops on the rectangle line take 6 mins each so 24 minutes in total on the train. Add to this the additional 5 minutes platform waiting time to give a total journey time of 29 minutes.

Question 154: C

- Baxton to Archite via Barts using only the Rectangle line takes (5 + 6 +6+ 6 +6=) 29 minutes.
- Baxton to Woopole on the Rectangle line, then Oval to Archite via Keyton takes (5 + 6 + 1 + 5 + 8 + 8 + 8 =) 41 minutes
- Baxton to Archite on the Oval line only takes (5 + (8 x 4) =) 37 minutes
- Baxton to Woopole on the Oval line, then Rectangle to Archite via Barts takes (5 + 8 + 1 + 5 + 6 + 6 + 6 =) 37 minutes
- As the bus takes 27-31 minutes, it is not possible to tell from between the options which will be slower/quicker so option **C** is the right answer.

Question 155: D

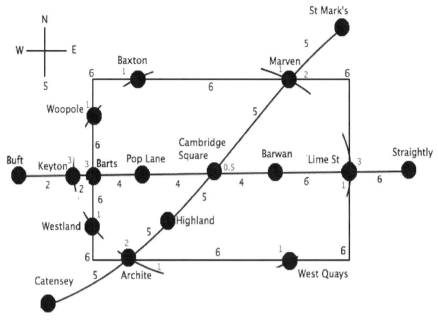

Remember the 5-minute platform wait. We are not told that the St Mark's express train from end to end is no longer running so we must assume that it is, which takes 5 minutes (plus the wait at St Mark's to go to Catensey).

Then, there is a 5 minute wait at Catensey to Archite, and a 2 + 5 minute changeover at Archite onto the Rectangle line which then takes 6 minutes to West Quays. 5 + 5 + 5 + 5 + 2 + 5 + 6 = 33 minutes. Via Lime St the journey takes 5 + 5 + 5+ 2 + 5 + 6+ 6 = 29 minutes.

Question 156: D

From the information:

- "Simon's horse wore number 1."
- "..the horse that wore 3, which was wearing red.."
- "the horse wearing blue wore number 4."

We can plot the information below:

Place	Owner	Number	Colours
	Simon	1	
		2	
		3	Red
		4	Blue

In addition: "The horse wearing green; Celia's, came second"

Which means Celia's horse must have worn number two because it cannot have worn number 1 because that is Simon's horse. Also it cannot have worn number three or four because they wore red and blue respectively. So we can plot this further deduction:

Place	Owner	Number	Colours
	Simon	1	
2nd	Celia	2	Green
		3	Red
		4	Blue

We also know that

- "Arthur's horse beat Simon's horse"
- "Celia's horse beat the horse that wore number 1." i.e. Simon's

We know Celia's horse came second, and that both Celia's and Arthur's horses beat Simon's. This means that Simon's horse must have come last. So;

Place	Owner	Number	Colours
4th	Simon	1	
2nd	Celia	2	Green
		3	Red
		4	Blue

And knowing that:

- "Only one horse wore the same number as the position it finished in."

The horses wearing numbers 3 and 4 must have placed 1st and 3rd respectively.

Place	Owner	Number	Colours
4th	Simon	1	
2nd	Celia	2	Green
1st		3	Red
3rd		4	Blue

"Lila's horse wasn't painted yellow nor blue"

So Lila's must have been red, and Simon's yellow. Leaving the only option for Arthur's to be blue. So we now know:

Place	Owner	Number	Colours
4th	Simon	1	Yellow
2nd	Celia	2	Green
1st	Lila	3	Red
3rd	Arthur	4	Blue

Question 157: C

Year 1 – 40 x 1.2 = 48

Year 2 – 48 x 1.2= 57.6

Year 3 – 57.6 x 1.1= 63.36

Year 4 – 63.36 x 1.1 = 69.696.

Question 158: C

To minimise the total cost to the company, they want the wage bills for each site to be less than £200,000. Working this out involves some trial and error; you can speed this up by splitting employees who earn similar amounts between the sites e.g. Nicola and John as they are the top two earners.

Nicola + Daniel + Luke = £198,500 and John + Emma + Victoria = £199,150

Question 159: C

Remember that pick up and drop off stops may be the same stop, therefore the minimum number of stops the bus had to make was 7. This would take 7 x 1.5 = 10.5 minutes.

Therefore the total journey time = 24 + 10.5 = 34.5 minutes.

Question 160: A

The best method here is to work backwards. We know the potatoes have to be served immediately, so they should be finished roasting at 4pm, so they should start roasting 50 minutes prior to that, at 3:10. We also know they have to be roasted immediately after boiling, so they should be prepared by 3:05, in order to boil in time. She should therefore start preparing them no later than 2:47, though she could prepare them earlier.

The chicken needs to be cooked by 3:55 to give it time to stand, so it should begin roasting at 2:40, and Sally should begin to prepare it no later than 2:25.

You can construct a rough timeline:

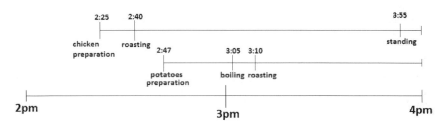

We can see from this timeline that from 2:40 onwards, there will be no long enough period of time in which there is a free space in the cooker for the vegetables to be boiled. They therefore must be finished cooking at 3:05.

The latest time prior to this that Sally has time to prepare them (5 minutes) is at 2:40, between preparing the chicken and the potatoes. She should therefore begin preparing the vegetables at 2:42, then begin boiling at 2:47, so they can be finished cooking by 2:55, in time for the potatoes to boil at 3:05.

Chicken: 2:25

Potatoes: 2:47

Vegetables: 2:42

Question 161: C

The quickest way to do this is via trial and error. However, for the sake of completion: let each child's age be denoted by the letter of their name, and form an equation for their total age:

$P + J + A + R = 80$

The age of each child can be written in terms of Paul's age.

P = 2J, therefore $J = \frac{P}{2}$

$A = \frac{P+J}{2}$

Now substitute in $J = \frac{P}{2}$ to get in terms of P only: $A = \frac{P+\frac{P}{2}}{2} = \frac{P}{2} + \frac{P}{4} = \frac{3P}{4}$

$R = P + 2$

Thus $P + \frac{P}{2} + \frac{3P}{4} + P(+2) = 80$

Simplify to give: $\frac{13P}{4} = 78$

$13P = 312$ Thus, $P = 24$

Substitute P = 24 into the equations for the other children to get: J = 12, A = 18, R = 26

Question 162: A

The total number of buttons is $71 + 86 + 83 = 240$. The total number of suitable buttons is $22 + 8 = 30$. Thus, she will have to remove a maximum of 210 buttons in order to guarantee picking a suitable button on the next attempt.

Question 163: E

This question requires you to calculate the adjusted score for Ben for each segment. If Ben has a 50% chance of hitting the segment he is aiming for, we can assume he hits each adjacent segment 25% of the time. Thus:

$$Adjusted\ Score\ =\ \frac{Segment\ aimed\ at}{2}\ +\ \frac{First\ Adjacent\ Segment}{4}\ +$$

$$\frac{Second\ Adjacent\ Segment}{4}$$

$$Adjusted\ Score\ =\ \frac{Segment\ aimed\ at}{2}\ +\ \frac{Sum\ of\ Adjacent\ Segments}{4}$$

E.g. if he aims at segment 1: He will score $\frac{1}{2} + \frac{18+20}{4} = 10$

Now it is a simple case of trying the given options to see which segment gives the highest score. In this case, it is segment 19: $\frac{19}{2} + \frac{7+3}{4} = 12$

Question 164: C

The total cost is £8.75, and Victoria uses a £5.00 note, leaving a total cost of £3.65 to be paid using change.

Up to 20p can be paid using 1p and 2p pieces, so she could use 20 1p coins to make up this amount.

Up to 50p can be paid using 5p and 10p pieces, so she could use 10 5p pieces to make up this amount. This gives a total of 30 coins, and a total payment of £0.70.

Up to £1.00 can be paid using 20p pieces and 50p pieces. Thus, she could use up to 5 20p pieces, giving a total of 35 coins used, and a total payment of £1.70.

The smallest denomination of coin that can now be used is a £1.00 coin. Hence Victoria must use 2 £1.00 coins, giving a total of 37 coins, and a total payment of £3.70. However, we know that the total cost to pay in change was £3.65, and that Victoria paid the exact amount, receiving no change. Thus, we must take away coins to the value of 5p, removing the smallest number of coins possible. This is achieved by taking away 1 5p piece, giving a grand total of 36 coins.

Question 165: B

The time could be 21:25, if first 2 digits were reversed by the glass of water (21 would be reversed to give 15). **A** cannot be the answer, because this would involve altering the last 2 digits, and we can see that 25 on a digital clock, when reversed simply gives 25 (the 2 on the left becomes a 5 on the right, and the 5 on the right becomes a 2 on the left). **C** cannot be the answer, as this involves reversing the middle 2 digits. As with the right two digits, the middle 2 digits of 2:5 would simply reverse to give itself, 2:5. **D** could be the time if the 2nd and 4th digits were reversed, as they would both become 2's. However, the question says that 2 *adjacent* digits are reversed, meaning that the 2nd and 4th digits cannot be reversed as required here. **E** is not possible as it would require all four numbers to be reversed.

Question 166: B

We can see from the question that Lorkdon is a democracy and therefore cannot have been invaded by a democracy because of the treaty (we are assuming this treaty is upheld, as said in the question). Thus, Nordic (which has invaded Lorkdon) *must* be a dictatorship. Now, we can see that Worsid has been invaded by a dictatorship, *and* has invaded a dictatorship. The question states that no dictatorship has undergone both of these events. Thus, we know that Worsid cannot be a dictatorship. We also know from the question that each of these countries is *either* a dictatorship or a democracy. Thus, Worsid must be a democracy.

Question 167: C

The total price of all of these items would usually be £17. However, with the DVD offer, the customer saves £1, giving a total cost of £16. Thus, the customer will need to receive £34 in change.

Question 168: B

To answer this, we simply calculate how much total room in the pan will be taken up by the food for each guest:

- 2 rashers of bacon, giving a total of 14% of the available space.
- 4 sausages, taking up a total of 12% of the available space.
- 1 egg takes up 12% of the available space.

Adding these figures together, we see that each guest's food takes up a total of 38% of the available space.

Thus, Ryan can only cook for 2 guests at once, since 38% multiplied by 3 is 114%, and we cannot use up more than 100% of the available space in the pan.

Question 169: C
To calculate this, let the total number of employees be termed "Y".
We can see that £60 is the total cost for providing cakes for 40% of "Y".
We know that £2 is required for each cake. Thus, we can work out that 30 must be 40% of Y.
$0.4Y = 60/2$
$0.4Y = 30$
$Y = 75$
Thus, we can calculate that the total number of employees must be 75.

Question 170: E
The normal waiting time for treatment is 3 weeks. However, the higher demand in Bob's local district mean this waiting time is extended by 50%, giving a total of 4.5 weeks.

Then, we must consider the delay induced because Bob is a lower risk case, which extends the waiting time by another 20%. 20% of 4.5 is 0.9, so there is a delay of another 0.9 weeks for treatment.
Thus, Bob can expect to wait 5.4 weeks for specialist treatment on his tumour.

Question 171: D
In the class of 30, 40% drink alcohol at least once a month, which is 12. Of these, 75% drink alcohol once a week, which is 9. Of these, 1 in 3 smoke marijuana, which is 3.

In the class of 30, 60% drink alcohol less than once a month, which is 18. Of these, 1 in 3 smoke marijuana, which is 6.
Therefore the total number of students who smoke marijuana is $3 + 6 = 9$.

Question 172: C
The sequence can either be thought of as doubling the previous number then adding 2, or adding 1 then doubling. Double 46 is 92, plus 2 is 94.

Question 173: B
If the mode of 5 numbers of 3, it must feature at least two threes. If the median is 8, we know that the 3rd largest number is an 8. Hence we know that the 3 smallest numbers are 3, 3, and 8. Because the mean is 7, we know that the 5 numbers must add up to 35. The three smallest numbers add up to 14. Hence, the two largest must add up to 21.

Question 174: E

The biggest difference in the weight of potatoes will be if the bag with only 5 potatoes in weighs the maximum, 1100g, and the bag with 10 potatoes weighs the minimum, 900g. If there are 5 equally heavy potatoes in a bag weighing 1100g, each weighs 220g. If there are 10 equally heavy potatoes in a 900g bag, each weighs 90g. The difference between these is 130g.

Question 175: D

There are 60 teams, and 4 teams in each group, so there are 15 groups. In each group, if each team plays each other once, there will be 6 matches in each group, making a total of 90 matches in the group stage. There are then 16 teams in the knockout stages, so 8 matches in the first round knockout, then 4, then 2, then 1 final match when only two teams are left. Hence there are 105 matches altogether (90 + 8 + 4 + 2 + 1 = 105).

Question 176: A

We know the husband's PIN number must be divisible by 8 because it has been multiplied by 2 3 times and had a multiple of 8 added to it. The largest 4 digit number which is divisible by 8 is 9992. Minus 200 is 9792. Divide by 2 is 4896. Hence the largest the husband's last 4 card digits can be is 4896. Minus 200 is 4696. Divide by 2 is 2348. Hence the largest my last 4 card digits can be is 2348. Minus 200 is 2148. Divide by 2 is 1074. Hence the largest my PIN number can be is 1074.

Question 177: C

If the first invitation is sent as early as possible, it will be sent on the 50th birthday. It will be accepted after 2 reminders and hence conducted at 50 years 11 months. The time between each screening will be 3 years 11 months. Hence, the second screening will be at 54 years 10 months. The third screening will be at 58 years 9 months. Hence, the fourth screening will be at 62 years 8 months.

Question 178: A

Ellie has worked for the company for more than five but less than six whole years. At the end of each whole year she receives a pay rise in thousands equal to the number of years of her tenure. Therefore at the end of the first year the raise is £1,000, then at the end of the second year it is £2,000 and so on to year 5. Thus the total amount of her pay comprised by the pay rises is £15,000, so the basic pay before accounting for these rises was £40,000 - £15,000 = £25,000.

Question 179: B

The trains come into the station together every 40 minutes, as the lowest common multiple of 2, 5 and 8 is 40. Hence, if the last time trains came together was 15 minutes ago, the next time will be in 25 minutes.

Question 180: C

If you smoke, your risk of getting Disease X is 1 in 24. If you drink alcohol, your risk of getting Disease X is 1 in 6. Each tablet of the drug halves your risk. Therefore a drinker taking 1 tablet means their risk is 1 in 12, and taking 2 tablets means their risk is 1 in 24, the same as someone who smokes.

Question 181: A

There are 10 red and 8 green balls. Clearly the most likely combination involves these colours only. Since there are more red balls than green, the probability of red-red is greater than green-green. However, there are **two** possible ways to draw a combination, either the red first followed by green or green first followed by red. The probability of red-red = $\left(\frac{10}{20} x \frac{9}{19}\right) = \frac{9}{38}$.

The probability of red and green = $\left(\frac{8}{20} x \frac{10}{19}\right) + \left(\frac{10}{20} x \frac{8}{19}\right) = \frac{8}{38} + \frac{8}{38} = \frac{16}{38}$.
Therefore the combination of red and green is more likely.

Question 182: B

The least likely combination of balls to draw is blue and yellow. You are much more likely to draw a green ball than either a blue or yellow one because there are many more in the bag. Since the draw is taken without replacement, yellow and yellow is impossible because there is only one yellow ball.

Question 183: F

Since there is only 1 blue and 1 yellow ball, it is possible to take 18 balls which are red or green. You would need to take 19 of the 20 balls to be certain of getting either the blue ball or the yellow ball.

Question 184: C

The smallest number of parties required would theoretically be 3 – Namely Labour, the Liberal Democrats and UKIP, giving a total of 355 seats. However, the Liberal Democrats will not form a coalition with UKIP, so this will not be possible. Thus, there are 2 options:

➤ Labour can form a coalition with the Greens and UKIP, which is not contradictory to anything mentioned in the question. This would give a total of 325 seats, and would thus need the next 2 largest parties (The Scottish National Party and Plaid Cymru) in order to get more than 350 seats, meaning 5 parties would need to be involved.

➤ Alternatively, Labour can form a coalition with the Liberal Democrats and the Green Party. This would give a total of 340 seats. Only one more party (e.g. the Scottish National Party) would be required to exceed 350 seats, giving a grand total of 4 parties.

Thus, the smallest number of parties needed to form a coalition would be 4.

Question 185: E

360 appointments are attended and only 90% of those booked are attended, meaning there were originally 400 appointments booked in and 40 have been missed. 1 in 2 of the booked appointments were for male patients, so 200 appointments were for male patients. Male patients are three times as likely to miss booked appointments, so of the 40 that were missed, 30 were missed by men. Given that of 200 booked appointments, 30 were missed, this means 170 were attended.

Question 186: B

If every one of 60 students studies 3 subjects, this is 180 subject choices altogether. 60 of these are Maths, because everyone takes Maths. 60% of 60 is 36, so 36 are Biology. 50% of 60 is 30, so 30 are Economics and 30 are Chemistry. 60+36+30+30=156, so there are 24 subject choices left which must be Physics.

Question 187: B

If 100,000 people are diagnosed with chlamydia and 0.6 partners are informed each, this is 60,000 people, of which 80% (so 48,000) have tests. 12,000 of the partners who are informed, as well as 240,000 who are not (300,000 – 60,000) do not have tests. This makes 252,000 who are not tested. We can assume that half of these people would have tested positive for chlamydia, which is 126,000. So the answer is 126,000.

Question 188: C

Tiles can be added at either end of the 3 lines of 2 tiles horizontally or at either end of the 2 lines of 2 tiles vertically. This is a total of 10, but in two cases these positions are the same (at the bottom of the left hand vertical line and the top of the right hand vertical line). So the answer is $10 - 2 = 8$.

Question 189: C

Harry needs a total of 4000ml + 1200ml = 5200ml of squash. He has 1040ml of concentrated squash, which is a fifth of the total dilute squash he needs. So he will need 4 parts water to every 1 part concentrated squash, therefore the resulting liquid is 1/5 squash and 4/5 water.

Question 190: C

There are 24 different possible arrangements (4 x 3 x 2 x 1), which means that there are 23 other possible arrangements than Alex, Beth, Cathy, Daniel.

Question 191: F

A is incorrect because the distance travelled is only 10 miles. B is incorrect because the distance travelled is 19 miles. C is incorrect because no town is visited twice. D is incorrect because Hondale and Baleford are both visited twice. E is incorrect because no town is visited twice. Therefore F is the correct answer.

Question 192: C

Georgia is shorter than her Mum and Dad, and each of her siblings is at least as tall as Mum (and we know Mum is shorter than Dad because Ellie is between the two), so we know Georgia is the shortest. We know that Ellie, Tom and Dad are all taller than Mum, so Mum is second shortest. Ellie is shorter than Dad and Tom is taller than Dad, so we can work out that Ellie must be third shortest.

Question 193: A

Danielle must be sat next to Caitlin. Bella must be sat next to the teaching assistant. Hence these two pairs must sit in different rows. One pair must be sat at the front with Ashley, and the other must be sat at the back with Emily. Since the teaching assistant has to sit on the left, this must mean that Bella is sat in the middle seat and either Ashley or Emily (depending on which row they are in) is sat in the right hand seat. However, Bella cannot sit next to Emily, so this means Bella and the teaching assistant must be in the front row. So Ashley must be sat in the front right seat.

Question 194: C

The dishwasher is run 2+p times a week, where p is the number of people in the house. Let the number of people in the house when the son is not home be s, and when the son is home it is s+1. In 30 weeks when the son is home, she would buy 6 packs of dishwasher tablets. In 30 weeks when the son is not home, she would buy 5 packs of dishwasher tablets. So 1.2 times as many packs of dishwasher tablets are bought when he is home. So 2+s+1 is 1.2 time 2+s.

i.e. $2.4 + 1.2s = 2 + s + 1$

Therefore 0.2s = 0.6

s = 3

When her son is home, there are s + 1 = 4 people in the house.

Question 195: A

No remaining days in the year obey the rule. The next date that does is 01/01/2015 (integers are 0, 1, 2, 5). This is 6 days later than the specified date.

Question 196: B

If each town is due North, South, East or West of at least 2 other towns and we know that one is east and one is north of a third, then they must be arranged in a square. So Yellowtown is 4 miles east of Bluetown to make a square, which means it must be 5 miles north of Redtown. So Redtown is 5 miles south of Yellowtown.

Question 197: B

Jenna pours 4/5 of 250ml into each glass, which is 200ml. Since she has 1500ml of wine, she pours 100ml into the last glass, which is 2/5 of the 250ml full capacity.

Question 198: E

The maximum number of girls in Miss Ellis's class with brown eyes and brown hair is 10, because the two thirds of the girls with brown eyes could also all have brown hair. The minimum number is 0 because it could be that all the boys, and the third of the girls without brown eyes, all had brown hair, which would be 2/3 of the class.

Question 199: E

A negative "score" results from any combination of throws which includes a 1 but from no other combination. Given that a negative score has a 0.75 probability, a positive or zero score has a 0.25 probability. Therefore throwing two numbers that are not 1 twice in a row has a probability of 0.25. Hence, the probability of throwing a non-1 number on each throw is $\sqrt{0.25} = 0.5$. So the probability of throwing a 1 on an individual throw is $1 - 0.5 = 0.5$.

Question 200: C

We can work out from the information given the adult flat rate and the charge per stop. Let the charge per stop be s and the flat rate be f. Therefore: $15s + f = 1.70$

$8s + f = 1.14$

We can hence work out that:

$7s = 0.56$, so $s = 0.08$. Hence, $f = 0.50$

Megan is an adult so she pays this rate. For 30 stops, the rate will be 0.08 x 30 + 0.50 = 2.90.

Question 201: B

We found in the previous question that the flat rate for adults is £0.50 and the rate per stop is £0.08. We know that the child rate is half the flat rate and a quarter of the "per stop" rate, so the child flat rate is £0.25 and the rate per stop is 2p. So for 25 stops, Alice pays:

0.02 x 25 + 0.25 = 0.75

Question 202: C

We should first work out how many stops James can travel. For £2, he can afford to travel as many stops as £1.50 will take him once the flat rate is taken into account. The per stop rate is 8p per stop, so he can travel 18 stops, so he will need to go to the 18th stop from town. So he will need to walk past 7 stops to get to the stop he can afford to travel from.

Question 203: D

The picture will need a 12 inch by 16 inch mount, which will cost £8. It will need a 13 inch by 17 inch frame, which will cost £26. So the cost of mounting and framing the picture will be £8 + £26 = £34.

Question 204: C

Mounting and framing an 8 by 8 inch painting will cost £5 for the mount and £22 for the frame, which is £27. Mounting and framing a 10 by 10 inch painting will cost £6 for the mount and £26 for the frame, which is £32. The difference is £32 - £27 = £5.

Question 205: B

We found in the last question that mounting and framing a 10 by 10 inch painting will cost £6 for the mount and £26 for the frame, which is £32 total. We can calculate that each additional inch of mount and frame for a square painting costs £2.50; £2 for the frame and £0.50 for the mount. So an 11 inch painting will cost £34.50 to frame and mount, a 12 inch £37, a 13 inch £39.50, a 14 inch £42. The biggest painting that can be mounted and framed for £40 is a 13 inch painting.

Question 206: D

Recognise that the pattern is *"consonants move forward by two consonants; vowel stay the same"*. This allows coding of the word MAGICAL to PAJIFAN to RALIHAQ.

Forward two			Forward	two
M	$\Rightarrow$	O (skips to) P		$\Rightarrow$ R
A	$\Rightarrow$	Stays the same		$\Rightarrow$ A
G	$\Rightarrow$	I (skips to) J		$\Rightarrow$ L
I	$\Rightarrow$	Stays the same		$\Rightarrow$ I
C	$\Rightarrow$	E (skips to) F		$\Rightarrow$ H
A	$\Rightarrow$	Stays the same		$\Rightarrow$ A
L	$\Rightarrow$	N		$\Rightarrow$ Q

Question 207: C

If f donates the flat rate, and k denotes the rate per km, we can use the information to form equations: $f + 5k = £6$ and $f + 3k = £4.20$

Solve these simultaneously:

$(f + 5k) - (f + 3k) = £6 - £4.20$

Thus, $2k = £1.80$ and $k = £0.90$

Therefore, $f + (5 \times 0.90) = £6$

So, $f + £4.50 = £6$

So, $f = £1.50$

$7k$ will be $£1.50 + 7 \times £0.90 = £7.80$

Question 208: C

The increase from 2001/2 to 2011/12 was 1,019 to 11,736, which equals a linear increase of 10,717 admissions.

So, in 20 years, we would expect to see an increase by 10,717 x 2 = 21,434. Add this to the number in 2011 to give 33,170 admissions.

Question 209: A

As the question uses percentages, it does not matter what figure you use. To make calculations easier, use an initial price of £100. When on sale, the dress is 20% off, so using a normal price of £100, the dress would be £80. When the dresses are 20% off, the shop is making a 25% profit. Therefore: £80 = 1.25 x purchase price.

Therefore, the purchase price is: $\frac{80}{1.25}$ = £64. Thus, the normal profit is £100 - £64 = £36. I.e. when a dress sells for £100, the shop makes £36 or 36% profit.

Question 210: C

1. Incorrect. There must be 6 general committee clinical students, plus the treasurer, and 2 sabbatical roles, none of whom can be preclinical, so there must be a maximum of 11 preclinical students.
2. Correct. There must two general for each year plus welfare and social officers, totalling to 6.
3. Incorrect. The committee is made up of 20 students, 2 roles are sabbatical, so there are 18 studying students, therefore there can be 3 from each year.
4. Correct. There are 18 studying students on the committee, and there must be 6 general committee members from pre-clinical, plus welfare and social, therefore there must be a minimum of 8 pre-clinical students, so there must be 10 clinical students.
5. Incorrect. You need to count up the number of specific roles on the committee, which is 5, and there must be 2 students from each year, which is 12. This leaves 3 more positions, which the question doesn't state can't be first years. Therefore there could be up to 5 first years.
6. Incorrect. There must be at least 2 general committee members from each year. However, the worked answer to 5 shows there are 15 general committee members which are split across the 6 years, and so there must be an uneven distribution.

Question 211: B

Remember 2012 was a leap year. Work through each month, adding the correct number of days, to work out what day each 13th would be on.

If a month was 28 days, the 13th would be the same day each month, therefore to work this out quickly, you only need to count on the number of days over 28. For example, in a month with 31 days, the 13th will be 3 weekdays (31-28) later.

Thus if 13th January is a Friday, 13th February is a Monday, (February has 29 days in 2012), 13th March is a Tuesday and 13th April is a Friday.

Question 212: E

There are 18 sheep in total. The question states there are 8 male sheep, which means there are 10 female sheep before some die. 5 female sheep die, so there are 5 female sheep alive to give birth to lambs. Each delivers 2 lambs, making 10 lambs in total. There are 4 male sheep and 5 mothers so the total is 10 + 4 + 5 = 19 sheep.

Question 213: D

We can see from the fact that all the possible answers end "AME" that the letters "AME" must be translated to the last 3 letters of the coded word, "JVN", under the code. J is the 10th letter of the alphabet so it is 9 letters on from A (V is the 21st letter of the alphabet and M is the 13th, and N is the 14th letter of the alphabet and E is the 5th, therefore these pairs are also 9 letters apart). Therefore P is the code for the letter 9 letters before it in the alphabet.

P is the 16th letter of the alphabet, therefore it is the code for the 7th letter of the alphabet, G. Therefore from these solutions the only possibility for the original word is GAME.

Question 214: C

Let x be the number of people who get on the bus at the station. It is easiest to work backwards. After the 4th stop, there are 5 people on the bus. At the 4th stop, half the people who were on the bus got off (and therefore half stayed on) and 2 people got on. Therefore, 5 is equal to 2 plus half the number of people who were on the bus after the 3rd stop. So half the number of people who were on the bus after the 3rd stop must be 3. Therefore, after the 3rd stop, there must have been 6 people on the bus.

We can then say that 6 is equal to 2 plus half the number of people who were on the bus after the 2nd stop. Therefore there were 8 people on the bus after the 2nd stop.

We can then say that 8 is equal to 2 plus half the number of people who were on the bus after the 1st stop. Therefore there were 12 people on the bus after the 1st stop.

We can then say that 12 is equal to 2 plus half the number of people who got on the bus at the station. Therefore the number of people who got on the bus at the station is 20.

Question 215: B

We know from the question that I have purchased small cans of blue and white paint, and that blue paint accounted for 50% of the total cost. Since a can of blue paint is 4 X the price of a can of white paint, we know I must have purchased 4 cans of white paint for each can of blue paint.

Each can of small paint covers a total of 10m^2, and I have painted a total of 100m^2, in doing so using up all the paint. Therefore, I must have purchased 10 cans of paint. Therefore, I must have purchased 2 cans of blue paint and 8 cans of white paint. So I must have painted 20m^2 of wall space blue.

Question 216: E

The cost for x cakes under this offer can be expressed as: $x(42-x^2)$

Following this formula, we can see that 2 cakes would cost 76p, 3 cakes would cost 99p, and 4 cakes would cost 104p. As the number of cakes increases beyond 4, we see that the overall price actually drops, as 5 cakes would cost 85p and 6 cakes would cost 36p. This confirms Isobel's prediction that the offer is a bad deal for the baker, as it ends up cheaper for the customer to purchase more cakes. It is clear that 6 cakes is the smallest number for which the price will be under 40p, and the price will continue to drop as more cakes are purchased.

Question 217: C

Adding up the percentages of students in University A who do "Science" subjects gives: $23.50 + 6.25 + 30.25 = 60\%$.

60% of 800 students is 480, so 480 students in University A do "Science" subjects.

Adding up the percentages of students in University B who do "Science subjects" gives:

$13.25 + 14.75 + 7.00 = 35\%$. 35% of 1200 students is 420, so 420 students in University B do "Science" subjects. Therefore: $480 - 420 = 60$.

60 more students in University A than University B take a "Science" subject.

Question 218: C

Let the number of miles Sonia is travelling be x. Because she is crossing 1 international border, travelling by Traveleasy Coaches will cost Sonia:

£$(5 + 0.5x)$

Travelling by Europremier coaches will cost Sonia: £$(15 + 0.1x)$.

Because we know the cost is the same for both companies, the number of miles she is travelling can be found by setting these two expressions equal to each other: $5 + 0.5x = 15 + 0.1x$

This equation can be rearranged to find that: $0.4x = 10$;

Therefore: $x = 10/0.4 = 25$

Question 219: E

To find out whether many of these statements are true it is necessary to work out the departure and arrival times, and journey time, for each girl

Lauren departs at 2:30pm and arrives at 4pm, therefore her journey takes 1.5 hours

Chloe departs at 1:30pm and her journey takes 1 hour longer than 1.5 hours (Lauren's journey), therefore her journey takes 2.5 hours and she arrives at 4pm

Amy arrives at 4:15pm and her journey takes 2 times 1.5 hours (Lauren's journey), therefore her journey takes 3 hours and she departs at 1:15pm.

Looking at each statement, the only one which is definitely true is **E**: Amy departs at 1:15pm and Chloe departs at 1:30pm therefore Amy departed before Chloe.

D *may* be true, but nothing in the question shows it is *definitely* true, so it can be safely ignored.

Question 220: B

First consider how many items of clothing she can take by weight. The weight allowance is 20 kg. Take off 2 kg for the weight of the empty suitcase, then take off another 3 kg (3 x 1000g) for the books she wishes to take. Therefore she can fit 15kg of clothes in her suitcase. To find out how many items of clothing this is, we can divide 15 kg = 15000g by 400g:

15000/400 = 150/4 = 37.5.

So she can pack up to 37 items of clothing by weight.

Now consider the volume of clothes she can fit in. The total volume of the suitcase is:

50cm x 50cm x 20cm = 50000 cm^3

The volume of each book is:

0.2m x 0.1m x 0.05m = 1000 cm^3

So the volume of space available for clothes is:

50000 – (3 x 1000) = 47000 cm^3

To find out how many items of clothing she can fit in this space, we can divide 47000 by 1500:

47000/1500 = 470/15 = 31.3

So she can pack up to 31 items of clothing by volume.

Although she can fit 37 items by weight, they will not fit in the volume of the suitcase, so the maximum number of items of clothing she can pack is 31.

Question 221: D

We can work out the Answer by considering each option:

Bed Shop A: £120 + £70 = £190

Bed Shop B: £90 + £90 = £180

Bed Shop C: £140 + (1/2 x £60) = £170

Bed Shop D: (2/3) x (£140+£100) = (2/3) x (£240) = £160

Bed Shop E: £175

Therefore the cheapest is Bed Shop **D**.

Question 222: C

The numbers of socks of each colour is irrelevant, so long as there is more than one of each (which there is). There are only 4 colours of socks, so if Joseph takes 5 socks, it is guaranteed that at least 2 of them will be the same colour.

Question 223: D

Paper comes in packs of 500, and with each pack 20 magazines can be printed. Each pack costs £3.

Card comes in packs of 60, and with each pack 60 magazines can be printed. Each pack costs £3 x 2 = £6.

Each ink cartridge prints 130 sheets, which is 130/26 = 5 magazines. Each cartridge costs £5.

The lowest common multiple of 20, 60 and 5 is 60, so it is possible to work out the total cost for printing 60 magazines. Printing 60 magazines will require 3 packs of paper at £3, 1 pack of card at £6 and 12 ink cartridges at £5. So the total cost of printing 60 magazines is:

$(3 \times 3) + 6 + (12 \times 5) = £75$. The total budget is £300 ; £300/£75 = 4

So we can print 4x60 magazines in this budget, which is 240 magazines.

Question 224: E

We can express the information we have as: $\frac{1}{4} - \frac{1}{5} = \frac{1}{20}$

So the six additional lengths make up 1/20 of Rebecca's intended distance. So the number of lengths she intended to complete was: 20 x 6 = 120.

Question 225: B

Sammy has a choice of 3 flavours for the first sweet that he eats. Each of the other sweets he eats cannot be the same flavour as the sweet he has just eaten. So he has a choice of 2 flavours for each of these four sweets. So the total number of ways that he can make his choices is: $3 \times 2 \times 2 \times 2 \times 2 = 48$

Question 226: C

Suppose that today Gill is x years old. It follows that Granny is 15x years old. In 4 years' time, Gill will be (x+4) years old and Granny will be 15x+4 years old. We know that in 4 years' time, Granny's age is equal to Gill's age squared, so:

$15x + 4 = (x + 4)^2$

Expanding and rearranging, we get:

$x^2 - 7x + 12 = 0$

We can factorise this to get:

$(x - 3)(x - 4)$

So x is either 3 or 4. Gill's age today is either 3 or 4 so Granny is either 45 or 60. We know Granny's age is an even number, so she must be 60 and hence Gill must be 4. So the difference in their ages is 56 years.

Question 227: C

If Pierre is telling the truth, everyone else is not telling the truth. But, also in this case, what Qadr said is not true, and hence Ratna is telling the truth. So we have a contradiction. So we deduce that Pierre is not telling the truth.

Therefore, Qadr is telling the truth, and so Ratna is not telling the truth. So Sven is also telling the truth, and hence Tanya is not telling the truth. So Qadr and Sven are telling the truth and the other three are not telling the truth.

Question 228: D

Angus walks for 20 minutes at 3 mph and runs for 20 minutes at 6 mph. 20 minutes is one-third of an hour. So the number of miles that Angus covers is: 3 × 13 + 6 × 13 = 6

Bruce covers the same distance. So Bruce walks 12 × 3 miles at 3 mph which takes him 30 minutes and runs the same distance at 6 mph which takes him 15 minutes. So altogether it takes Bruce 45 minutes to finish the course.

Question 229: B

Although you could do this quickly by forming simultaneous equations, it is even quicker to note that 72 x 4 = 288. Since Species 24601 each have 4 legs; it leaves a single member of species 8472 to account for the other 2 legs.

Question 230: E

None of the options can be concluded for certain. We are not told whether any chicken dishes are spicy, only that they are all creamy. Whilst all vegetable dishes are spicy, some non-vegetable dishes could also be spicy. There is no information on whether dishes can be both creamy and spicy, nor on which, if any, dishes contain tomatoes. Remember, if you're really stuck, draw a Venn diagram for these types of questions.

Question 231: C

At 10mph, we can express the time it takes Lucy to get home as:

60 x 8/10 = 48

Since Simon sets off 20 minutes later, his time taken to get home, in order to arrive at the same time, must be:

48 – 20 = 28

Therefore his cycling speed must be:

48/28 x 10 = 17 mph

Question 232: A

The total profit from the first transaction can be expressed as:

2000 x 8 = 16,000p

The total profit from the second transaction is:

1000 x 6 = 6,000p

Therefore the total profit is 22,000p or £220 before charges. There are four transactions at a cost of £20 each, therefore the overall profit is:

£220 – (20 x 4) = £140

Question 233: C

For the total score to be odd, there must be either three odd or one odd and two even scores obtained. Since the solitary odd score could be either the first, second or third throw there are four possible outcomes that result in an odd total score. Additionally, there are the same number of possibilities giving an even score (either all three even or two odd and one even scores obtained), and the chance of throwing odd or even with any given dart is equal. Therefore, there is an equal probability of three darts totalling to an odd score as to an even score, and so the chance of an odd score is ½.

Question 234 C

This is a compound interest question. £5,000 must be increased by 5%, and then the answer needs to be increased by 5% for four more iterations. After one year: £5,000 x 1.05 = £5,250

Increasing sequentially gives 5512, 5788, 6077 and 6381 after five years. Therefore the answer is £6,381

Question 235: D

If in 5 years' time the sum of their ages is 62, the sum of their ages today will be:

$62 - (5 \times 2) = 52$

Therefore if they were the same age they would both be 26, but with a 12 year age gap they are 20 and 32 today. Michael is the older brother, so 2 years ago he would have been aged 30.

Question 236: A

Tearing out every page which is a multiple of 3 removes 166 pages. All multiples of 6 are multiples of 3, so no more pages are torn out with that instruction. Finally, half of the remaining pages are removed, which equates to an additional 167 pages. Therefore 333 pages are removed in total. The total surface area of these pages is $15 \times 30 \times 333 = 149,850cm^2 = 14.9m^2$. At $110gm^2$, $14.9m^2$ weighs $14.9 \times 110 = 1,650g$ ($1,648g$ unrounded).

Question 237: D

The cost of fertiliser is 80p/kg = 8p/100g. At 200g the incremental increase in yield is 65 pence/m. At each additional 100g it will be reduced by 30%, therefore at 300g/m it is 45.5p, at 400g/m it is 31.8p, at 500g/m it is 22.3p, at 600g/m it is 15.6p, at 700g/m it is 10.9p, and at 800g it is 7.6p. So at 800g the gain in yield is less than the cost of the fertiliser to produce the gain, and so it is no longer cost effective to fertilise more.

Question 238: D

Statements **A**, **C** and **E** are all definitely true. Meanwhile, statement **B** may be not true but is not definitely untrue, as this depends on the number of cats and rabbit owned.

Only statement **D** is definitely untrue. The type of animal requiring the most food is a dog, and as can be seen from the tables, Furry Friends actually sells the most expensive dog food, not the cheapest.

Question 239: C

The largest decrease in bank balance occurs between January 1st and February 1st, totalling £171, reflecting the amount spent during the month of January, £1171. However, because there is a pay rise beginning on March 10th, we need to consider that from April onwards, the bank balance will have increased by £1100, not £1000. This means that the same decrease in bank balance reflects £100 more spending if it occurs after March.

This means that 2 months now have seen more spending than February. Between March 1st and April 1st, the bank balance has decreased by £139.

With the salary increase, the salary is now £1100, so the total spending for the month of March is £1239. This is greater than the total spending during the month of January.

Similarly, the month of April has also seen more spending than January once the pay rise is considered, a total of £1225 of spending. However, this is still less than the month of March.

Question 240: C

If Amy gets a taxi, she can set off 100 minutes before 1700, which is 1520.

If Amy gets a train, she must get the 1500 train as the later train arrives after 1700, so she must set off at 1500.

Since Northtown airport is 30 minutes from Northtown station, there is no way Amy can get the flight and still arrive at Northtown station by 1700. Therefore Amy should get a taxi and should leave at 1520.

Question 241: C

We can decompose the elements of the multiplication grid into their prime factors, thus:

	C	D
A	2 x 2 x 2 x 3 x 7	2 x 2 x 2 x 2 x 3 x 3 x 5
B	7 x 17	2 x 3 x 5 x 17

bc = 7 x 17, so one of b and c must be 7 and the other must be 17. b must be 17 because bd is a multiple of 17 and not of 7, and c must be 7 because ac is a multiple of 7 and not of 17. ac is 168, so a must be 168 divided by 7, which is 24. ad is 720 so d must be 720 divided by 24, which is 30. Hence the answer is 30.

Alternatively approach the question by eliminating all answers which are not factors of both 720 and 510.

Question 242: E

48% of the students are girls, which is 720 students. Hence 80 is 1/9 of the girls, so 1/9 of boys are mixed race. The remaining 780 students are boys, so 87 boys are mixed race to the nearest person. There is a shortcut to this question. Notice that 80 girls are mixed race, and the proportion is the same for boys. As there are more boys than girls we know the answer is greater than 80. Option E 90 is the only option for which this holds true.

Question 243: D

Don't be fooled – this is surprisingly easy. We can see that between Monday and Thursday, Christine has worked a total of 30 hours. We can also calculate how long her shift on Friday was supposed to be. She is able to make up the hours by working 3 extra hours next week, and 5 hours on Sunday. Thus, the Friday shift must have been planned to be 8 hours long. Adding this to the other 30 hours, we see that Christine was supposed to work 38 hours this week.

Question 244: C

130°. Each hour is 1/12 of a complete turn, equalling 30°. The smaller angle between 8 and 12 on the clock face is 4 gaps, therefore 120°. In addition, there is 1/3 of the distance between 3 and 4 still to turn, so an additional 10° must be added on to account for that.

Question 245: B

The total price of all of these items would usually be £17. However, with the DVD offer, the customer saves £1, giving a total cost of £16. Thus, the customer will need to receive £34 in change.

Question 246: E

A. Incorrect. UCL study found eating more portions of fruit and vegetables was beneficial.
B. Incorrect. This is a possible reason but has yet to be fully investigated.
C. Incorrect. Fruit and vegetables are more protective against cardiovascular disease, and were shown to have little effect on cancer rates.
D. Incorrect. Inconclusive – people who ate more vegetables generally had a lower mortality but unknown if this is due to eating more vegetables or other associated factors.
E. Correct. Although this has previously been the case, this study did not find so. 'they recorded no additional decline for people who ate over 5 portions'.
F. Incorrect. The 5% decline per portion was only up to 5 portions and no additional reduction in mortality for 7 than 5 portions.
G. Incorrect. Study only looks at cancers in general and states need to look into specific cancers.

Question 247: C

Deaths in meta-analysis = 56423/800000 = 0.07 or 7%
1% lower in UCL study so 6%
6% of 65,000 = 65000 x 0.06 = 3,900

Question 248: B

A. Eating more fruit and vegetables doesn't particularly lower overall risk but need research into specific cancer risk.

B. The UCL research alone found that increasing the number of fruit and vegetable portions had a beneficial effect, even though this wasn't the overall conclusion when combined with results from the meta-analysis.

C. The results were not exactly the same but showed similar overall trends.

D. Although this may be true, there is no mention of this in the passage.

E. Fruit and vegetables are protective against cardiovascular disease, but not exclusively. They also reduce the rates of death from all causes.

F. The UCL study is in England only and the meta-analysis a combination of studies from around the world.

G. Suggested by the UCL research, but not the meta-analysis, so not an overall conclusion of the article.

Question 249: E

Work out percentage of beer and wine consumption then the actual value using the total alcohol consumption figure:

Belarus: $17.3 + 5.2 = 22.5\%$;
$0.225 \times 17.5 = 3.94$

Lithuania: Missing figure $100 - 7.8 - 34.1 - 11.6 = 46.5$
$46.5 + 7.8 = 54.3\%$
$0.543 \times 15.4 = 8.36$

France: $18.8 + 56.4 = 75.2\%$
$0.752 \times 12.2 = 9.17$

Ireland: $48.1 + 26.1 = 74.2$
$0.742 \times 11.9 = 8.83$

Andorra: missing figure $100 - 34.6 - 20.1 = 45.3$
$34.6 + 45.3 = 79.9\%$
$0.799 \times 13.8 = 11.0$

Question 250: D

Russia:
2010 – Total = 11.5+3.6 = 15.1. Spirits = 0.51 x 15.1 = 7.7
2020 – Total = 14.5. Spirits = 0.51 x 14.5 = 7.4
Difference = 0.3 L

Belarus:
2010 – Total = 14.4 + 3.2 = 17.6. Spirits = 0.466 x 17.6 = 8.2
2020 – Total = 17.1. Spirits = 0.466 x 17.1 = 8.0
Difference = 0.2 L

Lithuania:
2010 – Total = 15.4. Spirits = 0.341 x 15.4 = 5.3
2020 – Total = 16.2. Spirits = 0.341 x 16.2 = 5.5
Difference = 0.2 L

Grenada:
2010 – Total = 12.5. Spirits % = 100 – 29.3 – 4.3 – 0.2 = 66.2%. Spirits = 0.662 x 12.5 = 8.3
2020 – Total = 10.4. Spirits = 0.662 * 10.4 = 6.8
Difference = 1.5 L

Ireland:
2010 – Total = 11.9. Spirits = 0.187 x 11.9 = 2.2
2020 – Total = 10.9. Spirits = 0.187 x 10.9 = 2
Difference = 0.2L

Question 251: C

Work out 4.9 as a percentage of total beer consumption in Czech Republic and search other rows for similar percentage.

4.9/13 = 0.38, approx. 38% which is very similar to percentage consumption in Russia (37.6).

Question 252: B

We can add up the total incidence of the 6 cancers in men, which is 94,000. Then we can add up the total incidence in women, which is 101,000. As a percentage of 10 million, this is 0.94% of men and 1.01% of women. Therefore the difference is 0.07%.

Question 253: C

Given there are 1.15 times as many men as women, the incidence of each cancer amongst men needs to be greater than 1.15 times the incidence amongst women in order for a man to be more likely to develop it. The incidence is at least 1.15 higher in men for 3 cancers (prostate, lung and bladder).

Question 254: D

If 10% of cancer patients are in Sydney, there are 10,300 prostate/bladder/breast cancer patients and 9,200 lung/bowel/uterus cancer patients in Sydney. Hence the total number of hospital visits is 10,300 + 18,400, which is 28,700.

Question 255: A

The proportion of men with bladder cancer is 2/3 and women 1/3.

Question 256: D

First we work out the size of each standard drink. 50 standard drinks of vodka is equivalent to 1250ml, so one drink is 25ml or 0.025 litres. 11.4 standard drinks of beer is 10 pints of 5700ml, so one standard drink is 500ml or 0.5 litres. 3 standard drinks of cocktail is 750ml so one is 250ml or 0.25 litres. 3.75 standard drinks of wine is 750ml, so one is 200ml or 0.2 litres.

We can then work out the number of units in each drink. Vodka has 0.025 x 40 = 1 unit, Beer has 0.5 x 3 = 1.5 units, Cocktail has 0.25 x 8 = 2 units and Wine has 0.2 x 12.5 = 2.5 units. Since the drink with the most units is wine, the answer is D.

Question 257: B

We found in the last question that vodka has 1 unit, beer has 1.5, cocktail has 2 and wine has 2.5. Hence in the week, Hannah drinks 23.5 units and Mark drinks 29 units. Hence Hannah exceeds the recommended amount by 9.5 units and Mark by 9 units.

Question 258: D

We found that vodka has 1 unit, beer has 1.5, cocktail has 2 and wine has 2.5. Hence it is possible to make 5 combinations of drinks that are 4 units: 4 vodkas, 2 cocktails, 2 vodkas and a cocktail, 1 vodka and 2 beers, or a wine and a beer.

Question 259: D

The total number of males in Greentown is 12,890. Adding up the rest of the age categories, we can see that 10,140 of these are in the older age categories. Hence there are 2750 males under 20.

Question 260: C

Given that in the first question we found the number of males under 20 is 2,750, we can then add up the totals in the age categories (apart from 40-59) in order to find that 15,000 of the residents of Greentown are in other age categories. Hence 9,320 of the population are aged 40-59. We know that 4,130 of these are male, therefore 5,190 must be female.

Question 261: C

The age group with the highest ratio of males:females is 20-39, with approximately 1.9 males per females (approximately 3800:2000). As a ratio of females to males, this is 1:1.9.

Question 262: C

There are 4 instances where the line for Newcastle is flat from one month to the next per year, hence in 2008-2012 (5 years) there are 20 occasions when the average temperature is the same from month to month. During 2007, there are 2 occasions, and during 2013 there are 3.

Question 263: A

The average temperature is lower than the previous month in London for all months from August to December, which is 5 months. However, in August and November in Newcastle, the average temperature remains the same as the previous month. Hence there are only 3 months where the average temperature is lower in both cities.

Hence from 2007 to 2012, there are 18 months where the average temperature is lower than the previous month. During 2013, the only included month where the temperature is lower in both cities than the previous month is September. Hence there are 19 months in total when the temperature is lower in both cities than the previous month.

Question 264: B
Firstly work out the difference between average temperatures for each month (2, 3, 1, 2, 1, 3, 3, 2, 2, 5, 1, 0). Then sum them to give 25. Divide by the number of months (12) to give $2^{1}/_{12}$, which is 2°C to the nearest 0.5°C.

Question 265: D
There is not enough information to tell which month the highest sales are in. We know it increases up to a point and decreases after it, but as we don't know by how much we cannot project where the maximum sales will be.

Question 266: B
Given that by observation, Q2 and Q3 both account for 1/3 of the sales and Q4 accounts for 1/4, this leaves that Q1 accounts for 1/12 of sales. 1/12 of £354,720 is £29,560.

Question 267: A
Quarter 2 accounts for 1/3 of the sales, which is £60,000 in sales revenue. If a tub of ice cream is sold for £2 and costs the manufacturer £1.50, this means profit is 1/4 of sales revenue. Hence £15,000 profit is made during Q2.

Question 268: D
A. and B – Incorrect. Both *could* be true but neither is *definitely* true as it is dependent on the relative number of families with each number of children, which is not given in the question. Therefore we cannot know for certain whether these statements are true.

C – Incorrect. C is definitely *untrue* as half of the families spend £400 a month on food, which totals £4800 a year.

D – Correct. This option is true as 1/6 of families with 1 child and 1/6 of families with 3 children spent £100 a month on food.

E   Incorrect. This option is definitely untrue as the average expenditure for families with 2 children is actually £400 a month.

Question 269: B

2210 out of 2500 filled in responses, meaning that 290 did not. 290 as a percentage of 2500 is roughly 12% (11.6%) of the school that did not respond.

Question 270: C

The percentage of students that saw bullying and reported it was 35%, so 65% of those who saw it did not which is equivalent to 725 students. Of this 725, 146 which roughly equals 20%, gave the reason that they did not think it was important.

Question 271: B

Of the students who told a teacher, 286 did not witness any action. Of those who did notice action, i.e. 110, only 40% noticed any direct action with the bully involved. 40% of 110 is 44, so the correct answer is B.

Question 272: D

"427 cited fears of being found out" which means about 59% out of the 725 students that did not tell about the bullying, cited that it was because they worried about others finding out.

Question 273: F

North-east: 56 per 100,000 on average. This means that there must be a higher proportion of women than this and a lower proportion of men, such that the average is 56/100,000

We must make the reasonable assumption that there are the same number of men and women in the population as the question asks us to approximate.

Therefore there are 18.6/50,000 men and 37.3/50,000 women

This scales to 74.4/100,000 women which is roughly 74/100,000.

Question 274: C

8 million children – question tells to approximate to 4 million girls and 4 million boys.

Girls: 20% eat 5 portions fruit and vegetables a day. 20% of 4 million: 4 x 0.2 = 0.8 million

Boys: 16% eat 5 portions of fruit and vegetables a day. 16% of 4 million: 4 x 0.16 = 0.64 million

Number of more girls: 800,000 – 640,000 = 160,000.

Question 275: B
A. Incorrect. Women: 13619+10144+6569 = 30332. Men: 16818 + 9726 + 7669 + 6311 = 40524
B. Correct. Flu + pneumonia, lung cancer and chronic lower respiratory diseases = 15361 + 13619 + 14927 = 43907
C. Incorrect. More common cause of death but no information surrounding prevalence.
D. Incorrect. Colon cancer ranking 8 for both.

Question 276: A

The government has claimed a 20% reduction, so we are looking for an assessment criterion which has reduced 20% from 2013 to 2014. We can see that only "Number of people waiting for over 4 hours in A&E" has reduced by 20%, so this must be the criterion the government has used to describe "waiting times in A&E".

Question 277: B

Rovers must have played 10 games overall as they played each other's team twice. They lost 9 games scoring no points and so must have won 1 game, which scores 3 points.

Question 278: A

To have finished between City and United, Athletic must have got between 23 and 25 points. Hence they must have got 24 points because no team got the same number of points as another. Athletic won 7 games which is 21 points, so they must have also got 3 points from drawing 3 games. This accounts for all 10 games they played, so they did not lose any games.

Question 279: C

United won 8 games and drew 1, which is 25 points. Rangers drew 2 games and won none, which is 2 points. Therefore the difference in points is 23.

Question 280: C

Type 1 departments reached the new target of 95% at least three times since it was introduced. All the other statements are correct.

Question 281: C

Total attendances in Q1 08-9: 5.0 million
Total attendances in Q1 04-5: 4.5 million
The difference = 0.5 million
0.5/5 x 100 = 10% increase

Question 282: C

There are 16 quarters in total since the new target came into effect.
$4/16 = 0.25$, so the target has been hit 25% of the time i.e. missed 75% of the time.

Question 283: C

Ranjna must leave Singapore by 20:00 to get to Bali by 22:00. The latest flight she can therefore get is the 19:00. Thus, she must arrive in Singapore by 17:00 (accounting 2 hours for the stopover). The flight from Manchester to Singapore takes 14 hours. Manchester is 8 hours behind Singapore so she must leave Manchester 22 hours before 17:00 on Wednesday i.e. by 19:00 on Wednesday. Thus, the latest flight she can get is the 18:00 on Wednesday.

Question 284: D

The 08:00 flight will arrive at Singapore for 22:00 on Monday (GMT) or 06:00 Tuesday Singapore time. She then needs a 2 hour stopover, so earliest connecting flight she can get is 08:30 on Tuesday. The flight lands in Bali at 10:30. She then spends 1 hour and 45 minutes getting to her destination – arriving at 12:15 Tuesday.

Question 285: C

A. Incorrect. The graph is about level, and certainly not the steepest gradient post 2007.
B. Incorrect. Although there has been a general decline, there are some blips of increased smoking.
C. Correct.
D. Incorrect. The smoking rate in men decreased from 51% in 1974 to 21% in 2010. Thus, it decreased by more than a half.
E. Incorrect. The percentage difference between men and women smokers has been minimal in the 21st century.

Question 286: D

For this type of question you will have to use trial and error after you've analysed the data pattern to find the correct answer.   The quickest way to do this is to examine outliers to try and match them to data in the table e.g. the left-most point is an outlier for the X-axis but average for the y-axis. Also look for any duplicated results in the table and if they are present on the graph, e.g. Hannah and Alice weigh 68 kg but this can't be found on the graph.

Question 287: C

This is pretty straightforward; the point is at approximately 172-174 cm in height and 164 -166 cm in arm span. Matthew is the only student who fits these dimensions.

Question 288: C

This is straightforward – just label the diagram using the information in the text and it becomes obvious that C is the correct answer.

Question 289: C

Since we do not know whether they went to university or not, we must add the number of women with children who work and those who went to university, 2, to the number of women with children who work but did not go to university, 1 (2 + 1 = 3).

Question 290: C

To work this out we must add up all the numbers within the rectangle, 4 + 6 + 1 + 2 + 11 + 12 + 7 + 15 = 58

Question 291: E

To work this out we must calculate the number of men plus women who have children and work i.e. 11 + 5 + 2 = 18

Question 292: C

To solve this we must work out the total number of people who had children i.e. 3 + 6 + 5 + 11 + 1 + 2 =28. Then we work out the total number of people who went to university, but that do not also have children so that these are not counted twice: 13 + 12 = 25. Then we add these two numbers together, 28 + 25 = 53 and subtract the number of people who fell into both categories i.e. 53 - (5 + 11 + 2) = 35

Question 293: C

To work this out we must add up all the numbers outside the rectangle that also fall within both the circle and the square, which is 5

Question 294: D + E

This question asks for identification of the blank space, which is the space within the triangle, the rectangle and the square i.e. indicating working women who went to university but did not have children. This also reveals non-working men who did not have children and did not go to university.

Question 295: C

The normal price of these items would be £18.50 (£8 + £7 + £3.50). However, with the 50% discount on meat products, the price in the sale for these items will be £9.25. Thus, Alfred would receive £10.75 of change from a £20 note.

Question 296: C

The number of games played and points scored is a red herring in this question. The important data is 'Goals For' and 'Goals Against'. As this is a defined league and the teams have only played each other, the 'Goals For' column must equal the 'Goals Against' column.

Total Goals For = 16 + 11 + 8 + 7 + 8 + 4 = 54

Total Goals Against = 2 + Wilmslow + 7 + 9 + 12 + 14 = 44 + Wilmslow

For both columns to be equal, Wilmslow must have a total of 54 − 44 = 10 Goals Against.

Question 297: C

Working with the table it is possible to work out that the BMIs of Julie and Lydia must be 21 and 23, and hence their weights 100 and 115 lbs. Thus Emma's weight is 120 lbs, and her BMI must be 22, making her height equivalent to 160 cm.

Question 298: C

Working through the results, starting with the highest and lowest values, it is possible to plot all values and decipher which point is marked.

Question 299: D

The average production across the year is at least 7 million barrels per day. Multiplying this by 365 gives around 2,550 million barrels per year. All other options require less than 7 million barrels daily production to be produced, and it is clear there is at least 7 million barrels per day. Therefore the answer is 2,700 million. Alternatively we can estimate using 30 days per month, and multiplying the amount of barrels produced per day in each month by 30. 6+7+7+7.5+7.5+7+7.5+8+8.5+8.5+8+9 = 91.5, multiplying by 30 elicits just over 2,700 million barrels.

Question 300: C

Use both graphs. For July, multiply the oil price by the amount sold in the month, and multiply by the number of days in the month. Thus, July = 7.5 million barrels x $75 per barrel x 31 days = $17,400 million = $17.4 billion

Final Advice

Arrive well rested, well fed and well hydrated

The TSA is an intensive test, so make sure you're ready for it. You'll have to sit this at a fixed time (normally at 9AM). Thus, ensure you get a good night's sleep before the exam (there is little point cramming) and don't miss breakfast. If you're taking water into the exam then make sure you've been to the toilet before so you don't have to leave during the exam. Make sure you're well rested and fed in order to be at your best!

Move on

If you're struggling, move on. Every question has equal weighting and there is no negative marking. In the time it takes to answer on hard question, you could gain three times the marks by answering the easier ones. Be smart to score points- especially in section 2 where some questions are far easier than others.

Make Notes on your Essay

Oxford admission tutors may ask you questions on your TSA essay at the interview. Given that the interview will normally be 4 – 6 weeks after your TSA, it is essential that you make short notes on the essay title and your main arguments after the exam so that don't get caught off guard during the final hurdle.

Afterword

Remember that the route to a high score is your approach and practice. Don't fall into the trap that *"you can't prepare for the TSA"*– this couldn't be further from the truth. With knowledge of the test, time-saving techniques and plenty of practice you can dramatically boost your score.

Work hard, never give up and do yourself justice.
Good luck!

Acknowledgements

We would like to express our gratitude to the many people who helped make this book possible, especially the 10 TSA Tutors who shared their expertise in compiling the huge number of questions and answers. We are also grateful to the numerous editors who painstakingly provided valuable feedback throughout the authoring process.

About Us

Infinity Books is the publishing division of *Infinity Education*. We currently publish over 85 titles across a range of subject areas – covering specialised admissions tests, examination techniques, personal statement guides, plus everything else you need to improve your chances of getting on to competitive courses such as medicine and law, as well as into universities such as Oxford and Cambridge.

Outside of publishing we also operate a highly successful tuition division, called UniAdmissions. This company was founded in 2013 by Dr Rohan Agarwal and Dr David Salt, both Cambridge Medical graduates with several years of tutoring experience. Since then, every year, hundreds of applicants and schools work with us on our programmes. Through the programmes we offer, we deliver expert tuition, exclusive course places, online courses, best-selling textbooks and much more.

With a team of over 1,000 Oxbridge tutors and a proven track record, UniAdmissions have quickly become the UK's number one admissions company.

Visit and engage with us at:
Website (Infinity Books): www.infinitybooks.co.uk
Website (UniAdmissions): www.uniadmissions.co.uk
Facebook: www.facebook.com/uniadmissionsuk
Twitter: @infinitybooks7

Your Free Book

Thanks for purchasing this Ultimate Book. Readers like you have the power to make or break a book –hopefully you found this one useful and informative. *UniAdmissions* would love to hear about your experiences with this book. As thanks for your time we'll send you another ebook from our Ultimate Guide series absolutely <u>FREE</u>!

How to Redeem Your Free Ebook

1) Either scan the QR code or find the book you have on your Amazon purchase history or your email receipt to help find the book on Amazon.

2) On the product page at the Customer Reviews area, click 'Write a customer review'. Write your review and post it! Copy the review page or take a screen shot of the review you have left.

3) Head over to www.uniadmissions.co.uk/free-book and select your chosen free ebook!

Your ebook will then be emailed to you – It's as simple as that! Alternatively, you can buy all the titles at

<u>www.uniadmissions.co.uk/our-books</u>

Printed in Great Britain
by Amazon